THE COMPLETE
ILLUSTRATED COMPANION

XENA: WARRIOR PRINCESS: THE COMPLETE ILLUSTRATED COMPANION

Standard edition 1 84023 622 1
Creation edition 1 84023 697 3
Diamond edition 1 84023 710 4

Published by Titan Books
A division of Titan Publishing Group Ltd
144 Southwark Street, London, SE1 0UP

First edition March 2003
2 4 6 8 10 9 7 5 3 1

In Memory of Kevin Smith.

This book would have been impossible without the following: the cast and crew of Xena: Warrior Princess and Hercules: The Legendary Journeys; Darryl Curtis and the staff and contributors of Xena: Warrior Princess Magazine; Robert Weisbrot; Diane Denesowicz; Barbara Powell; my editors Jo Boylett, Adam Newell and Sholto Brown; and the worldwide community of Xena fans.

The publisher would like to thank Christina Macphail, David Wilson-Nunn and all those involved with the production of this book at Universal Studios Consumer Products.

All pictures in this book were previously cleared for publication in Xena: Warrior Princess Magazine.

No writers, editors or designers were harmed during the production of this book, although several deadlines were sacrificed.

Did you enjoy this book? We love to hear from our readers. Please email us at: readerfeedback@titanemail.com or write to Reader Feedback at the above address. To subscribe to our regular newsletter for up-to-the-minute news, great offers and competitions, email: titan-news@titanemail.com

Titan Books' film and TV range are available from all good bookshops or direct from our mail order service. For a free catalogue or to order, phone 01536 764646 with your credit card details, or write to Titan Books Mail Order, AASM Ltd, Unit 6, Pipewell Industrial Estate, Desborough, Northants, NN14 2SW. Please quote reference XC/IC

A CIP catalogue record for this title is available from the British Library.

Printed and bound in Great Britain by MPG, Bodmin, Cornwall.

XENA
WARRIOR PRINCESS ™

THE COMPLETE
ILLUSTRATED COMPANION

K. STODDARD HAYES

TITAN BOOKS

CONTENTS

"Everyone can relate to a story of redemption... I think that has an appeal. And I also think that, at the time we started, there were no kick-ass women shows." — Rob Tapert

Xena was born in a haunted cabin in the woods... Well, sort of. Producer Robert Tapert and director Sam Raimi began their professional careers by making the funky horror film *The Evil Dead*, with their friend Bruce Campbell as the star. Produced on a shoestring, it was released in 1983, and its blend of humour and horror quickly made it a cult hit. Fast forward to 1992, when Dan Filie, a Senior Vice President for Development at Universal Television, invited Renaissance Pictures — Raimi and Tapert's production company — to produce a series of telefilms. Filie, it seems, was an *Evil Dead* fan, and was looking for a similar mix of humour and action for Universal Television's new syndication package, the Action Pack.

The following year, Renaissance Pictures formed a New Zealand division, Pacific Renaissance, to produce a series of TV movies for Universal. The movies updated a classic hero with a modern style of storytelling, and in doing so brought new life to the fantasy genre. The hero was, of course, Hercules. From the début of Renaissance's first film, *Hercules and the Amazon Women*, he was a smash success. The *Hercules* telefilms soon evolved into *Hercules: The Legendary Journeys*, a syndicated television series which carried forward the audience following and the ratings success of the films. Eager to build on that success, even before production was finished on *Hercules'* first season, the producers and the parent studio began looking for ways to expand this new world of adventure.

While Raimi returned to his first love, films, executive producer Tapert took the reins. He was a fan of Hong Kong martial arts epics, and wanted to do an episode featuring a woman warrior who would fight in the Hong Kong style. At about the same time, *Hercules* head writer and co-executive producer John Schulian had a story idea about a beautiful woman who would come between Hercules and his best friend Iolaus. The two ideas eventually merged — and Xena had arrived. At the urging of co-producer David Eick, the story of the Warrior Princess was soon expanded into a three-episode arc to conclude *Hercules'* first season. "She was based on characters from Hong Kong movies — conflicted villainesses who had some good elements and some bad elements," says Tapert, recalling the influences on the development of Xena. "[They] brought an attitude to the character. We were able to take it and make a story of redemption, making it a bad character who was searching for redemption. And that was the spin on a new female superhero that no one had done before."

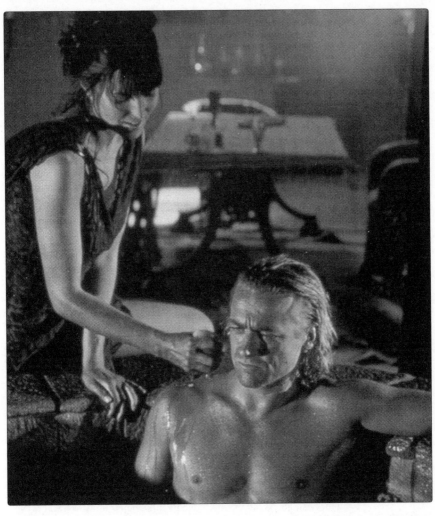

The original plan for the Warrior Princess was to have her die in battle (of course!) at the end of her *Hercules* story arc, presumably redeeming herself with her sacrifice. But at Universal Studios, Dan Filie was already considering making a spin-off series from the studio's newest success. *Vanishing Son,* which was paired with *Hercules* as the second half of the Action Pack at that time, was not maintaining the audience brought in by the Renaissance series. Consequently, Tribune Stations, which represented a fifth of the syndicated market, only wanted to renew *Hercules.* Universal understandably didn't want to give up the strong ratings lead-in provided by its new hit show to a series from a rival studio. They decided it would be better to follow *Hercules* with a show that would appeal to the same audience, and Filie definitely liked the idea of the Warrior Princess.

Lucy Lawless seduces Michael Hurst in her first appearance as Xena.

Once the possibility of a spin-off series had been attached to the Xena character, casting suddenly loomed as a huge issue. It's hard to believe now, but Lucy Lawless was far from the studio's first choice for the role. Indeed, she very nearly didn't get it.

Lawless originally read for the part of Amazon Queen Hippolyta in *Hercules and the Amazon Women*. Her audition impressed the producers greatly, but both they and the studio also liked Roma Downey, and though Lawless had modest credits in her native New Zealand she was completely unknown in the US. She was eventually cast as Hippolyta's lieutenant, Lysia, instead — a role in which she first demonstrated the dangerous edge that would be so essential to Xena. Later, she appeared in the *Hercules* episode 'As Darkness Falls', playing the sly temptress Lyla, a character whose humour and vivacity demonstrated to the producers that Lawless' range could stretch far beyond the menace she had displayed as Lysia.

Though David Eick and New Zealand casting director Diana Rowan urged that Lawless be cast as Xena, her lack of recognition still stood in the way. Universal, with its eye on that possible spin-off, wanted an actress already known to American audiences, whose name would help draw viewers to *Hercules* and to the new series, if it was greenlit. The role was consequently offered to Vanessa Angel, who had been considered for both Hippolyta and Deianeira, and who already had her own series with Universal, *Weird Science*. Both the studio and the producers recognised that casting an actress already committed to an existing series meant that the *Xena* spin-off was a dead proposition, but the decision was made anyway.

Then fate, in the form of the flu, stepped in. Angel came down with a bad case of it over the Christmas holidays, and was unable to travel to New Zealand. Shooting on 'The Warrior Princess' episode of *Hercules* was scheduled to begin on 5 January 1995, and as always with TV production schedules, there was no slack for sick days. The producers had to find another star, and fast. Still thinking of an American actress, they ran through a list of five other candidates, all of whom declined the opportunity to travel to New Zealand for the part. With no options and no time left, the producers decided to try Lucy Lawless. But they couldn't find her!

Lawless, with her husband and daughter, had gone off on a camping trip with no set itinerary, touring the country and stopping at random to visit various relatives along the way. After all, nothing in the way of work or casting ever happened over the New Year... So while Lawless enjoyed her holiday, the producers at Renaissance frantically tried to locate her with phone calls to her agent, her home, her parents, and various friends and relatives all over the country.

Lawless' parents weren't in when Diana Rowan called their house, but fortunately, as chance — or fate — would have it, her brother had just stopped by for a few minutes to pick up some mail. He called her in-laws, and they

THE ILLUSTRATED COMPANION

called other relatives who Lawless had mentioned she might visit. It turned out that Lawless *was* with them, having decided on the spur of the moment to drop in that day. Did she want the role? Happily, after all the trouble tracking her down, Lawless' answer was an emphatic yes!

Only two days before shooting was to begin, Lawless flew to Auckland. She had her brown hair dyed black so that she would appear more menacing and as different as possible from Lyla and Lysia (and it didn't hurt that the jet black hair made a startling contrast to her brilliant blue eyes and ivory skin). She was also rushed into costume fittings so that the outfit designed for Vanessa Angel could be remade for her. Only days after getting that first call, Lawless walked on camera for the first time as Xena, Warrior Princess.

Lawless didn't hear about the possibility of a spin-off until 'The Gauntlet' was in production, and she was initially sceptical about anything so big coming of the role. Even though the original cut of 'The Gauntlet' was lightened up in editing and post production, it was still by far the darkest *Hercules* episode to date — foreshadowing the later development of intense drama and serious themes in both series.

The episode first aired in May 1995, and the fans loved it, especially Lawless' performance as a conflicted warrior at a turning point. Their enthusiasm was an important factor in convincing the studio and the syndication market that a successful new series might be developed from the character.

The pairing of Lawless and Renee O'Connor proved crucial to Xena's success.

But it would take more than just a few popular episodes to sell the idea of this particular *Hercules* spin-off. Female action heroines had never been a great success on television, and studio executives are not well known for taking risks. However, Xena's dark past put an original spin on the standard female superhero genre, and studio executives are always on the lookout for the next great idea — if they can be sure it will be a hit. The popularity of *Hercules* also helped to sell the spin-off, as did the Renaissance producers' promise that *Xena: Warrior Princess* would not be just a *Hercules* clone, but a new show with a new look. Finally, a demo tape edited from Hong Kong movie fight sequences helped to convince Tribune, *Hercules'* main distributor, of the appeal of *Xena's* action style. With their support, the new series was confirmed.

To help get *Xena: Warrior Princess* on the right road from the start, Universal brought in seasoned television and film writer R. J. Stewart (whose credits include *Remington Steele*) to help develop the series. Stewart helped Tapert develop a back story for Xena that made her a bit less of a villain, and more of a hero gone wrong. It's the story of a girl who first started fighting to protect her village from a warlord, and then simply went too far down that path (as was later detailed in the episodes 'Remember Nothing', 'Death Mask' and 'Destiny').

Stewart was especially excited by the dramatic possibilities of Xena's history. "I recognised right away that there'd never been a hero on television who had such a dark past," he says. "She was a monster and now she's had this major conversion to good, and I wanted the pilot to be about the consequences of that to her life. I've always said that the biggest monster Xena ever fights is the one inside of her. The opportunity to revive that — the idea that the dark Xena is still inside her and could come back — gave a great tension to the series."

Xena's bloody past is one of the major story elements that distinguishes the spin-off from *Hercules*, and provided the new twist promised by the show's creators to its syndication market. Hercules, like most superheroes, may have his flaws and his weaknesses, but he has always been a good guy, fighting for truth and justice. In contrast, Xena is a superhero whose life was filled with hatred, bloodshed and terrible crimes. This provides the opportunity for all kinds of drama absent from *Hercules*, or your usual wholesome superhero story. Xena carries the guilt of her past, and she's always trying to atone for it, and indeed, wondering if she ever can.

Added to the burden of guilt is the question of whether the Warrior Princess could ever return to being that evil, violent monster. Just as Xena herself, Gabrielle, and others who love her, fear her dark side and want to contain it, there are just as many (Ares, Callisto and Alti, for a start) who want to see the dark Xena reborn so that they can exploit her power. Half of the dramatic conflict in the show hangs on the question of just how much

influence Xena's dark side has at any given time.

Another major dramatic difference between *Xena* and *Hercules* lay in the decision to give Xena a permanent companion, instead of a part-time sidekick like Herc's buddy Iolaus. In contrast to Hercules, who is an open and accessible guy, the producers saw Xena as a taciturn character who reveals little of what she is thinking or feeling — hence the need for another character to do all the talking.

It fell to R. J. Stewart to develop the character of Gabrielle as he wrote the script for the series pilot, 'Sins of the Past'. It was he who hit on the idea of making the worldly Warrior Princess' new best friend an innocent young girl who had never before left home. Making her very sharp-witted (not to mention as quick with her tongue as Xena is with a chakram) gave the sidekick a chance to be more than just a tag-along.

Finding the right Gabrielle turned out to be as lengthy a process as finding the right Warrior Princess. When Tapert saw Stewart's script, he immediately thought of Renee O'Connor, who had proved her appeal playing the young Deianeira opposite Sorbo's Hercules in *Hercules and the Lost*

O'Connor made her début as Deianeira in Hercules and the Lost Kingdom.

Opposite Page: Xena's elaborate Hercules armour was replaced with elegant copper and leather for the series.

Kingdom. Yet with a series at stake, the producers felt they had to be sure. This meant an exhaustive casting process in which US casting director Beth Hymson-Ayer saw about 400 young actresses, selected some fifty who were interviewed by the producers, and finally narrowed the field to half a dozen who tested for the role. They might as well have saved themselves the trouble — O'Connor continued to shine above all the competition, and was duly cast as Gabrielle.

The decision to create a sidekick, the inspiration of pairing the Warrior Princess with an innocent bard, and the chemistry between Renee O'Connor and Lucy Lawless all combined to create the most important element in *Xena*'s enduring success. Fans came back again and again to see what would happen in the odd-couple friendship between the two. From the beginning, the interplay between the two characters was the heart of the series and the key to its wide appeal. It was also the source of endless new dramatic stories, as their relationship developed, taking some remarkable ups and downs.

Premièring in September 1995, the new series landed not just on its feet, but at a dead run. Before the end of its first season, *Xena: Warrior Princess* had achieved a major ratings victory by becoming the highest rated new syndicated series on television. By the end of its second season, *Xena* had become the highest rated of *all* syndicated action series, toppling even the ratings colossus *Baywatch*. A television legend had been born. ⚔

THE ORIGINAL WARRIOR PRINCESS: THE BRIDE WITH WHITE HAIR

Executive producer Rob Tapert's main inspiration for bringing a woman warrior into *Hercules: The Legendary Journeys* was the 1993 Hong Kong film *The Bride With White Hair.*

The film had won both critical and popular acclaim, not only for its exciting fight choreography, but also for its beautiful cinematography, and especially for the drama and tragedy of the story it tells. Produced and directed by Ronnie Yu and based on an old Chinese legend, it is a tale of star-crossed lovers from opposite sides of a bitter feud. Hong Kong star Brigitte Lin plays Lien, a woman who was raised by wolves and is now the chief assassin of a powerful faction. Leslie Cheung plays Yi Hang, the heir to a clan which Lien's faction is determined to wipe out of existence. When Yi Hang first sees Lien, he is captivated by her beauty and courage. He later rescues her when she is wounded, nurses her back to health, and the two fall in love and pledge their devotion to each other. Though they try to escape the hatred of their respective clans, conspiracy and tragedy overtake them. In one sequence, Lien is forced to endure an ordeal very similar to the titular scene in *Xena*'s 'The Gauntlet'.

"Each week is a battle to get a new show out... you always feel the pressure of having to think, 'How can I entertain people in a new way?'" — Rob Tapert

New Zealand's spectacular landscape was an essential element in the look of Xena.

Xena: Warrior Princess entered production in mid-1995, in Auckland, New Zealand. Many creative and technical aspects of the show had already been established during the filming of the *Hercules* telefilms and the thirteen-episode first season of *Hercules: The Legendary Journeys*. Most important was New Zealand itself, chosen by producer Eric Gruendemann when he was first scouting locations for *Hercules*. The country offered then (as now) remarkable scenery and a favourable exchange rate, as well as an up-and-coming film and television industry. Gruendemann had settled on Auckland, rather than Wellington or Christchurch, primarily because it had a larger talent pool for film and television projects.

Most production departments and many key personnel for *Xena* were already on the job because of *Hercules*. They included producer Chloe Smith in New Zealand, producer Liz Friedman and post-production supervisor Bernadette Joyce in Los Angeles, production designer Robert Gillies, costume designer Ngila Dickson, make-up and hair supervisor Francia Smeets, Peter Bell's stunt team, Kevin O'Neill's visual effects team at Flat Earth Productions and score composer Joseph LoDuca.

As for the tone of the new series, *Xena* inherited from *Hercules* the contemporary dialogue and an often humorous tone, along with the freedom to play fast and loose with myth and history, and the cartoon treatment of many fight scenes. At the same time, the producers wanted to be very sure that *Xena: Warrior Princess* had a style and character all its own, for both business and creative reasons. After all, one of the strong points in selling *Xena* to Tribune and other syndication markets had been the promise that the new show would not be just a clone of *Hercules*. So the producers took *Xena* in new directions in several critical areas.

The character of Xena had been created partly to provide an opportunity to show off some Hong Kong martial arts-style action. Consequently, the stunt fighting in *Xena: Warrior Princess* was deliberately choreographed to showcase this approach. Xena leaps on and off tall structures, flips over the heads of adversaries, runs sideways along walls or the chests of the bad guys, and even fights high in the air in spirit battles with adversaries like Alti. All this had an impact on the production: Hong Kong-style action involves much more work with wire, harness and crane, and also uses more weapons, especially for the main characters. Whereas Herc and Iolaus fight barehanded with kicks and punches, Xena and Gabrielle have a whole stock of weapons, beginning with Xena's trademark chakram and Gabrielle's staff. Before production started, Lucy Lawless spent a few weeks in Los Angeles, getting some kung fu training from martial arts master Douglas Wong, as well as learning how to fight with sword and staff.

Another difference from *Hercules* was evident in the look of the show. Rob Tapert wanted *Xena* to be shot with much quicker cuts and more camera motion. Again, production-wise, this means that more set-ups were required for different shots and camera angles, meaning less time for perfection. The result is a show that visually, at least, moves faster. Compared to the polished cinematic look of *Hercules*, *Xena* has a rougher, more spontaneous look.

Doug Lefler, who had started with Renaissance as a second unit director on the *Hercules* telefilms and directed the *Hercules* series première, 'The Wrong Path', was also given the task of directing *Xena*'s première episode, 'Sins of the Past'. He recalls another parameter set early on for the new show: "When *Xena* started, it was supposed to be different from *Hercules* in the sense that they were not going to have Flat Earth working on it. It was going to be more of an action show, and the only visual effects were going to be in-

KEEP YOUR EYE ON THE CINEMATOGRAPHER

Donald Duncan, *Xena*'s director of photography, employed a whole repertoire of camera tricks to create *Xena*'s snappier visual look.

1 Take many different shots. Where *Hercules* might do fifteen different shots in a day, *Xena* might shoot thirty, giving less time to each shot, but providing the editors with a much wider range of shots to cut into a scene. A scene made up of many shorter shots cut together has a much faster visual pace than a scene made of fewer, longer shots.

2 Keep the camera moving. Constant motion — tracking around characters or action, moving in or out — gives the feeling that the audience is in a scene, instead of just watching it from a distance.

3 Use Steadicams as often as possible. The Steadicam, which is mounted on a special harness worn by the cameraman, allows for even greater movement and intimacy, as it can track characters around corners, up stairs and into tight places that a dolly-mounted camera can't go.

4 Vary the film speed. Shooting an action shot at twenty-two frames per second, instead of the usual twenty-four, creates an illusion of speed when the film is played back at twenty-four. Slowing the speed from twenty-four to twenty-two frames during the take ('ramping up') creates a fight that gradually speeds up, while speeding up the film during the take ('ramping down') produces a slow motion effect.

camera visual effects, like forced perspective. So they wanted the pilot episode to be a prototype of how they would do it."

Many Xena episodes after 'Sins of the Past' do maintain this approach, and the lack of computer-generated creatures and effects adds much to the realistic feeling of the show. But of course, before the end of the first season, strict observance of the rule was abandoned in favour of adding CGI effects for creatures like the flying dragon of 'Prometheus', the harpies of 'Mortal Beloved' and the skeleton dryads of 'Girls Just Wanna Have Fun'. Eventually an entire episode, 'Fallen Angel', was produced with backgrounds entirely created in a computer.

Film editor Robert Field was among those brought on board for Xena. Field already had a long and successful career creating film trailers for Universal Studios, eventually becoming head of the trailer department. So when Tapert was looking for an editor with experience in trailers to create the opening montage sequences for the *Hercules* telefilms, Universal gave him Field's name. At the time he created the *Hercules* montage, Field was ready to move into editing longer forms. A year later, when Xena became a series, he was invited back to become one of its editors, a job he shared with Jim Prior.

Hudson Leick plays Renaissance producer Liz Friedman in the Hercules *episode 'Yes Viriginia, There Is a Hercules'.*

Field and Prior alternated editing duties for each episode of *Xena* (check the end credits of any episode to see which of the two edited it). On average, they had eighteen or twenty hours of footage from main and second units for each forty-four-minute episode. The amount of footage for any one scene varied hugely, depending on both the nature of the scene and the director's approach: the frenetic ladder fight in 'Callisto' had over 145 shots, while the laid back hot tub scene in 'A Day in the Life' had only three.

One of Field's first tasks as editor had a special impact on the series. He created the opening title sequence for *Xena*, producing in just two days an exciting first cut montage that was used, shot for shot and unchanged, until the sixth season. His long experience with trailers also gave him the skill to write a narration that was concise, dramatic and evocative, and which any *Xena* fan can quote by heart: "In a time of ancient gods, warlords and kings, a land in turmoil cried out for a hero. She was Xena, a mighty princess forged in the heat of battle. The power — the passion — the danger! Her courage will change the world."

MUSIC

For the musical tracks, Joseph LoDuca gave the Warrior Princess a different sound from the heroic-fantasy symphonic sound he had developed for Hercules. While the *Hercules* theme features a fanfare of brass and strings, *Xena*'s theme begins with the wild and eerie sound of a Bulgarian bagpipe, then incorporates syncopated percussion and a female chorus. The voices are those of the Bulgarian Women's Chorus, whose distinctive sound was admired by Rob Tapert long before *Xena* and *Hercules*. Tapert suggested the Chorus to LoDuca for Xena's *Hercules* episodes, and they followed Xena to her own series. For the *Xena* main title music, LoDuca actually wrote an 'Ode to the Warrior Princess' and had it translated into Bulgarian. The voices chanting in a language alien to most of us creates a sense of a faraway time and place better than any orchestral effects could.

Throughout the series, LoDuca drew on a wide range of international music to find inspiration and instruments for each episode's score. Eastern European music had a strong influence on *Xena*'s basic sound, but he also worked with musical cultures as diverse as China ('The Debt, Part I' and 'The

JOSEPH LODUCA'S BULGARIAN LYRICS FOR THE 'ODE TO THE WARRIOR PRINCESS'

Jenata iazdi samotna	The Warrior Princess rides alone.
Neinoto minalo srazi ia	Her past drives her from shame.
Sreshtu voiskite ot tumen sviat	Against the forces of a dark world
Vouva za dobro tia	She fights for good, not for fame.
Rogovi zuunove idvat	Horns sound her coming, blare her name.
"Napraite put na voina!"	"Make way the Warrior! Cheer!"
Tupani biat vuv ritum	Drums beat a rhythm.
Princhesata e pak tuka!	Let villains beware,
	the Warrior Princess is here!

Debt, Part II'), seventies pop music ('Lyre, Lyre, Hearts on Fire') and Hasidic chant (for Xena's funeral dirge, first heard in 'The Path Not Taken'). Though he travelled the world musically to find evocative and exciting sounds for both *Xena* and *Hercules*, physically LoDuca worked almost entirely from his state-of-the-art music studio at his home in Michigan, using computer technology to compose and synchronise the music, and print out the score, and the internet to get it to the studios for sound mixing. He visited the set only occasionally, for example to work with the actors on their vocal parts for 'Lyre, Lyre, Hearts on Fire'.

WRITING

From the start, R. J. Stewart headed the writing staff of *Xena*. He was soon joined by Steven L. Sears and Chris Manheim, and the team of Adam Armus and Nora Kay Foster. These five would be the main writers for the first four seasons, with producer Liz Friedman also contributing heavily to the creative mix by working closely with the writers. Friedman, who had been with Renaissance since before the New Zealand days, worked as producer for both *Hercules* and *Xena*.

Kevin Smith and Alexandra Tydings team up for divine comedy in 'The Quill Is Mightier'.

Sears, whose earlier credits include *Riptide* and *The A-Team*, pitched the idea that became 'Dreamworker' at his first meeting with Renaissance's producers. Hired originally as creative consultant, he quickly stepped into the shoes of the departing Babs Greyhofsky to become *Xena's* supervising producer in the first season.

Manheim had written for *Eight is Enough, Murder She Wrote* and *Columbo*. She was invited to pitch for *Xena* by Sears, who was represented by the same agency. She wrote two freelance scripts in the first season ('The Prodigal' and 'Altared States'), before becoming story editor in the second season.

Armus and Foster made their first sale to Renaissance with the *Hercules* script 'The March to Freedom', and eventually wrote scripts for all of Renaissance's New Zealand-based series. Though their first *Xena* script was the dramatic 'Chariots of War', they quickly found their niche in comedy, writing comic classics including 'For Him the Bell Tolls', 'The Xena Scrolls' and 'Fins, Femmes and Gems'.

The writers found that the possibilities of a *Xena* script were almost infinite. "There is so much we can do on *Xena*: we can do melodrama, we can do soap opera, we can do comedy," said Stewart in an interview early in 2000. "At the core of it all is adventure and jeopardy. And the greatest thing is that we can do fantasy and mythology, which really liberates you… we're so free to explore just about anything. The writer then has to go off and do the hard work. You can give a bad writer the greatest idea in the world and it will suck, and you can give a terrific writer a pretty mediocre idea and they can make it into something special."

Because of the huge pre-production effort of preparing costumes, sets and make-up, Renaissance did have one practice on *Xena* that is unusual in television: beatsheets (an outline of a script, usually running to about ten pages). Very early drafts of scripts also went out to all the production departments, to allow them as much creative input as possible and as much time as possible for pre-production work. Chris Manheim explains: "Television is a collaborative medium. Everyone is on board and at Renaissance Pictures this is particularly so, because everyone gets the beatsheets and everyone knows what is going on — the costumiers, set developers, props, everyone. This means that no one is left out of the production process, and it creates a much better product."

On *Xena*, a script would begin with a story meeting (actually, lots of story meetings). Throughout the series, most ideas originated with either Rob Tapert or R. J. Stewart. At the start, the idea might be no more than a simple concept such as, "Everything Gabrielle writes in her scrolls comes true." At the story meetings, the entire writing staff would discuss the new idea and develop a beatsheet outlining the action of the episode, with no dialogue or description. The story would then be assigned to a writer, who would write the

first draft of the script, fleshing out the scenes with action and dialogue.

In any given year, members of the writing staff wrote about fourteen scripts of the twenty-two needed, while freelancers wrote about eight. The first draft would then be discussed in another story meeting and changes suggested. The script might be rewritten, once, twice or even more, depending on how difficult it was to work out the story.

Freelance scripts were nearly always rewritten by Stewart. (Staff rewrites of freelance scripts are pretty standard in television, mainly because a freelancer's knowledge of a series or feel for the characters can't compare with that of the staff.) A rewrite, however, might be anything from a few scene changes here and there, to a complete overhaul of the whole script.

Lawless, Tilly and some extras in action.

CASTING

Actors for *Xena*, like those for *Hercules*, were cast from both Los Angeles and New Zealand. Los Angeles casting was done by the casting agency of Beth Hymson-Ayer, whose credits before *Xena* and *Hercules* included American television hits like *LA Law* and *21 Jump Street*. Hymson-Ayer was responsible

for such great casting finds as Alexandra Tydings (Aphrodite) and Hudson Leick (Callisto).

New Zealand casting was handled by Diana Rowan, best known before *Xena* for casting the acclaimed film *The Piano*. Since only lead guest stars merited the expense of paying an actor's travel from Los Angeles, Rowan was responsible not only for casting major characters, but for all smaller speaking parts. Rowan's greatest casting find was, of course, Lucy Lawless.

In casting both *Hercules* and *Xena* from the relatively small talent pool of New Zealand, Rowan had two main challenges: "Can this person do an American accent?" and, very often, "Can we get away with using this actor again in a different role?" The answer to the first question was generally "Yes", as actors working in New Zealand have to be able to do a variety of accents in order to get enough work. Even when New Zealand creeps into the voices of the characters, the accent often only adds to the charm of the setting. The answer to the second question usually ended up being "Yes" out of necessity — there just aren't that many actors in New Zealand! In the fantastic setting of *Xena*, with a little help from creative costume and make-up, doubling up on roles never seems to hamper the audience's willing suspension of disbelief. The sight of Karl Urban in Caesar's Roman armour, or Alison Bruce in Kahina's flowing desert robes, easily persuades one to overlook the fact that their faces have appeared before on different characters.

In choosing actors, the casting directors had to consider not only the looks and personality required for a particular part, but also what physical skills the part might call for. In casting Callisto, for example, the actress chosen not only had to convince an audience she could hold her own against Xena, she also had to look at home on a horse in a simple riding scene.

In casting extras, the first consideration was often what sort of general ethnic look was wanted for a particular scene, whether Chinese for the Chin-set episodes, Indian for the India trilogy or Germanic for the Ring trilogy. Extras casting director Tracy Hampton found New Zealand's ethnic diversity made this aspect of her job much easier. Hampton was also responsible for casting many stunt and body doubles, who had to be able to imitate the way the actors moved. What the extras might have to do in a scene was another consideration. A village battle scene with people running and falling called for extras who could keep up with both the physical demands and the complex directions required.

Like most film and television productions, *Xena* used two production units to film its episodes. The main unit was responsible for all footage involving the principal actors, such as scenes with dialogue and any action footage where the actor's face was visible. The second unit was responsible for everything else: stunts and stunt double work, long shots of characters in the distance played by body doubles, background and establishing shots of a scene, and insert shots that show a close detail of some aspect of the scene,

such as a character's hand picking up a weapon. The second unit also travelled to South Island to get scenic footage of the mountains and wild places.

SHOOTING/LOCATIONS

For *Xena*, the main unit worked Monday through Friday, and usually completed its part of an episode in seven or eight days. The second unit, overlapping with the main unit, worked Tuesday through Saturday and took

The headland and black sands of Bethells Beach were a favourite location.

I'M SURE I'VE SEEN THAT BEACH BEFORE...

Xena used locations all over New Zealand, though the vast majority were within an hour or so of Auckland.

Perhaps the most famous is the black sands of Bethells Beach, where Caesar crucifies Xena in 'Destiny' and where Xena receives her god-killing power during Eve's baptism in 'Motherhood' (to mention just a couple of the many uses of a particularly beautiful location). Among those farther afield were Lake Taupo, some four hours south of Auckland, where much of 'The Debt' and 'Adventures in the Sin Trade' were shot, and the sand dunes near Dargaville, two hours north of Auckland, which provided the Sahara for 'Destiny'. Many of the scenic shots, especially for wild and mountainous areas, came from South Island.

Hercules and Xena also shared a constantly changing and expanding series of outdoor sets in a former safari park near Auckland. These sets could be rebuilt or redressed to suit the needs of any episode. The walled city used for the siege of Troy in one episode might become a gladiatorial arena or an Athenian fort in another. An Indian village in one episode might be redressed as an Amazon village the next week.

Interior scenes were shot in sets built inside 300,000 square feet of warehouse converted to a sound stage. Sets and props were constantly being recycled, both to save time in the tight production schedule and to keep costs down. Boat scenes were shot on a motorised barge, which was redressed to resemble everything from a Greek sailing ship to a Japanese sampan.

about eight days per episode. Hence an average episode of *Xena* took about sixteen days of production between the two units.

While *Xena*, like *Hercules*, was photographed in New Zealand, the writing team worked in Los Angeles, where Renaissance Pictures is based. Los Angeles was also the location of almost all post-production work, including editing, sound mixing and special effects.

SEASON ONE

The first episode of *Xena: Warrior Princess*, 'Sins of the Past', lays a solid foundation for the series with a balance of action, humour, drama and characterisation. It also begins the exposition of several themes that are central to the series. The choice between the way of violence and the path of peace is set forth not only in 'Sins of the Past', but also in 'Chariots of War', 'Dreamworker' and 'The Path Not Taken' during season one. It's a theme that arises in many later episodes, and indeed becomes the focus of the entire fourth season. Closely tied to that theme is the question of redemption and forgiveness. In 'Sins of the Past', this relates only to Xena, as she tries to convince her family that she has changed, but later it becomes an important issue for Gabrielle, Ares and Callisto, among others.

Xena and Gabrielle's friendship quickly became the central theme of Xena.

The series' central theme, the tapestry into which everything else is woven, is of course the friendship between Xena and Gabrielle. The moment Xena accepts Gabrielle's companionship with the words, "All right, *friend*," they begin a six-year odyssey that takes them, and us, through experiences and emotions that no one could have imagined at the start of the journey. There may not be, anywhere else in television, an exploration of friendship that is so intimate, so profound and so immensely varied, ranging as it does from the trauma of deaths, betrayals and attempted murders, to the scatological comedy of head lice and the sheer silliness of a pie fight.

Other episodes in the first season (there are twenty-four, instead of the usual twenty-two for a syndicated series) explore a range of genres. There is the treasure-hunt of 'A Fistful of Dinars', a cross between Westerns and *Raiders of the Lost Ark*, the M*A*S*H-style realism of 'Is There a Doctor in

The Troy set, built for 'Beware Greeks Bearing Gifts', was redressed for many later episodes.

the House?' and the farcical comedy of 'Warrior... Princess' — where Lucy Lawless makes her first foray into dual roles, playing both Xena and Princess Diana. Autolycus and Salmoneus pay their first visits to the series in 'The Royal Couple of Thieves' and 'The Black Wolf' respectively. In 'Hooves and Harlots', the Amazons make a spectacular entrance into *Xena's* world, where they subsequently play a far more important role than they did in *Hercules*.

The production teams also began to stretch their wings, with stunt sequences such as the chariot chase in 'Chariots of War' and the ladder fight in 'Callisto', and the construction of a castle and a full size Trojan horse for 'Beware Greeks Bearing Gifts'.

Several directors who became *Xena* regulars make their débuts in the first season. Among them are Charles Siebert, Garth Maxwell, Josh Becker and T. J. Scott. Becker began his *Xena* career fortuitously with the serio-comic 'A Fistful of Dinars', and went on to direct a number of classic comedy episodes such as 'For Him the Bell Tolls'. Scott, known for his innovative visual style, set the tone for his work on *Xena* by tracking his cameras all over the castle set of Troy in 'Beware Greeks Bearing Gifts', and shot 'Is There a Doctor in

the House?' entirely with a Steadicam, in only five days.

Before the end of the first season, three of *Xena*'s most important supporting characters have been introduced. Ares had previously featured on *Hercules*, but was always disguised in one way or another. It takes the dangerous beauty of the Warrior Princess to draw out the real Ares — the suave, seductive and ruthless God of War portrayed by Kiwi actor Kevin Smith. His pairing with Lucy Lawless resulted in on-screen chemistry that, throughout the series, is second only to the chemistry of Lawless with Renee O'Connor. A single episode, 'Callisto', introduces the other two essential characters, both of whom provide interesting contrasts to the Warrior Princess: Joxer the definitely not mighty, and Callisto, the first truly terrifying *Xena* villain.

R. J. Stewart came up with the idea of Callisto as a reaction to the Warrior Princess' reformed character: "I was driving to work one day thinking, 'Boy, Xena got off easy. She did all these terrible things, [and now] she doesn't have to deal with the consequences.' So I thought, 'What if she comes face to face with somebody she did wrong to? What if that somebody has become evil and is trying to out-bad the old Xena?' Then I said, 'What if that someone is a beautiful woman?' By the time I got into work, I had a great story to pitch to people. It really went rather effortlessly from there. The first draft worked, T. J. [Scott, who directed 'Callisto'] totally got it, and they cast the right gal."

The role of Joxer was conceived as a character who could bring to *Xena* the same type of comic relief that Salmoneus brought to *Hercules*. In the person of Ted Raimi, that goal was once again fulfilled far beyond the original conception. Though Joxer's dorkiness makes him the character that some fans most love to hate, Raimi brought to the warrior wannabe both his whimsical charm and an endlessly inventive comic talent that allowed the writers to feature him in a number of notable episodes.

One final and indispensable detail had also become a permanent part of production by the middle of the first season. It actually began on *Hercules*, when producer Liz Friedman and post production supervisor Bernadette Joyce were working on 'As Darkness Falls' (an episode which, coincidentally, also features Lucy Lawless' first guest appearance on the series). "I was on the mix stage with Bernie Joyce, our really fabulous head of post [production] and I said to her, 'I wish we could say, 'No centaurs were harmed during the making of this picture','" remembers Friedman, recalling the magic moment. "She said, 'We can!' So it was like my fourth grade joke that I thought was so funny, and now somebody was telling me I could do it."

The first *Xena* disclaimer, for 'Cradle of Hope', is the half-serious 'No babies were harmed during the production of this motion picture.' The second — 'Iolaus was harmed during the production of this motion picture. However, the Green Egg Men went on to live long and prosperous lives' — for 'Prometheus', is a harbinger of the silliness that follows. It is also a hint of

the occasional truthfulness of the disclaimers, since Michael Hurst had broken his arm during production. At first, not every episode of *Xena* or *Hercules* got one, but after 'The Black Wolf', every single *Xena* episode carries a disclaimer of one sort or another. "Bernie and I came up with one for every episode," says Friedman. "All that mattered was it had to make me laugh. Other people would suggest stuff and, frankly, if I didn't think it was funny, I didn't use it. It was my little area where I got to have control and be a bit of a dictator, and of course they escalated more and more as we went along."

The disclaimers were an instant hit with the fans, causing an immeasurable amount of wear on video recorders as tapes were rewound and played back at slower speed to read the latest silliness. They also led to countless fan complaints about the practice of showing end credits on a split screen, which often rendered the fine print of the disclaimers too small to read. The disclaimers spread deep into *Xena* fandom, with imitations springing up on fan websites, in books and even in the official *Xena* magazine, which carried a disclaimer in the masthead of every issue — in suitably tiny print!

SEASON TWO

The second year confirms Ted Raimi's Joxer, Kevin Smith's Ares and Hudson Leick's Callisto as semi-regular characters who have tremendous impact on *Xena* storylines for most of the subsequent seasons. It also sees T. J. Scott pushing the visual style of *Xena* a bit further over the edge with the "rock-horror video" look of the Halloween episode, 'Girls Just Wanna Have Fun'. And the writing team pushed the story format right out of the BC era for the first time, by putting Lawless, O'Connor, Raimi and Smith in 1940s Macedonia for 'The Xena Scrolls'.

One very special second season episode not only brought Aphrodite into the *Xena*verse, it also introduced the series' most famous (or infamous) musical track: the Joxer song. "We were on the set of 'For Him the Bell Tolls' and Josh [Becker, the episode's director] said, 'You're trapped in that dungeon with Renee, so you should try and find something to really bug Gabrielle... Why don't you just do a song?'" recalls Ted Raimi. "I came up with one thing, Josh came up with another thing, and so finally it was done. Joe LoDuca's a very talented composer but that's one thing that Josh and I came up with on our own." LoDuca continues the story: "That's been a fun running gag from the first time it got introduced. They actually wrote a stanza, and then I added verses to it, and the writers took a look at it and said, 'Well, okay. How about this?' So there would be another version, and it's turned into an ongoing joke. Ted made an appearance at a convention out in California, and everybody was singing along and knew all the words!"

Silly songs aside, the major challenge of the second season (beyond the normal grind of producing twenty-two film-quality television episodes in forty-

five weeks) arose in October 1996, when Lucy Lawless had a riding accident while rehearsing for a skit on *The Tonight Show* in New York. She broke her pelvis, putting her in the hospital and off camera, halfway around the world in the middle of the production season.

Scriptwriter Paul Robert Coyle, who was then freelancing for Renaissance, was called in to help cover Lawless' absence with some essential script changes. "They were having emergency meetings in every room!" he recalls. "Adam [Armus] and Nora Kay [Foster] were doing a show in one room with Steve Sears, while Rob and Liz Friedman were with somebody else in another room. I went in with R. J., who said, 'Here's what we want to do with 'Ten Little Warlords'. We've already shot the previous episode, 'Intimate Stranger', which is a [Xena/Callisto] body swap episode. We're going to alter the ending so that Xena did not get into her regular body, and carry that storyline over to your show.' So I was given the mandate to rewrite my show with Hudson Leick. Over ninety per cent of that story remained the same in the script; I just had to remember that the characters were seeing Hudson and reacting to her as if she was Callisto."

Xena goes AD for the first time in 'The Xena Scrolls'.

Leick plays Xena in Callisto's body in 'Intimate Stranger' and 'Ten Little Warlords'.

Charles Siebert, who directed 'Ten Little Warlords', also pulled extra duty during the crisis — because of his long experience as an actor, he stepped in to play Sisyphus in the same episode. "It was a time of very interesting and clever improvisation," Siebert remembers. "As Ray [Henwood, who had played Sisyphus in 'Death in Chains'] wasn't available, someone said to me, 'Well, you're an actor. Why don't you do it?' I thought, 'That's the last thing I need!' I thought acting in and directing the same episode of *Xena* would be a pain in the arse. Every time I wanted to set up a shot, I had to go and get my beard re-glued!"

Several other episodes were scripted to work around this emergency. In 'The Quest', Bruce Campbell portrays both Xena and Autolycus, as the spirit of the dead Xena enlists the King of Thieves to steal her body and the

ambrosia to restore her to life. 'For Him the Bell Tolls' focuses almost entirely on Gabrielle and Joxer — Xena's scenes at the beginning and end of the episode were shot partly with body doubles, and partly weeks later, when Lawless had returned to the set. 'Here She Comes… Miss Amphipolis' was deliberately light on fight sequences, to allow for Lawless' continuing recovery. All these episodes are examples of how a good creative team can produce genius out of practical necessity. Chris Manheim has ultimately positive memories of the time: "It was a great bonding experience, with everyone pulling together."

SEASON THREE

The third season of *Xena* is memorable chiefly for the Rift between Xena and Gabrielle over Gabrielle's daughter Hope. Steven Sears credits Rob Tapert with shaking things up to this extent: "We got to our third season and he said, 'Let's not fall into a slump — let's change it!' And boy did we change it!"

The Rift between Xena and Gabrielle reaches its nadir in 'The Bitter Suite'.

Having spent two years establishing that Xena and Gabrielle will not only die for each other, they can't live without each other, the writers spent the third season turning the relationship on its head. A series of events and betrayals, beginning with the rise of the evil god Dahak and the birth of the demonic Hope, brings the story to the moment in 'The Bitter Suite' when Xena and Gabrielle — best of friends and soulmates — try to kill each other.

'The Bitter Suite' was the greatest departure yet from the series' established style and format, and remains a standout for its operatic style and huge production numbers, as well as its dramatic impact on the story of the Rift. It took longer to shoot than any other *Xena* episode except 'Fallen Angel'. Instead of the usual sixteen days of production in main and second units, *Xena's* first musical episode took over twenty days — not counting all the time involved in pre and post production, scripts, sets, creating the elaborate costumes, rehearsing and recording the music and soundtracks.

Editor Robert Field recalls that the episode was among the most challenging to edit as well: "They were never able to shoot the entire song in a master take. Bits of the song were recorded in different takes, and I was forced not only to cut the footage so that it made sense visually, but also to edit the music together so that the song was correct." Then when composer LoDuca replaced some 'temp' musical and vocal tracks with the final recordings, Field had to re-cut some sequences to match the performers' lips with the new vocal tracks. It took him four-and-a-half weeks just to produce the first cut. He let Jim Prior edit the next musical episode, 'Lyre, Lyre, Hearts on Fire'.

In the middle of this intense story arc, the creative staff sent their characters on a dramatic and philosophical quest, farther afield than they had ever been, for the landmark two-part episode 'The Debt'. The story takes Xena and Gabrielle all the way to China, introduces Xena's mentor Lao Ma (Jacqueline Kim), and explores Taoist themes and a huge chunk of Xena's backstory. It was one of the series' most elaborate productions. Field, who considers the two-parter one of *Xena's* finest stories, recalls that it took him five-and-a-half weeks to edit. Set design, costumes, make-up, stunts and special effects all worked overtime to create the world of ancient China in an epic that includes barbarian cavalry battles, beautiful Chinese palaces, high-flying mental powers and a horrendous prison hip-deep in filthy water.

1997 also saw Renaissance Pictures venturing into new territory with the production of an animated feature based on both hit series. *Hercules & Xena — The Animated Movie: The Battle for Mount Olympus* was released direct to video in January 1998. The story, unrelated to any series plotlines, involved the Olympian mischief typical of a *Hercules* episode, with the abduction of Alcmene and the vengeful Hera releasing some Titans. Kevin Sorbo, Lucy Lawless, Michael Hurst, Renee O'Connor, Kevin Smith and Alexandra Tydings all voiced their usual series roles. Among the other voice actors were Alison Wall and Ted Raimi who provided voices for some of the Titans. The

music and songs earned composer Joseph LoDuca and songwriters Michele Brourman and Amanda McBroom a 1998 Annie Award nomination (recognising excellence in animation). However, critical and fan reception was lukewarm, and copies of the video and DVD are now hard to get hold of.

The third season ends with another two-part episode, 'Sacrifice', which brings together all the major characters in a complex story of betrayal, religious propaganda and violence. The episode's final moments, featuring Gabrielle's fall with Hope into a fiery chasm, make up *Xena*'s first big end-of-season cliff-hanger.

SEASON FOUR

With its tale of the Rift, the third season had established the dramatic possibilities of carrying a single story thread through a whole year, woven in and out of stand-alone episodes. The fourth season repeats this pattern. Its story arc begins and ends with the searing image of Xena and Gabrielle being crucified, and the key arc episodes of the season focus on the conflict between the way of the warrior and the way of peace.

The fourth season introduces Claire Stansfield as the fans' favourite evil shamaness, Alti.

Two important new characters make their début: the prophet Eli and the evil shaman Alti. Alti's first episode, the memorable two-part season première 'Adventures in the Sin Trade', also introduces the Siberian Amazons with their fur and bead costumes, and reveals another large slice of Xena's past. Claire Stansfield's Alti is passionate, ruthless and magnetic, and proved an instant hit with fans. Her popularity led to Alti's return in four more episodes and created a mini-career on the side for Stansfield, who continues to be a very popular guest at *Xena* conventions.

Opposite Page: Alti's vision of the crucifixion of Xena and Gabrielle comes true in 'The Ides of March'.

However, perhaps the best-remembered aspect of the fourth season is the controversy that centred on a single episode: the Hindu-themed 'The Way' (first aired in the week of 22 February 1999). In that episode — the third of a

TWO HINDU VIEWS OF 'THE WAY'

The World Vaishnava Association spearheaded the protest against 'The Way'.

The Association sent a letter to Pacific Renaissance shortly before 'The Way' aired, asking that the episode not be broadcast unless WVA approved of its portrayal of Krishna. American Hindus Against Defamation sent a similar letter, less strongly worded, on the same date. Both letters are on AHAD's website, www.hindunet.org/anti_defamation.

In early March 1999, Tusta Krishnadas, the Press Secretary of the World Vaishnava Association, posted an editorial on VNN.org, Vaisnava News Network. Titled 'Xena's Message To The Viewers', the article provides a detailed analysis of 'The Way'. It condemns Xena's behaviour toward Krishna throughout the episode as arrogant and condescending instead of properly humble, and concludes that 'The Way' teaches that Krishna "is at the beck and call of the proud and the faithless." The article also complains that the episode conveys the "subtle message" that Krishna and Hanuman give their blessing to lesbian relationships, stating, "it is common knowledge that Xena is a lesbian icon, a lesbian hero, and that lesbians make up a large part of the viewing audience." It goes on to assert that presenting Krishna as a fictionalised character might lead non-Hindus to believe that Krishna and other gods are fictional instead of real, and that their worshippers are therefore ignorant and superstitious.

Hinduism Today, a US monthly magazine, also reported on 'The Way' and the attendant controversy in its regular television column in the June 1999 issue. The column reports the opinions of several of the magazine's regular correspondents from different parts of the country. All give favourable reviews, finding that Krishna is portrayed with love and reverence, that he is treated with respect even by Xena, who doesn't like gods, and that it is obvious the producers made an effort to research Hinduism. Says one correspondent: "It conveyed the philosophy of non-violence and love very well. It brought Hindu ideas into the mainstream, reaching an audience that might not be exposed otherwise." The column concludes by quoting Dr Ravi Palat of Auckland University, a consultant for the episode, who is puzzled by the protest because, as he observes, the Indian film industry has made "hundreds" of movies portraying Hindu deities as fictional characters.

Opposite Page: O'Connor strikes an angelic pose for 'Fallen Angel'.

trilogy set in India — Xena and Gabrielle encounter the Hindu gods Krishna and Hanuman, and the demon king Indrajit. Certain elements of the worldwide Hindu community were offended by the episode, and began a campaign to censor it, even before it had aired. The uproar forced Renaissance to announce in April 1999 that the episode would be withdrawn from syndication, much to the dismay of many viewers (especially those in Britain, where the episode had not yet been shown).

In an interview published in November of that year, Rob Tapert gave his perspective: "The World Vaishnava Organisation were trying to make a play with this controversy to become the guardians of Hindu philosophy and religion. They took our show as their political cause and used it to make themselves watchdogs for the Hindu community. They were able to turn this into a Renaissance Pictures/Indian community relationship, which we couldn't allow it to become, because that wasn't the intent."

R. J. Stewart, who wrote the episode, reported later in the year that far from all Hindus were unhappy with what they had seen: "I'm going to a banquet of Hindus and I will be guest of honour. It has actually been very rewarding, since the original crisis. That was a nightmare, but it's been rewarding to see that other Hindus appreciated the episode."

At the end of August 1999, little more than six months after it first aired, a new version of 'The Way' was released. Despite fan fears that the episode would suffer from heavy editing, the only cut made was a shot of Xena giving a ferocious head butt to the Hindu monkey god Hanuman. A new disclaimer was added to the beginning of the episode: 'The producers of the following episode took liberties with Hindu deities and historical timelines, but their sole intent was to illustrate the beauty and power of the Hindu religion.' A thirty-second public service announcement was also added to the end credits.

The fourth season reaches its climax in 'The Ides of March' with one of the series' finest dramatic moments: the sequence intercutting the assassination of Caesar with the crucifixion of Xena and Gabrielle. Their deaths, on camera, provide the series with its most compelling cliff-hanger, and left fans wondering for an entire summer how the characters would be brought back from the dead, without any of the usual television cheating...

SEASON FIVE

Season four's cliff-hanger is resolved with the Emmy-winning fifth season première, 'Fallen Angel'. With its elaborate costumes and make-up for archangels and demons, extensive stunt work and the exclusive use of CGI for the celestial backgrounds, 'Fallen Angel' was the series' most time-consuming episode ever to produce.

Both on and off camera, the fifth season of *Xena* brought greater changes than any other year. A number of long-time production personnel left, for a variety of reasons. The greatest changes were felt in the writing staff. Producer

*A pregnant
Lawless and
O'Connor
ham it up on
the set of
'God Fearing
Child'.*

Steven L. Sears, who had been one of *Xena*'s primary writers, left to produce
his own series, *Sheena*. Meanwhile, with *Hercules* ending and Renaissance's
new Back2Back pair of shows (*Cleopatra 2525* and *Jack of All Trades*) just
starting, R. J. Stewart left to launch *Cleopatra 2525* and *Hercules* writers
Roberto Orci and Alex Kurtzman moved over to *Xena*. The writing staff then
shifted yet again when Orci and Kurtzman went over to *Jack of All Trades*,
while Stewart returned to *Xena*. Adam Armus and Nora Kay Foster also moved
on after writing their last comic script, 'Lyre, Lyre, Hearts on Fire'. Finally,

the team of George Strayton and Tom O'Neill joined the writing staff. Liz Friedman, who had done a great deal of work with the writers during her time on the show, resigned as producer, first to join the writing staff of *Hercules* for its final eight episodes and then to freelance.

On the crafts side of production, costume designer Ngila Dickson surrendered the Renaissance costume shop in order to produce costumes for the blockbuster *Lord of the Rings* film trilogy — a project for which, at the time of writing, she has already earned one Oscar nomination, for *The Fellowship of the Ring*. Dickson's shoes were filled by Jane Holland, whose baptism of fire was to costume 'Fallen Angel'.

On camera, the writers and the crew faced a far bigger challenge than Lucy Lawless' injury in the second season. Lawless was pregnant for much of the production year, forcing the producers to make the choice that always accompanies the pregnancy of a main actor in a television series: conceal the pregnancy from the cameras or write it into the story?

Challenging as it may be to conceal an advanced pregnancy from the sharp-eyed TV audience (as was done, for example, for Gillian Anderson in the second season of *The X-Files*), this is usually a much simpler dramatic option than giving an established character a baby. However, *Xena's* producers chose the much bolder step of allowing the Warrior Princess to become pregnant and have a baby, a decision that would profoundly alter the course of the series for the rest of its run.

Once this decision had been made, cast and crew grappled with the challenge of shooting an action-adventure series with a leading lady whose hours on camera, and whose ability to do action sequences, diminished from week to week. A number of strategies were adopted to cope with the Xena 'shortage', especially in fight sequences. In 'Animal Attraction' and 'God Fearing Child', the climactic fights are performed by the main guest stars, Alison Bruce and Kevin Sorbo. In 'Them Bones, Them Bones', fighting skeletons replace the on-camera bodies of Xena and Alti. In 'Little Problems', Xena spends much of the episode, including a fight, in the body of a little girl. Meanwhile Gabrielle completes her transition to warrior bard, as Renee O'Connor took over more of the action in a leaner, meaner leather costume.

During production of the final season, Rob Tapert considered the results of all the changes during season five. "I can look at the fifth season and say there are some things that I really liked and was proud of, but I think that in some ways it was a disappointing season," he said of his mixed feelings. "When R. J., Steve and all those people were leaving, I had some scripts that just sucked, and because I was launching *Cleo*, no one was watching the fort on the China episodes that went through, and I was incredibly disappointed in that. And then I made some really bad judgement calls in doing 'Punch Lines', for which I had absolutely the wrong director. I knew it was a bad script going forward, and nothing could ever fix it. Everything in my mind after

'Them Bones' to 'Antony and Cleopatra' was such an uneven mish-mash of stuff that I personally can't say I was satisfied with it.

"There was a bunch of stuff that I'll cop all the blame for: 'Lyre, Lyre' (which I still personally like a lot), that was a tremendous disaster in terms of ratings and in terms of fan interest. That surprised me. I actually liked 'God Fearing Child', 'Eternal Bonds' and 'Amphipolis Under Siege', but the fans didn't rate them particularly well. 'Married with Fishsticks' was also a huge fumble on my part. I had to cover an episode with Xena not being there, and I wanted to try to create a *Simpsons*-like world against the background of live action Florida kitsch, which just exploded."

Despite Tapert's misgivings, season five is marked by a number of outstanding and unusual episodes, beginning with 'Fallen Angel'. Another standout episode in terms of production values is the comic musical 'Lyre, Lyre, Hearts on Fire'. Though not as big a ratings or popular success as 'The Bitter Suite', it brings back Xena's mother Cyrene, Joxer and his twin brother Jace, and the lovesick Draco in hot pursuit of Gabrielle — all singing and dancing to classic pop tunes. Like its musical predecessor, the episode required huge effort to prepare the musical numbers, took longer than usual to produce and resulted in a new soundtrack CD.

Xena also hit a major landmark in the middle of the season, with the airing of its hundredth episode, 'Seeds of Faith', which features Callisto's final appearance and an epic confrontation between Ares and Eli. The landmark was accompanied by considerable media attention and the highest ratings of the season (a rating of 4.3, tied with 'Fallen Angel').

The season that begins with the war between Heaven and Hell ends with the Twilight of the Olympian Gods, and another radical — and controversial — dramatic choice. Once Xena's child was born, the writers had to work out the story beats that would incorporate this child into the 'family' created by the relationship of Xena and Gabrielle. One possibility they considered was having Gabrielle leave to become a mercenary, because she couldn't accept that while her daughter had been evil, Xena's was not. Xena and Eve would then have followed Gabrielle, trying to stop her from pursuing the path of violence that Xena had once chosen. "We finally decided we didn't want to drive a wedge between Xena and Gabrielle and play a whole season on Gabrielle being pissy about losing," says Rob Tapert of the decision not to pursue another rift storyline.

Tapert credits Kurtzman and Orci with the plot twist that was ultimately chosen: "As we were getting closer to working out the end, they were adamant that we should do a Rumpelstiltskin-type story, with Xena and Gabrielle going to sleep for twenty-five years and the daughter being an adult [when they woke]." The twenty-five year jump is capped by the conclusion of the Twilight of the Gods arc, when Xena, in defence of her now grown daughter, wipes out nearly all of the Olympian gods.

This storyline was and still is controversial among fans, with some delighted by the dramatic possibilities and the excitement of such a dramatic shift, while others are disappointed that Xena lost a chance to raise her daughter, and that so many regular recurring characters must be supposed dead or gone.

SEASON SIX

As production began on the sixth season, rumours began to spread that this would probably be *Xena*'s last. This was confirmed in an official announcement from Rob Tapert and Studios USA domestic television president Steve Rosenberg on 16 October 2000, shortly after the season began airing. "*Xena* has been an outstanding performer for us since its September 1995 début," Rosenberg said, "finishing No. 1 among all first run syndicated dramas for the past four consecutive seasons. We want to see it go to the top… The series has been nothing short of groundbreaking in redefining the female action hero on television and has inspired a host of imitators across the television landscape." Tapert added, "*Xena* has been a labour of love for

Xena's sixth and final season opened with 'Coming Home', by fan-turned-writer Melissa Good.

everyone associated with it. We've been unusually lucky in having the freedom to explore everything we've ever wanted to try — from high action dramas to slapstick comedies to musicals."

In an interview published a few weeks before the announcement was made, Tapert had already commented on the direction of the final season: "I don't think we're going to play a huge arc in the new season as we've done in the past few seasons. I've received numerous letters [from people who] felt the Xena/Gabrielle relationship was screwed up in the fifth season, in that they didn't talk to one another, and Gabrielle never brought up the issue of her evil daughter. So what we're going to try to do going into the sixth season is to make sure that the relationship between Xena and Gabrielle, within the confines of doing an action show, is still front and centre."

Season six brought more changes in the production staff, with Francia Smeets moving on, leaving Jane O'Kane to take over the job of make-up and hair supervisor. Director of photography Donald Duncan, and long-time Renaissance co-executive producer Eric Gruendemann also took their leave of *Xena* at the end of the fifth season.

Two new writers joined the writing staff for *Xena*'s final year. Joel Metzger had sold a script to Renaissance for *Cleopatra 2525* before being given a rewrite of 'The Haunting of Amphipolis'. The producers were so pleased with his work on the rewrite that they offered him a staff position. Emily Skopov came aboard in a similar way. She was actually talking to the producers about writing for *Cleopatra 2525* and *Jack of All Trades*, when she was given the freelance assignment for 'Heart of Darkness'. She had only completed the outline for that episode when she was taken on staff.

The writing team also got a new freelance voice from an unprecedented source: fan fiction. The idea was Rob Tapert's, because he wanted to show appreciation of the fans by getting a fan involved in an episode. Steven Sears, though now producing *Sheena*, had maintained his contacts both with Renaissance and with *Xena*'s fans. He recommended popular fan fiction writer Melissa Good, with whom he had become acquainted at conventions and through email. After talking with Good and reading some of her *Xena* fiction, Tapert offered her the story which became the episode 'Legacy'. Good went on to write 'Coming Home', which ended up airing first for production and scheduling reasons.

The huge changes at the end of the fifth season story arc left the writers with relatively few recurring characters to generate new stories — the survivors included Ares, Aphrodite and the new characters Virgil and Eve, introduced at the end of the previous year. All the other old standbys — Joxer, Cyrene, Caesar, Alti, the Amazons and Centaurs, could only be introduced in one-time scenarios. In essence the writers had to recreate a world for Xena and Gabrielle to inhabit. As a result, in *Xena*'s sixth season the stories and the characters travel farther afield than ever, with episodes set in North Africa, the

The monsters
Grindl and
Grinhilda
were among
KNB FX's
more
remarkable
creations.

Germanic world of the Norse gods and Beowulf, the twentieth century and, finally, ancient Japan.

A third musical episode was also under consideration for the final season. Despite the time, effort and expense involved in another musical, Tapert really wanted to do one and pursued the idea actively until well into the production year, even having Melissa Good work on a script. Ultimately the episode was cancelled, mainly over difficulties in securing song rights.

Xena: Warrior Princess wrapped production on 31 March 2001. The production of the final episode, 'A Friend in Need', was surrounded by secrecy, though some information inevitably leaked out ahead of broadcast. The rumour that Xena would die at the hands of Samurai warriors, later confirmed by producers, caused a groundswell of fan concern even before the final episode aired.

'A Friend in Need' premièred at a special screening on 19 June at the Museum of Television and Radio in Beverly Hills, California. Rob Tapert, R. J. Stewart, Lucy Lawless and Renee O'Connor attended, along with an audience of several hundred, composed of press and fans. It was then broadcast in many American markets as a two-hour movie on 23 June.

Opposite Page: Xena reaches the end of her journey in 'A Friend in Need'.

The final episode of Xena provoked more critical debate than any previous story. Ratings for the second hour were the highest for the season, but while some critics praised 'A Friend in Need', others were disappointed. The US *TV Guide*'s 'Cheers & Jeers' column gave it "**Jeers** to a charnel conclusion." It complained that taking the series finale to Japan was "like locating the final episode of *Gunsmoke* onboard a pirate ship", and added that Xena's "gruesome death" was far worse: "We don't object to Xena going down fighting. But we liked her too much to see her butchered."

Among fans, the reaction was equally mixed. Some felt it was a sad but fitting end to the Warrior Princess' life, and found the episode moving and effective. Many others were bitterly disappointed at being denied a happy ending for Xena and Gabrielle. Some fans echoed *TV Guide* in their distress at the violent images of Xena's death, which they found unnecessarily brutal for such a beloved character.

In comments at the première screening, Tapert and his colleagues defended their choices. "People have had a very mixed reaction, but the finale was really based on where the series started, and it seemed to complete her journey looking for redemption," commented Tapert. "What people are finding most troubling is that Xena is dead and the great love story between them doesn't carry on in the traditional sense. But I thought the benefits of Xena passing the mantle on to Gabrielle was an important part of the journey." The producers had known that Xena's death would upset many fans, but felt strongly that it was the right choice. "I really thought Xena's death was appropriate," said Stewart, the episode's writer. "You don't really want to upset people, but we knew it would be emotional for the right reasons." Lawless concurred: "It was the strongest choice dramatically. This show never took the easy way out. I don't know why people want a neat, pat, set ending. It's not the way we started the show, it's not the way we did it on a day-to-day basis."

Tapert explained some of the thinking behind the decision: "When the series began, it was unique. Xena was introduced on *Hercules* as a villain with a very high body count [who] finds her mission, which is to redeem herself. We've always withheld that [ability to] forgive herself for what she's done. She's had to pay a great price — she was a war criminal, as painted on *Hercules*. So flash forward to six years later. We wanted to do a Japanese ghost story, and Xena is gonna be the ghost. We thought, 'How are we gonna bring her back to life again for the seventy-eighth time? Wait a minute — ultimate redemption may be here if she's *not* brought back to life.'"

With the end of Xena, Pacific Renaissance closed its doors after eight years in New Zealand, in which over 300 hours of television were produced. Plans for Xena movies, which had been under discussion for some time, were tabled during sixth season production, and later, in his comments about Xena's death, Tapert affirmed that there is always a way to bring someone back in Xena's universe. With or without new movies, Xena lives on. ⚔

THE WARRIOR PRINCESS

Written by: John Schulian

Directed by: Bruce Seth Green

Guest stars: Michael Hurst (Iolaus), Lucy Lawless (Xena), Elizabeth Hawthorne (Alcmene)

Air date: 13 March 1995 [this is the Monday of the week the episode first aired in syndication in the US.]

First Sight: Xena's chakram makes a dramatic entrance when she throws it and cuts the throat of her lieutenant, Estragon.

The vicious Warrior Princess, Xena, sets a trap for Hercules by tricking Iolaus into falling in love with her and turning him against his best friend. When Iolaus attacks Hercules, Xena expects that the demi-god will kill him, and then, in his distress, be easy prey for her soldiers.

In her first appearance as the Warrior Princess (having already played two other characters in *Hercules*), Lawless seems far more subtle, manipulative and talkative than the blunt and somewhat taciturn Xena of the series — perhaps because this Xena is also playing a part for most of the episode. There is also some impressive stunt work as Iolaus and a bad guy fight over and under a very placid horse.

Iolaus to Xena, in the middle of a fight

"You sure know how to show a guy a good time!"

Disclaimer: No disclaimer.

THE GAUNTLET

Written by: Robert Bielak

Directed by: Jack Perez

Guest stars: Robert Trebor (Salmoneus), Lucy Lawless (Xena), Matthew Chamberlain (Darphus)

Air date: 1 May 1995

When Xena saves a baby from a massacre ordered by her lieutenant, Darphus, he challenges her leadership and forces her to walk a gauntlet of soldiers. She survives and escapes, only to encounter Hercules, who spares her life after a duel. Salmoneus, having witnessed the baby incident, urges them to work together to stop Darphus. Xena refuses at first, but returns to join the fight.

Xena's insistence on saving the baby foreshadows (unintentionally) her giving up of her own child to protect him. The gauntlet scene resembles a similar scene in the Hong Kong action movie *The Bride with White Hair*. For the final cut of this episode, Salmoneus' part was beefed up and the violence was cut down to alleviate the grim tone. Dean O'Gorman (cousin Iloran) went on to star as the young Iolaus in *Young Hercules*.

Salmoneus, describing his captivity

"They humiliated me, they took my entire line of kitchen ware!"

Disclaimer: No disclaimer.

UNCHAINED HEART

Written by: John Schulian
Directed by: Bruce Seth Green
Guest stars: Michael Hurst (Iolaus),
Robert Trebor (Salmoneus), Lucy
Lawless (Xena), Matthew Chamberlain
(Darphus)
Air date: 8 May 1995

Xena, Hercules and Salmoneus learn that Darphus is back from the dead, and has Ares' hell hound Graegus to help him. On their way to stop him, the two heroes and their "official biographer" are joined by Iolaus, who spurns Xena until she saves his life in battle. After Salmoneus is captured, the three heroes invade Darphus' stronghold, rescue Salmoneus from Graegus' lair, and feed Darphus to the hell hound, who explodes into flame. After a last Herculean kiss, Xena rides off into the sunset in search of her redemption. Cue opening credits for a new television series…

Matthew Chamberlain later appears in *Xena* as Orpheus ('Girls Just Wanna Have Fun') and Crassus ('When in Rome'). In early outlines for this episode, Xena dies a heroic death in battle.

Xena to Salmoneus

"Are you a biographer or a comedian?"
"How about love slave? I'm versatile!"
"You're delusional!"

Disclaimer: No vicious beasts intent on taking over the world were harmed during the production of this motion picture.

'Unchained Heart'.

SINS OF THE PAST

Story by: Robert Tapert

Teleplay by: R. J. Stewart

Directed by: Doug Lefler

Guest stars: Darien Takle (Cyrene), Jay Laga'aia (Draco) [In season one, Renee O'Connor's 'Also Starring' credit ran after the episode title, it was subsequently incorporated into the series main title.]

Air date: 4 September 1995

First Sight: The first time we see Xena put 'the pinch' on someone and do her spin kick across her enemies' chests.

Renouncing her violent past, the Warrior Princess buries her weapons, only to retrieve them so she can rescue some villagers (including the feisty young Gabrielle) from a war band. In search of adventure, Gabrielle follows Xena home to Amphipolis, where Xena's mother and neighbours reject the warrior's offer of help against the warlord Draco. When Draco invades, Xena challenges him to a duel, which she wins with the help of Gabrielle and the villagers. Reconciled with her mother, she goes on her way with a new companion — Gabrielle.

An entertaining introduction to Xena's mother Cyrene, Gabrielle and her family, and the hunky warlord Draco. Rob Tapert plays a bearded villager whose head is stepped on by Draco in the duel and several production crew members also double as extras in the scene.

Xena to the Cyclops

"*You should find another line of work.*"

"*Like what? I'm a blind Cyclops, for cryin' out loud!*"

'Sins of the Past'.

Disclaimer: No disclaimer.

CHARIOTS OF WAR

Story by: Josh Becker & Jack Perez
Teleplay by: Adam Armus & Nora Kay Foster
Directed by: Harley Cokeliss
Guest stars: Nick Kokotakis (Darius), Jeff Thomas (Cycnus), Stuart Turner (Sphaerus)
Air date: 11 September 1995

Xena is wounded rescuing a peaceful village from a warlord's attack, and is rescued in turn by the widowed Darius and his young children. Meanwhile, Gabrielle befriends the warlord's son Sphaerus who is torn between desire for his father's approval and revulsion at his violence. As the warlord presses for a slaughter, Xena has to choose between the lure of peaceful family life and fighting to defend the innocent.

This episode's most memorable scene is a disturbing portrayal of Ancient Greek battle surgery with a hot poker. The chariot chase is a precursor to the climactic chase in 'The Return of Callisto'. Sphaerus is the first of many young men who will share a mutual attraction with Gabrielle early in the series.

Gabrielle to Xena

"I learned something really important today."
"That you can find goodness in unlikely places?"
"Yeah. And that I really, really hate chariots!"

Disclaimer: No disclaimer.

DREAMWORKER

Written by: Steven L. Sears
Directed by: Bruce Seth Green
Guest stars: Nathaniel Lees (Manus), Desmond Kelly (Elkton)
Air date: 18 September 1995

First Sight: A merchant shows Gabrielle where to wear a breast dagger. We'll see that dagger again...

Gabrielle is kidnapped by the priests of Morpheus, to be the God of Dreams' bride. When they try to force her to go through trials that will rob her of her blood innocence, she outwits them by talking and tricking her adversaries into fighting each other. Meanwhile, with help from a former priest called Elkton, Xena enters the dream world to try to rescue Gabrielle, but has to face shadows of her victims and her own evil side before she can save her friend.

This is the first episode to hand the dramatic choice between fighting and non-violence to Gabrielle rather than Xena. The dilemma will be a central part of the bard's character arc.

Xena, to Gabrielle

"The moment you pick up a weapon, you become a target, and the moment you kill, everything changes"

Disclaimer: No disclaimer.

CRADLE OF HOPE

Written by: Terence Winter
Directed by: Michael Levine
Guest stars: Mary Elizabeth McLynn
(Pandora), Edward Newborn (Gregor),
Simon Prast (Nemos)
Air date: 25 September 1995

Catch the Baby, Round One:
During a fight, Xena and Gabrielle toss
the baby to each other over the bad
guys' heads, and Xena tosses him
straight up high in between kicks
and punches.

While King Gregor and his evil councillor Nemos search for an infant prophesied to inherit his throne, Xena and Gabrielle search for the mother of an abandoned baby. Along the way they rescue Pandora, the guardian of a dangerous box, and Xena infiltrates the castle as a dancing girl to find out what kind of man Gregor is.

A baby being put in a basket to escape execution recalls the story of Moses in the Old Testament Book of Exodus. In one fight scene, we see Xena's 'flame thrower' trick for the first time, when she chugs a swig of liquor then blows a fiery breath in Nemos' face.

Gabrielle
"Do you know there's a reward out for us? It's over a thousand dinars. I'm tempted to turn myself in."

Disclaimer: No babies were harmed during the production of this motion picture.

THE PATH NOT TAKEN

Written by: Julie Sherman
Directed by: Stephen L. Posey
Guest stars: Bobby Hosea
(Marcus), Stephen Tozer (Mezentius)
Air date: 2 October 1995

First Sight: Mezentius has the series'
first Ancient Greek hot tub.

An arms dealer kidnaps a princess so he can profit from a war between two feuding kingdoms. When Xena pretends to be the bad Warrior Princess so she can infiltrate his stronghold, she discovers that his lieutenant is her old lover, Marcus. Marcus stops Xena's rescue, but when his boss tries to shoot the innocent princess, he sacrifices himself to save her.

Xena and Marcus remember old times in a room full of weapons — how romantic! Lawless sings the dirge over Marcus' funeral; Xena's singing of this melody will become a regular feature of funerals in the series. This is the first Gabrielle-lite episode.

Marcus, to Xena
"You know, there is something different about you now. Before, you were so determined, like you always had something to prove. But now… it's like now you have the answer, when I've never even found the question."

Disclaimer: No disclaimer.

THE RECKONING

Written by: Peter Allan Fields

Directed by: Charles Siebert

Guest star: Kevin Smith (Ares)

Air date: 16 October 1995

Ares frames Xena for the murder of some villagers, and sets her up for a lynching, but it's all a plot to tempt her back to his service. Gabrielle sticks by Xena through the trial, a threatened lynching and even a whack on the head that should have killed her. Finally, Xena pretends she'll join Ares, and tricks him into bringing the murdered villagers back to life.

Kevin Smith makes the first of many appearances in *Xena* and *Hercules* as the God of War, and when Ares reveals his passion for Xena in a vision, she's tempted. Who wouldn't be? Meanwhile, Gabrielle shows that she can be a pretty good detective and advocate. Also, Argo finally gets a name instead of being just "my horse" or even "boy" (in 'Sins of the Past', when they obviously hadn't yet decided which sex *she* would be).

Xena to Gabrielle, after Gabrielle punches her

"What was that?"

"Payback for hitting me."

"Feel better?"

"I think I broke my hand. But I do feel better."

'The Reckoning'.

Disclaimer: No disclaimer.

THE TITANS

Written by: R. J. Stewart
Directed by: Eric Brevig
Guest stars: Mark Raffety
(Hyperion), Amanda Tollemache
(Theia), Edward Campbell (Crias),
Andy Anderson (Hesiod), Paolo
Rotondo (Phyleus)
Air date: 30 October 1995

When Gabrielle accidentally awakens three Titans, they mistake her for a goddess, until the power goes to her head. While Xena hatches a plan to stop the disgruntled Hyperion from awakening an army of Titans, Gabrielle sneaks into their cave on her own to find the chant that will turn them back to stone.

Gabrielle gets to show off the scholarly turn that makes her good bard material, when she teaches the villagers how to chant different styles of Greek poetry. By waking the Titans, she also reveals that she's a virgin. The camera effects that create the gigantic Titans are seamless: watch for a Titanic foot kicking through a wall in the same frame as three little mortals.

Xena, on hearing that Gabrielle is missing
"If the Titans caught her, we could be facing thousands by now. On the bright side, if anyone can stall, it's Gabrielle."

Disclaimer: No disclaimer.

PROMETHEUS

Written by: R. J. Stewart
Directed by: Stephen Posey
Guest stars: Kevin Sorbo
(Hercules), Michael Hurst (Iolaus)
Air date: 6 November 1995

Incidentally: Michael Hurst broke his arm during production, giving a double meaning to the Disclaimer.

When Hera chains Prometheus, humans lose their ability to heal themselves. In order to recover a sword which can break his chains, Xena has to undergo an oracle's trial and a deadly labyrinth. Then she and Gabrielle ally with Hercules and Iolaus to free Prometheus so that mankind will not lose his gifts. Since both Xena and Hercules know that whoever frees the Titan will die, they fight with each other along the way about who gets to be a hero.

The dragon was the first significant CGI creature used in *Xena* — perhaps Hercules brought it with him. There is also a precursor to the King Arthur moment in 'Gabrielle's Hope', when Xena draws the Sword of Hephaestus from a stone.

Xena to Hercules
"You're not using your head."
"Sometimes you go with your heart, not your head."

Disclaimer: Iolaus was harmed during the production of this motion picture. However, the Green Egg Men went on to live long and prosperous lives.

DEATH IN CHAINS

Story by: Babs Greyhosky and Adam Armus & Nora Kay Foster

Teleplay by: Adam Armus & Nora Kay Foster

Directed by: Charles Siebert

Guest stars: Kate Hodge (Celesta), Ray Henwood (Sisyphus), Leslie Wing (Karis), Kieran Hutchinson (Talus), Erik Thomson (Hades)

Air date: 13 November 1995

Costume Change: Gabrielle's midriff makes its début in this episode, as her long skirt and blue blouse are replaced with a short skirt and surplice top.

'Prometheus'.

Hades asks Xena to rescue his sister Death from King Sisyphus, who has captured her so he won't die. The trouble is, neither will anyone else, including the gravely ill, the fatally injured and a nasty outlaw that Xena has killed, and who plans to capture Death for himself. Sisyphus' wife tries to change his mind, while Xena and her friends sneak into the castle to rescue Death before she dies.

Xena and Talus certainly show their bravery when they are showered with rats as they crawl through a sewer. During shooting, the rats nestled into Lawless' cleavage and bare legs, an experience which she recalled with disgust in later interviews.

Hades, to Xena as she strikes a defensive pose
"Hey, relax. I'm a big fan."

Disclaimer: No Jumbo-Sized Cocktail Rats were harmed during the production of this motion picture.

HOOVES AND HARLOTS

Written by: Steven L. Sears
Directed by: Jace Alexander
Guest stars: Danielle Cormack
(Ephiny), David Aston (Tyldus),
Alison Bruce (Melosa), Mark
Ferguson (Krykus)
Air date: 20 November 1995

First Sight: Gabrielle gets her staff.

After trying to protect a dying Amazon princess and consequently inheriting the princess' Right of Caste — making her the heir to the Amazon Queen Melosa — Gabrielle learns Amazon martial arts from the tough young Amazon Ephiny. Meanwhile, Xena tries to stop a warlord from starting a war between the Amazons and the Centaurs.

A splendid entrance for the Amazons, with their tiny costumes and their huge and beautiful feathered battle masks (which, according to Danielle Cormack, were very difficult to work in). Xena and Melosa have a ripping duel with spinning chobos, while leaping on and off a tower. Alison Bruce also appears as Talia in 'Animal Attraction' and Kahina in 'Legacy'.

Ephiny to Gabrielle
"Come. Now."
"I'm sorry, you must have me mistaken for a pet."

Disclaimer: No Males, Centaurs, or Amazons were harmed during the production of this motion picture.

THE BLACK WOLF

Written by: Alan Jay Glueckman
Directed by: Mario Di Leo
Guest stars: Robert Trebor
(Salmoneus), Kevin J. Wilson
(Xerxes), Nigel Harbrow (Koulos),
Emma Turner (Flora), Ian Hughes
(Diomedes)
Air date: 8 January 1996

Xena gets herself thrown into prison on purpose in order to rescue a childhood friend who is part of an outlaw gang fighting a tyrant. Salmoneus gets himself thrown into prison by accident for "messing around with Gabrielle's tomatoes." Gabrielle starts food fights in order to get herself thrown into prison to help Xena, and invents a stylish new item of headgear in the process — Xena's chakram.

In his first appearance in *Xena*, Salmoneus is hawking tie-in merchandise. Since it's a tie-in to a notorious outlaw, one has to ask why the soldiers of King Xerxes didn't toss him in prison long ago. The Black Wolf is Xena's nod to prison films, Robin Hood and other noble outlaws. There is also a moment that recalls *Spartacus*, when several Black Wolf followers protect their leader's identity by claiming to be the Black Wolf.

Salmoneus, doing his sales pitch
"I call it a Black Wolf pack. Wolf. Pack. Get it?"

Disclaimer: No disclaimer. This is the last episode to have no disclaimer.

BEWARE GREEKS BEARING GIFTS

Story by: Roy Thomas & Janis Hendler

Teleplay by: Adam Armus & Nora Kay Foster

Directed by: T. J. Scott

Guest stars: Galyn Gorg (Helen), Scott Garrison (Perdicas), Cameron Rhodes (Deiphobus), Warren Carl (Paris)

Air date: 15 January 1996

Helen of Troy asks Xena to come to the city and help her end the war. Instead, they are caught up in the treacherous plotting of Helen's brother-in-law, who sells out Troy to the Greeks and tries to take Helen for himself.

Production designer Robert Gillies convinced director Scott that he would have only a four-inch model Trojan horse to work with, until he unveiled the full-sized critter. On the other hand, the Greeks rushing in the gates of Troy may well be the world's smallest invading army. As well as the fall of Troy, Gabrielle and Perdicas rekindle their flame in this episode, which will prove fatal for Perdicas in season two.

Eagle Eye: Watch for spiders crawling out of a skull.

Paris to Helen

"I don't know how all this happened. I just wanted to love you."

"No. You wanted to own me."

Disclaimer: No oversized Polynesian-style Bamboo Horses were harmed during the production of this motion picture. However, many wicker lawn chairs gave their lives.

'Beware Greeks Bearing Gifts'.

ATHENS CITY ACADEMY OF THE PERFORMING BARDS

Written by: R. J. Stewart
& Steven L. Sears

Directed by: Jace Alexander

Guest stars: Dean O'Gorman
(Orion/Homer), Graham Moore
(Polonius)

Air date: 22 January 1996

Incidentally: Is 'Stallonus' an ancestor of a certain modern star of movies long on action and short on plot?

I n the series' first clip show, Gabrielle enters a bard contest, but soon finds that her fiercest competition comes from the father of a fellow competitor, who thinks his son's chances are threatened by her ability to hold everyone spellbound with stories of Xena's adventures.

In addition to clips from previous episodes, clips from *Spartacus* and the Steve Reeves *Hercules* movies enhance the storytelling.

Gabrielle to Xena
"The family he had sought had travelled the world with him. The only family he had ever known, ever needed, was standing right beside him."
"Thanks for being my family. You're like a sister to me. Now go get your dream."

Disclaimer: The producers would like to acknowledge and pay tribute to Stanley Kubrick, Kirk Douglas and all those who were involved with the making of the film classic "SPARTACUS". Additional thanks to Steve Reeves.

A FISTFUL OF DINARS

Written by: Steven L. Sears
& R. J. Stewart

Directed by: Josh Becker

Guest stars: Jeremy Roberts
(Thersites), Peter Daube (Petracles)

Air date: 29 January 1996

Eagle Eye: Watch for a shadow moving the wrong way at sunrise. And that skull full of spiders pops up again, too.

X ena and Gabrielle join forces with a band of outlaws on a treasure hunt — not for the treasure, but to stop anyone from capturing the Ambrosia that can make a mortal into a god.

Jeremy Roberts has played several guest roles in *Hercules* and *Xena*, as well as *Buffy the Vampire Slayer*, *The X-Files* and many other television shows and movies. The title is a nod to the Clint Eastwood Western *A Fistful of Dollars*.

Temple priest, arresting Gabrielle and Thersites just as Xena and Petracles take out the temple guards
"Your doom is assured!… However, I could be mistaken!"

Disclaimer: No Ambrosia was spilled, spoiled or in any way harmed during the production of this motion picture. (Thanks to the indefinite shelf life of marshmallows.)

WARRIOR... PRINCESS

Written by: Brenda Lilly

Directed by: Michael Levine

Guest stars: Iain Rea (Philemon), Norman Forsey (King Lias), Latham Gaines (Mineus)

Air date: 5 February 1996

First Sight: Gabrielle's scrolls make their first appearance.

X ena switches places with her look-alike Princess Diana, to protect her from assassins. Xena curtseys abominably, gets her hair brushed 835 strokes and breaks Diana's harp when she's not using it as a bow. Diana rides Argo side-saddle, brushes her tail 835 strokes and has her first encounter with poverty, when she's not tying red bows to Xena's breastplate. Even in a gown, Xena catches the assassins and helps Diana match up with her true love instead of his stuffy brother.

In Lawless' first multi-role episode, she plays both Xena and the dainty Princess Diana. Among the many switched identity gags, Xena as Diana beats up a whole squad of bad guys and still manages to look angelic every time Philemon glances her way. At one point there is a glimpse of water being splashed from off camera onto a burning stunt man.

Diana to Gabrielle, and a little girl
"It's my round killing thing."
"Chakram."
"Bless you!"

Disclaimer: Neither Xena nor her remarkably coincidental identical twin, Diana, were harmed during the production of this motion picture.

'Warrior... Princess'.

MORTAL BELOVED

Written by: R. J. Stewart
Directed by: Garth Maxwell
Guest stars: Bobby Hosea
(Marcus), Paul Willis (Atyminius)
Air date: 12 February 1996

When the villain Atyminius steals Hades' Helmet of Invisibility, he turns the Underworld upside down. Fortunately, Marcus is allowed to return from the dead to help Xena recover the helmet, and they hunt Atyminius through this world and the next.

Xena and Marcus fight with some wild and weird computer generated Harpies in the Underworld. Erik Thompson reprises his role as Hades, and look out for Michael Hurst cameoing as Charon, the grouchy ferryman of the dead. Hades' Helmet of Invisibility will appear again in 'God Fearing Child'.

Charon, to Xena

"We got everything turned upside down: all the wicked are in the Elysian Fields, all the good guys are down in Tartarus, and now we got tourists already!"

Disclaimer: No Winged Harpies were harmed or sent to a fiery grave during the production of this motion picture.

THE ROYAL COUPLE OF THIEVES

Written by: Steven L. Sears
Directed by: John Cameron
Guest star: Bruce Campbell
(Autolycus)
Air date: 19 February 1996

Xena teams up with the self-styled 'King of Thieves' to recover a chest containing the world's most powerful weapon before it can fall into the hands of warlords. They masquerade as an assassin and a concubine, fall overboard, and Xena has a pressure point duel with the real assassin, before eventually recovering the chest — which proves to be the Ark of the Covenant.

The first of a pair of capers (the other one is season three's 'Vanishing Act') in which Xena and Autolycus use a masquerade to get the goods. In an unusual stunt sequence, Xena chases Autolycus through the streets of a town by running along the clothes-lines!

Autolycus, pretending to be a famous assassin

"Of course, the trick to killing someone with an apricot is in the wrist..."

Disclaimer: No Ancient and Inflexible Rules governing moral behaviour were harmed during the production of this motion picture.

THE PRODIGAL

Written by: Chris Manheim
Directed by: John T. Kretchmer
Guest stars: Tim Thomerson
(Meleager), Willa O'Neill (Lila)
Air date: 4 March 1996

Gabrielle returns home to Poteidaia to search for her lost nerve, but instead finds her sister angry at her desertion and the town threatened by a warlord, with a washed-up, drunken mercenary, Meleager the Mighty, as their only defence. Gabrielle uses Xena's lessons to sober up Meleager and teach her neighbours how to defend themselves.

The townspeople of Poteidaia defeat their enemies with a whole series of clever, rustic traps — including a perfectly timed slapstick frying pan in the face. Renee O'Connor and Willa O'Neill give us some effective sister bonding, while Tim Thomerson's first appearance as Meleager the Mighty is a delicious performance that recalls Lee Marvin's drunken gunfighter in *Cat Ballou*.

Gabrielle, creating a sexy diversion
"*Oh! Oh! Oh, Meleager! No wonder they call you 'The Mighty'!*"

Disclaimer: Meleager the Mighty, the generally tipsy and carousing warrior-for-hire, was not harmed during the production of this motion picture.

'The Prodigal'.

ALTARED STATES

Written by: Chris Manheim
Directed by: Michael Levine
Guest stars: David Ackroyd
(Anteus), David de Lautour (Icus),
Karl Urban (Maell)
Air date: 22 April 1996

Fighting With Fish, Round One:
Xena beats up Maell's followers with the
Catch of the Day.

While trying to prevent a pious father from sacrificing his young son to his monotheistic god, Xena and Gabrielle discover that the man's jealous older son has tricked his father into believing that he is the voice of god.

Abraham's sacrifice of Isaac is related in the Old Testament Book of Genesis, but that deep male voice telling Anteus to spare his son comes from the 1950s Biblical epics! Watch out for the twist at the end though — could this be the first 'appearance' in the *Xena*verse of the God of Eli? It definitely is the first appearance on *Xena* of actor Karl Urban, who is of course much better known for playing Cupid and Caesar.

Xena to Anteus
"I am asking you to spare your son."
"And teach him what? That faith is just for those times when it's convenient to believe? What's the good in sparing his life, if I rob him of the very thing that makes it worth living?"

Disclaimer: No Unrelenting or Severely Punishing Deities were harmed during the production of this motion picture.

TIES THAT BIND

Written by: Adam Armus & Nora
Kay Foster
Directed by: Charles Siebert
Guest stars: Tom Atkins (Atrius),
Kevin Smith (Ares)
Air date: 29 April 1996

Xena meets an ageing warrior who claims to be her long-lost father Atrius. However, after bonding with some rescues and childhood memories, Xena takes over a warlord's army and nearly massacres a village in revenge for their torture of her father, before 'Atrius' reveals that he's really Ares trying another scheme to win Xena back.

Gabrielle physically stands up to Xena for the first time in this episode, by hitting her with a pitchfork. Sometimes talking just isn't enough! In 'The Furies', Xena will claim that Ares is her father in order to exonerate her mother of her mortal father's murder. Maybe this episode is where she got the idea.

Xena, to Gabrielle
"We both have families we were born into. But sometimes families change, and we have to build our own. For me, our friendship binds us closer than blood ever could."

Disclaimer: No Fathers, Spiritual or Biological, were harmed during the production of this motion picture.

THE GREATER GOOD

Written by: Steven L. Sears

Directed by: Gary Jones

Guest stars: Robert Trebor (Salmoneus), Peter McCauley (Talmadeus)

Air date: 6 May 1996

Nearly Departed: Xena dies for the first time — or seems to.

'The Greater Good'.

S oft drink magnate 'Lord Seltzer', aka Salmoneus, seeks Xena's protection from a warlord. Unfortunately, Xena succumbs to a mysterious poison, and Salmoneus, Gabrielle and Argo have to become heroes in order to save Lord Seltzer's employees from the warlord.

Callisto makes her first appearance here, though we won't see her face until the next episode. Gabrielle and Argo get to kick butt in true Xena style — though Gabrielle's first attempt at Xena's war cry is a flop! This episode also features a huge water fight, and a mêlée that has not Xena, but Gabrielle at its centre. Robert Trebor and Renee O'Connor steal the show with their poignant reactions to Xena's apparent death.

Gabrielle to Xena

"Argo doesn't like me."

"Sometimes you have to have patience with things that annoy you."

"Oh, I never said she annoyed me."

"I wasn't talking to you."

Disclaimer: Excessive belching can cause brain damage and social ostracism. Kids, please don't give in to peer pressure. Play it safe.

CALLISTO

Written by: R. J. Stewart
Directed by: T. J. Scott
Guest stars: Hudson Leick
(Callisto), Ted Raimi (Joxer)
Air date: 13 May 1996

Eagle Eye: Watch for the world's tiniest sword.

T he savage Callisto lays waste to the countryside in order to blacken Xena's name and lure her into mortal combat, in revenge for the murders of her family by Xena's army. When Xena captures Callisto, she plays expertly on Xena's guilt until she can escape and then capture Gabrielle to bait a new trap. Meanwhile, warrior wannabe Joxer tries to prove he's worthy of Callisto's army.

In the most important episode of the first season, Callisto and Joxer make superb entrances, each in their own inimitable style: Callisto covers herself in blood and Joxer gets his butt kicked. Incidentally, the duel on the ladders is one of the most complex stunt sequences ever filmed for the series, consisting of over 145 different shots.

Xena to Callisto
"What happened to you was terrible. It was my fault and I'm sorry."
"Oh. Well. That makes all the difference! And now we can be the best of friends. [spits] That's what I think of your apology!"

Disclaimer: Joxer's nose was not harmed during the production of this motion picture. However, his crossbow was severely damaged.

'Callisto'.

DEATH MASK

Written by: Peter Allen Fields

Directed by: Stewart Main

Guest stars: Joseph Kell (Toris), Michael Lawrence (Cortese)

Air date: 6 June 1996

Breast Dagger Watch: Watch for it popping up again.

Xena reunites with her older brother Toris, who has infiltrated the army of the warlord who plundered Amphipolis and killed their brother Lyceus. But Xena soon finds she has her hands full trying to keep Toris from either murdering or being murdered before they can bring the warlord to justice.

Hats off to the casting department for finding Joseph Kell, whose remarkable resemblance to Lawless sells their relationship even more than their performances.

Malik to Xena

"Now, my dear, let's not waste time in senseless pleas for mercy or silly games. Right to it, shall we?"

"Have it your way. [Xena punches him] Right to it! I like that!"

Disclaimer: No messenger doves were harmed during the production of this motion picture. However, several are reportedly missing in action and search-and-rescue efforts are underway.

IS THERE A DOCTOR IN THE HOUSE?

Written by: Patricia Manney

Directed by: T. J. Scott

Guest stars: Ray Woolf (Marmax), Danielle Cormack (Ephiny)

Air date: 29 July 1996

Nearly Departed: Gabrielle dies for the first time, and is revived by Xena.

M*A*S*H meets the ancient world when Xena and Gabrielle rescue the pregnant Ephiny from a battlefield. They take refuge in a healing temple full of wounded, where Ephiny's Centaur son is born. Xena shows off some remarkably modern battlefield medicine and the women teach a wounded general a few things about peace.

Director Scott traded for the nine days he needed to shoot 'Callisto' by delivering this episode in only five days. Lucy Lawless said that Gabrielle's death scene was the first time she had ever "given it all up" as an actress, letting go of all control and being "really real and really raw".

Xena, frantically trying to revive Gabrielle

"Come on, breathe! You never ran from anything in your whole life! Come on, fight! Don't you leave me! Wake up! Wake up!"

Disclaimer: Being that war is hell, lots of people were harmed during the production of this motion picture (but since television is a dramatic medium of make-believe, all casualties removed their prosthetic make-up and went home unscathed).

ORPHAN OF WAR

Written by: Steven L. Sears

Directed by: Charles Siebert

Guest star: David Taylor (Solan)

Air date: 30 September 1996

Costume Change: Say goodbye to Gabrielle's brown surplice top, and hello to her green lace-up bodice.

Xena and Gabrielle travel to a Centaur village to stop a warlord from capturing the Ixion Stone, which holds all the evil of the first Centaurs. Xena is also reunited with her son, Solan, who has been raised by a Centaur without knowing who his mother is.

This is the first appearance of Solan, who will play a critical role in the Rift story arc during the third season. It's also the first time we hear of Borias, and the first mention of Xena's warlord title: 'Destroyer of Nations'.

Xena, giving the infant Solan to Kaleipus

"Take this child. He's my son, and the son of Borias.
If he stays with me, he'll become a target for all those who
hate me. And he'll learn things a child should never know.
He'll become like me."

Disclaimer: No Sleazy Warlords who deem it necessary to drink magic elixirs that turn them into scaly Centaurs were harmed during the production of this motion picture.

'Orphan of War'.

REMEMBER NOTHING

Story by: Steven L. Sears & Chris Manheim

Teleplay by: Chris Manheim

Directed by: Anson Williams

Guest stars: Aaron Devitt (Lyceus), Robert Harte (Maphius)

Air date: 7 October 1996

Eagle Eye: Watch for a loaf of bread seasoned with dog saliva and a cup of wine flavoured with spit.

The Fates place Xena in an alternate life in which she never became the Warrior Princess, and where she can stay as long as she doesn't spill blood. In that life, her brother Lyceus is still alive, but her mother is dead and Gabrielle is a warlord's embittered slave. Cue a battle against inevitable destiny, as Xena tries to rescue Gabrielle and fight the injustices around her without becoming a warrior again.

The Fates' proscription against drawing blood evidently doesn't prohibit other kinds of violence, as Xena can (and does) shove, punch and kick without changing her fate.

Gabrielle the slave, to Xena

"I don't know whether to thank you or to hate you. At least before, I had forgotten what a real life was. You showed me all that, gave me hope, made me think maybe it wasn't too late for me."

Disclaimer: Xena's memory was not damaged or… What was I saying?

THE GIANT KILLER

Written by: Terence Winter

Directed by: Gary Jones

Guest stars: Todd Ripton (Goliath), Antony Starr (David)

Air date: 14 October 1996

Xena meets up with an old friend, the giant Goliath, who has become a mercenary for the Philistines, but after Xena and Gabrielle rescue David and some other Hebrews from the Philistines, Xena and Goliath find themselves on opposite sides. Xena must help David to devise a way to kill her friend, while Gabrielle develops warm feelings for the handsome young bard David.

Once again, the scale effects for the giant are excellent, in particular a scene where Xena and Goliath are both running through the same ruins in the same shot, with Goliath smashing them as he passes. The Old Testament story of David and Goliath is told in 1 Samuel 17. Saul and David are the first historical persons to appear in *Xena*.

Gabrielle to Dagon, putting her head on the block on top of David's

"You're going to have to kill the both of us!"
"All right."
"What?"

Disclaimer: No Bible myths or icons were irreparably mangled during the production of this motion picture.

GIRLS JUST WANNA HAVE FUN

Written by: Adam Armus & Nora Kay Foster

Directed by: T. J. Scott

Guest stars: Ted Raimi (Joxer), Matthew Chamberlain (Orpheus), Anthony Ray Parker (Bacchus)

Air date: 21 October 1996

ena and Gabrielle go up against the dread god Bacchus, who has been turning village maidens into bloodsucking Bacchae. They're aided (if that's the right word) by Joxer, and by the head — just the head, mind you — of the famed musician Orpheus. Gabrielle and Xena both get bitten by the Bacchae before the fun is over.

Xena's first Halloween episode gives us T. J. Scott's rock-horror video camera effects and an Ancient Greek take on the vampire legend. The visual pairing of Joxer in his pointy hat and the straw stuffed dummy that supports Orpheus' head recalls the Scarecrow and Tin Man of *The Wizard of Oz*.

Joxer to Gabrielle, and Xena

"*A package, from Orpheus to Xena.*"

"*What is it?*"

"*It speaks for itself.*"

[*Xena pulls out Orpheus' still living head*]

Disclaimer: No Bloodsucking Bacchae were harmed during the production of this motion picture. However, a few Driads lost their heads.

'Girls Just Wanna Have Fun'.

THE RETURN OF CALLISTO

Written by: R. J. Stewart
Directed by: T. J. Scott
Guest stars: Hudson Leick
(Callisto), Ted Raimi (Joxer), Scott
Garrison (Perdicas)
Air date: 28 October 1996

Nearly Departed: Callisto sinks into quicksand and dies. The ending — Xena watches her sinking and ignores her pleas for help — was only determined late in the editing process.

G abrielle agrees to marry Perdicas just as Callisto escapes from prison. When Callisto murders Perdicas, Gabrielle demands that Xena teach her how to kill, so she can take revenge.

The second entry in the riveting story of Callisto brings Gabrielle face to face with her core values, reveals Joxer's courage and sends Callisto to Tartarus. T. J. Scott added the chariot race to give the script a spectacular finish.

Xena to Gabrielle

"Gabrielle, if you're taken over by hatred, Callisto wins."
"I got news for you. She's already won! The little innocent Gabrielle is dead, and there's no getting her back."

Disclaimer: Although Xena finally conquered her dark nemesis Callisto, it took her weeks to get the sand out of her leather unmentionables.

WARRIOR... PRINCESS... TRAMP

Written by: R. J. Stewart
Directed by: Josh Becker
Guest star: Ted Raimi (Joxer)
Air date: 4 November 1996

Catch the Baby, Round Two:
This time, the baby's in a basket hung from a rope, and zooms up and down over a fire as the fight pulls the rope this way and that.

A villain kidnaps Princess Diana and hires the trampy Meg to impersonate her. In the subsequent mayhem, the three look-alikes, Meg, Diana and Xena, have a field day posing as each other, Gabrielle gets thrown in prison and Joxer gets very confused about his love life.

Lawless adds Meg to Xena and Diana in a comic tour de force which she carries off so skilfully that we always know exactly which look-alike we're watching, no matter which costume she's in.

Joxer to Xena

"How am I supposed to know who the real Diana is?"
"Well, if you come across a woman and she looks exactly like me, and she displays any interest in you whatsoever as a man, that's the bad one."

Disclaimer: Neither Xena nor her remarkably coincidental identical twin, Diana, were harmed during the production of this motion picture. Meg, however, suffered minor injuries while preparing Aardvark nuggets for King Lias.

INTIMATE STRANGER

Written by: Steven L. Sears

Directed by: Gary Jones

Guest stars: Hudson Leick (Callisto), Ted Raimi (Joxer), Kevin Smith (Ares)

Air date: 11 November 1996

Breast Dagger Watch:
There it is, tied to Gabrielle's staff.

When, with some help from Ares, Callisto switches bodies with Xena and escapes from Tartarus, Hades lets Xena loose in Callisto's body to pursue her. Meanwhile Callisto plays havoc among Xena's friends and family, and has a tumble with Ares.

Lawless and Leick have great fun swapping roles in this episode. The warrior women go all out hand-to-hand in a fight that needs no special effects but the intensity of their hatred. Because Lawless needed time to recover from breaking her pelvis in a riding accident, the ending of this episode was rewritten to leave Callisto in Xena's body, allowing Hudson Leick to play the Warrior Princess for a while longer.

Gabrielle, to Xena

"This is such a mess! You wish you hadn't killed her, Joxer wishes he had killed her and I wish she'd never been born. I guess Callisto won after all."

Disclaimer: Argo was not harmed during the production of this motion picture. However, she is undergoing intensive psychotherapy to help her work through her resentment and feelings of distrust toward Xena.

'Intimate Stranger'.

TEN LITTLE WARLORDS

Written by: Paul Robert Coyle
Directed by: Charles Siebert
Guest stars: Ted Raimi (Joxer),
Charles Siebert (Sisyphus), Kevin
Smith (Ares), Hudson Leick (Xena
[Yes, you read that right!])
Air date: 18 November 1996

Fighting With Fish, Round Two:
Gabrielle picks a fight with some
fishmongers. Watch for a flying lobster.

Ares loses his sword, and with it his powers. In an effort to recover Ares' stolen weapon, he and Xena (still in Callisto's body) join King Sisyphus' contest to determine the new God of War. But Sisyphus' real plan is to take Ares' place and escape from Tartarus forever. Meanwhile, Joxer and Gabrielle kill a ferocious fan, er, monster.

Hudson Leick continues filling in for Lawless, and her portrayal of Xena is so accomplished that in remembering the episode, it's easy to forget Lawless wasn't in it until the last shot. Kevin Smith's performance as Ares develops exponentially, as the God of War experiences mortality for the first time (but not the last).

Ares
"I've been hanged, swung over a fire and nearly shish kebabed on razor sharp spikes. How do you mortals get through the day?"

Disclaimer: No one was harmed during the production of this motion picture. However, Xena's ability to recover her body was severely impeded by Lawless' unexpected mishap.

A SOLSTICE CAROL

Written by: Chris Manheim
Directed by: John T. Kretchmer
Guest stars: Joe Berryman
(Senticles), Peter Vere Jones
(King Silvas)
Air date: 9 December 1996

Eagle Eye: Watch for a Hercules action figure.

On Winter Solstice Eve, Xena and Gabrielle arrive in a kingdom where celebrating the Solstice has been forbidden by the king, Silvas, who has also sent his soldiers to evict an orphanage. With the help of the toymaker Senticles and the orphans, they masquerade as the Fates to teach the king the true meaning of Solstice.

Sound familiar? *Xena's* reworking of A *Christmas Carol* pulls out all the holiday treats and suggests an alternative origin for Santa Claus. Among the festive stunts is a fight with toys and Xena 'gift-wrapping' a squad of soldiers by throwing her chakram with long ribbons tied to it. Listen for 'Jingle Bells' when Gabrielle conks some soldiers with a handbell.

The disguised King Silvas, to a soldier trying to arrest him
"Don't be absurd. I am the king."
"Right, and I'm the Queen of the Amazons. Seize them!"

Disclaimer: Senticles was not harmed during the production of this motion picture. However, several chimneys are in dire need of repair.

THE XENA SCROLLS

Story by: Robert Sidney Mellette
Teleplay by: Adam Armus & Nora Kay Foster
Directed by: Charlie Haskell
Guest stars: Ted Raimi (Jacques S'er), Kevin Smith (Ares)
Air date: 13 January 1997

Macedonia, 1940. Treasure hunter Janice Covington (O'Connor), classical scholar Melinda Pappas (Lawless) and brush salesman... er free French officer Jacques S'er are in a race with the slimy villain John Smythe to find a treasure that "has the power to turn myth into history, history into myth" — the Xena Scrolls!

This fan favourite manages to transform the dreaded clip episode into first-rate entertainment. Lawless and O'Connor play the reverse of their usual characters, while Raimi's French accent puts Inspector Clouseau to shame. The producer in the tag is played by *Xena's* executive producer Rob Tapert — now we know where he *really* got the idea for *Xena: Warrior Princess*.

Jacques S'er to Janice Covington
"I could have kill' you in the blin' of an eye."
"A what?"
"Blin' — blin'! Don' you speak English?"

Disclaimer: No Hollywood producers were harmed during the production of this motion picture.

HERE SHE COMES...
MISS AMPHIPOLIS

Written by: Chris Manheim
Directed by: Marina Sargenti
Guest stars: Karen Dior (Miss Artiphys), Robert Trebor (Salmoneus)
Air date: 20 January 1997

Alternate Disclaimer: In loving memory of Keith K. Walsh*.
*Chris Manheim's brother and the inspiration for the Miss Artiphys character.

Salmoneus persuades Xena to enter his beauty pageant, so she can find out who's trying to start a war by killing the contestants. Xena wears a blonde wig and ribbons to mingle with the contestants, while Gabrielle wears a turban and a thick accent to take on the sponsors...

As a former Mrs New Zealand, Lawless is an experienced pageant contestant. Karen Dior is also known as female impersonator Geoff Gann. So does that passionate smooch Miss Artiphys lays on Xena count as subtext?

Gabrielle to Salmoneus, about the pageant
"A feeble excuse for men to exploit and degrade women."
"Since when did we need an excuse?"

Disclaimer: No ribbons were harmed during the production of this motion picture. However, several experienced severe motion sickness.

DESTINY

Story by: Robert Tapert

Teleplay by: R. J. Stewart & Steven L. Sears

Directed by: Robert Tapert

Guest stars: Ebonie Smith (M'lila), Karl Urban (Julius Caesar), Nathaniel Lees (Niklio)

Air date: 27 January 1997

Nearly Departed: Xena dies for real, for the first time. In the flashback, she is crucified for the first time but doesn't die.

'Here She Comes... Miss Amphipolis'.

In the present, Xena is critically injured, and Gabrielle takes her on a desperate journey to a special healer. In the flashback, Xena recalls her first meeting with Caesar, and the betrayal that made her into the 'Destroyer of Nations'.

Karl Urban's Caesar makes an imperious entrance. The costume department goes over the top with Caesar's Roman armour, Xena's pirate costume and that hot little red dress! M'lila (or her stunt double) shows off some real Hong Kong-style fighting, and the story of Xena's past includes where she learned her pressure points trick. And if the Roman guard with the hammer looks familiar, it's because he's played by Lawless' brother, Daniel Ryan.

Caesar, to Xena

"Where did you steal that dress? Maybe someday you can go back for the rest of it."

Disclaimer: Julius Caesar was not harmed during the production of this motion picture. However, the producers deny any responsibility for any unfortunate acts of betrayal causing some discomfort.

THE QUEST

Story by: Chris Manheim & Steven
L. Sears & R. J. Stewart

Teleplay by: Steven L. Sears

Directed by: Michael Levine

Guest stars: Bruce Campbell
(Autolycus), Melinda Clarke (Velasca),
Danielle Cormack (Ephiny), Michael
Hurst (Iolaus)

Air date: 3 February 1997

While Gabrielle plans an Amazon funeral for Xena, Xena's spirit jumps into Autolycus so that he can help her steal her body and the Ambrosia needed to revive her. Meanwhile, Velasca plots to take Gabrielle's place as Amazon Queen and ends up going for godhood.

Autolycus discovers a novel new use for an Amazon bodice pin in this episode. Bruce Campbell and Renee O'Connor both have fun playing Xena when she borrows their bodies, and that kiss between Gabrielle and the spirit of Xena certainly fired up the subtext!

Autolycus, to Xena in his body
"Well, nature's calling. How do you want to handle that?"

Disclaimer: Xena's body was not harmed during the production of this motion
picture. However, it took weeks for Autolycus to get his swagger back.

A NECESSARY EVIL

Written by: Paul Robert Coyle

Directed by: Mark Beesley

Guest stars: Melinda Clarke
(Velasca), Hudson Leick (Callisto)

Air date: 10 February 1997

Nearly Departed: Callisto falls into a
river of lava with Velasca.

When Velasca makes herself a god and attacks the Amazons, Xena decides she needs an immortal to fight a god. She makes a devil's bargain with the only one she's got — Callisto (who became an immortal in the *Hercules* episode 'Surprise'), who agrees to fight Velasca for a chance to capture some Ambrosia. While Gabrielle endures the anguish of being allied with her husband's murderer, Xena has to stay one step ahead of Callisto to keep her from turning on her supposed allies.

Hudson Leick gives another powerful performance, as Callisto relives her own worst memory when she makes Xena publicly confess to the murder of her parents. The battle on the rope bridge is spectacular, but one can't help wondering why on earth Xena told Gabrielle to give Callisto the Ambrosia.

Xena to Callisto
"You may be immortal, but I can still do damage. How'd you like to spend eternity in five pieces?"
"Oh, Xena, how I've missed you!"

Disclaimer: The reputation of the Amazon Nation was not harmed, despite Velasca's
overly radical adherence to an otherwise valid belief system.

A DAY IN THE LIFE

Written by: R. J. Stewart
Directed by: Michael Hurst
Guest stars: Murray Keane
(Hower), Alison Wall (Minya)
Air date: 17 February 1997

Hot Tub Watch: More subtext fun
with Xena and Gabrielle sharing a
hot tub.

Xena and Gabrielle go through an ordinary day: fighting before breakfast, fishing for breakfast, staving off admirers, having a bath, using frying pans for weapons, chakrams for fish knives and scrolls for toilet paper. Along the way, they happen to rescue two villages from a giant and a warlord's army, and they bicker — a lot!

A novel format, with headings in Greek and English opening each scene. Xena's kite battle with the giant Gareth was originally filmed for 'The Giant Killer'. Alison Wall later returns several times as Minya and also plays a twentieth century Xena fan in 'Send in the Clones'.

Soldier under the pinch to Xena, interrupting her argument with Gabrielle

"Uhh, could you guys talk about this some other time?"
"Oh, yeah, I've cut off the..."
"... Flow of blood to my brain. I've heard all about it. What do you want to know?"

'A Necessary Evil'.

Disclaimer: No Slippery Eels were harmed during the production of this motion picture, despite their reputation as a fine delicacy in select cultures of the known world.

FOR HIM THE BELL TOLLS

Written by: Adam Armus
& Nora Kay Foster

Directed by: Josh Becker

Guest stars: Ted Raimi (Joxer),
Alexandra Tydings (Aphrodite), Karl
Urban (Cupid)

Air date: 24 February 1997

A phrodite bets Cupid that she can make a great lover out of *any* man. So naturally she picks Joxer, and puts a spell on him so that every time he hears a bell ring he becomes a dashing hero. All the women duly swoon over him, including the very betrothed Princess Ileandra.

This is another episode produced during Lawless' hospitalisation, and instead of the Warrior Princess it gives us Cupid, Aphrodite, the Joxer song and a showcase for Ted Raimi's comic genius as he switches back and forth between Joxer the hero and Joxer the idiot. Who would ever have dreamt that Joxer could hold the hero's place in the climactic fight scene?

Xena, to Joxer

"The gods can't give us anything that isn't in our hearts. Aphrodite just used what was already there. The real Joxer may not be the best swordsman around, but he's always had the heart of a lion."

'For Him the Bell Tolls'.

Disclaimer: The producers wish to acknowledge the inspiration of Danny Kaye and pay tribute to the classic motion picture *The Court Jester*.

THE EXECUTION

Written by: Paul Robert Coyle
Directed by: Garth Maxwell
Guest stars: Tim Thomerson (Meleager), Tony Blackett (Arbus)
Air date: 7 April 1997

Gabrielle's old friend Meleager has been convicted of murder. Convinced of his innocence, Gabrielle breaks him out of jail and makes a run for it, while Xena goes in search of a witness, only to discover that the real criminal is the 'hanging judge' who's determined to punish *somebody*, whether they're guilty or not.

There are plenty of little delights in this straightforward whodunit, including Xena catching an arrow in her teeth and the executioner making a selection from his wardrobe of black robes. The old woman knitting is a nod to the character of Madame Defarge in Charles Dickens' A *Tale of Two Cities*.

Gabrielle to Xena, observing the old woman knitting beside the gallows
"When I'm that age, I hope I'm knitting socks!"
"Oh, don't worry about it. People in our line of work never get to be that age."

Disclaimer: By popular demand, "The Executioner" will bring back his comfortable lightweight cotton-flax blend robe in a variety of spring colors.

BLIND FAITH

Written by: Adam Armus & Nora Kay Foster
Directed by: Josh Becker
Guest star: Jeremy Callaghan (Palaemon)
Air date: 14 April 1997

A young aspiring bravo kidnaps Gabrielle in order to pick a fight with Xena, so he can make a name for himself by killing her. During the fight, Xena gets sprayed with sumac oil and starts to go blind. Meanwhile, Gabrielle has been sold to an evil prime minister who plans to use her in his scheme to inherit the throne by marrying her to the king — who's been dead for days.

The dead king's face during the 'wedding' to Gabrielle may be the creepiest sight in the whole series, but Gabrielle does learn the 'royal wave'. Jeremy Callaghan also plays Pompey in 'When in Rome' and 'A Good Day'.

Palaemon to Xena
"Admit it. I'm a very formidable foe."
"You're nothing but a stupid kid with a very limited life expectancy."

Disclaimer: Once again, Gabrielle's luck with men was harmed during the production of this motion picture.

ULYSSES

Written by: R. J. Stewart
Directed by: Michael Levine
Guest stars: John D'Aquino
(Ulysses), Rachel Blakely (Penelope)
Air date: 21 April 1997

Xena and Gabrielle encounter the legendary mariner on his way home from the Trojan War to reclaim his island kingdom and be reunited with his faithful wife Penelope. Xena helps Ulysses defeat the pirates preying on his home, but there is still one little obstacle in the way of happiness: Ulysses and Xena have fallen in love…

In this rewrite of the *Odyssey*, Poseidon makes his first appearance outside the credits, and a bunch of stunt men have a lot of fun jumping overboard. Although Xena and Gabrielle saw the end of the Trojan War only a few months ago, in Homer's epic Ulysses took ten years to get from Troy to Ithaca.

Xena to a miserable, seasick Gabrielle
"Don't lose your sense of humour. You're going to need it in rough seas."
"This isn't rough?"

Disclaimer: Despite Gabrielle's incessant hurling, Ulysses' ship was not harmed during the production of this motion picture.

THE PRICE

Written by: Steven L. Sears
Directed by: Oley Sassone
Guest stars: Paul Glover
(Menticles), Charles Mesure (Mercer)
Air date: 28 April 1997

Besieged in an Athenian fort by savage warriors of the Horde, Xena reverts to her ruthless warrior self, believing it's the only way to defeat a monstrous foe. But Gabrielle shows mercy to the wounded Horde warriors, and Xena realises that she can end the battle by challenging their chieftain to single combat.

Unusually for Xena, there are no fancy martial arts in sight in this relentless dramatisation of the brutality of war. The Horde warriors' fearsome war paint and headdresses make them look as savage and inhuman as Xena believes them to be. Charles Mesure later appeared as the Archangel Michael.

Xena to Gabrielle
"I let my fear and hatred blind me to everything."
"If I had been through what you've been through…"
"No. You understand hatred, but you have never given in to it."

Disclaimer: To show sympathy for the Horde, 'kaltaka' was only served upon request during the production of this motion picture.

LOST MARINER

Written by: Steven L. Sears
Directed by: Garth Maxwell
Guest stars: George Henare
(Hidsim), Nigel Harbrow (Basculis),
Tony Todd (Cecrops)
Air date: 5 May 1997

Incidentally: How does Xena's
chakram, which doesn't float, get
washed ashore after the wreck?

Xena and Gabrielle find themselves aboard the cursed ship of Cecrops, who is doomed to sail for eternity, hunted by Poseidon and pursued by pirates, unless he can be redeemed by love.

This remake of the Flying Dutchman legend and 'The Rime of the Ancient Mariner' pulls out all the watery special effects, including shipwrecks, tidal waves, the giant whirlpool Charybdis and Poseidon himself. Tony Todd, veteran of countless guest starring roles from *Hercules* to *Beverly Hills 90210*, commands the screen as always. Watching Gabrielle eat raw squid is enough to make anyone seasick!

Cecrops
"Oh, please! Who's going to love me? I'm not exactly the Catch of the Day: tall, dark and cursed for eternity!"

Disclaimer: Cecrops' Joie de Vivre was not harmed during the production of this motion picture.

A COMEDY OF EROS

Written by: Chris Manheim
Directed by: Charles Siebert
Guest stars: Ted Raimi (Joxer), Jay
Laga'aia (Draco), Karl Urban (Cupid)
Air date: 12 May 1997

Cupid's baby son Bliss steals daddy's bow and arrows, and causes merry mayhem: Xena's in love with Draco, Draco's in love with Gabrielle, Gabrielle's in love with Joxer and a flock of Hestian virgins are chasing Draco's men. Oh yes, and Joxer's in love with Gabrielle — but he wasn't hit by one of Cupid's arrows.

This episode gives Gabrielle two new suitors: Draco, the victim of a god-induced passion, and Joxer, whose genuine but unrequited love will become an important story arc. When Karl Urban first played Cupid for *Hercules*, he spent two months getting into shape for the role, not only to look like a god, but to have the stamina for sixteen-hour days in a large pair of wings.

Gabrielle to Draco
"Look! Cherries! I love cherries!"
"Me, too!"

Disclaimer: No Cherries were harmed during the production of this motion picture.

THE FURIES

Written by: R. J. Stewart
Directed by: Gilbert Shilton
Guest stars: Kevin Smith (Ares),
Darien Takle (Cyrene)
Air date: 29 September 1997

Ares persuades the Furies to punish Xena for not avenging her father's death, so they send a crazed Xena on a search for her father's murderer. However, Xena finds that the person she is looking for is her own mother, Cyrene, who killed Atrius to stop him sacrificing his little daughter to the God of War.

This episode features three riveting dramatic turns: a tormented but indomitable Cyrene, Ares at his most charismatic and persuasive, and an insane Xena who goes from kooky to terrifying to blazingly intense. We also get the Furies' almost non-existent costumes and a super stunt fight as Xena and Ares leap and swing from a row of spears sticking out of a wall.

Ares and Xena, to the Furies

"If you've noticed, she is crazy."

"Yeah, I'm completely out of my gourd, and I might cut mommy up later just for fun, but not because she killed my father."

Disclaimer: Xena's sanity was not harmed during the production of this motion picture. The Furies, however, will be opening their own lap-dancing variety show off-off-off Broadway soon.

'The Furies'.

BEEN THERE, DONE THAT

Written by: Hilary J. Bader

Directed by: Andrew Merrifield

Guest stars: Ted Raimi (Joxer), Joseph Murray (Neron), Deverik Williams (Tybelus), Rebekah Davies (Hermia)

Air date: 6 October 1997

Nearly Departed: Xena really dies for the second time, Gabrielle for the second and third times, Joxer for the first three times and Argo for the first time… but none of it counts because of the curse!

C upid curses a town to repeat the same day over and over again until a hero can save two star-crossed lovers from their feuding families. In the whole town, only Xena is aware that she and her friends have relived the same day — fifteen times — while she tries to break the curse.

The curse is broken by the longest chakram throw in *Xena* history, with a record 35 ricochets, including a pinball-style 21 bouncer in a doorway. There is also a black-humoured gag when Xena kills Joxer with her chakram.

Gabrielle to Xena

"So you're saying that today is actually yesterday for you, but for us today is today because we can't remember that yesterday was today, right?"
"Right."
"I don't get it."

Disclaimer: The rooster was not harmed during the production of this motion picture, although his feathers were severely ruffled. However, a little gel and mousse straightened out the mess.

THE DIRTY HALF DOZEN

Written by: Steven L. Sears

Directed by: Rick Jacobson

Guest stars: Kevin Smith (Ares), Charles Mesure (Darnell), Katrina Hobbs (Glaphyra), Jon Brazier (Walsim), Jonathan Roberts (Agathon)

Air date: 13 October 1997

Eagle Eye: Watch for Xena's sword getting broken.

X ena rounds up a band of convicts to help her stop Ares' latest warlord protégé, Agathon. In a scheme as elaborate as the Great Train Robbery, they have to break into his castle and destroy the forge where he's making weapons out of the Metal of Hephaestus.

A salute to every misfit heroes movie ever made, this episode also has one of the series' most spectacular explosions. Though the Metal of Hephaestus can break Xena's sword, her chakram slices and dices it. Jon Brazier also appears in 'Vanishing Act' as Tarsus (credited as 'John Brazier'). In an interview, Charles Mesure revealed that he played Darnell as "a really bad Kevin Smith impression."

Gabrielle to Xena, about the bickering convicts

"I don't think I've ever been a part of a true disaster before."
"You are such a cynic!"

Disclaimer: No Convicts were reformed during the production of this motion picture. Can't we all just get along?

THE DELIVERER

Written by: Steven L. Sears

Directed by: Oley Sassone

Guest stars: Karl Urban (Caesar), Jennifer Ward-Lealand (Boadicea), Marton Csokas (Khrafstar)

Air date: 20 October 1997

Incidentally: Jennifer Ward-Lealand is Michael Hurst's wife.

Xena rushes to Britannia to help Boadicea fight Caesar. Instead, she and Gabrielle come face to face with the evil god Dahak, who needs Gabrielle's child and her blood innocence to make his way into our world.

The drama cranks up to a new level in the wrenching scenes where Gabrielle kills for the first time and is subsequently engulfed in the flames of Dahak. Spectacular pyrotechnics embody the evil god's power and blow up his temple over our heroines' heads. This is the first episode in the multi-episode story arc unofficially known as the Rift.

Xena, to the Deliverer

"I thought your god was all powerful or something. All I've seen is a lame attempt at a religion and some fancy fireworks."

Disclaimer: Gabrielle was slightly well-done during the production of this motion picture. However, the producers would like to recommend a zesty barbecue sauce to bring out the full flavor of the episode.

GABRIELLE'S HOPE

Written by: R. J. Stewart

Directed by: Charles Siebert and Andrew Merrifield

Air date: 27 October 1997

Wild Banshees and the Knights of the Round Table pursue Gabrielle, who's carrying the child of Dahak. After a birth surrounded by ominous portents and the mysterious murder of one of the knights, Xena is convinced the baby girl is evil incarnate. But Gabrielle, insisting Hope is an innocent, flees the castle with Xena in grim pursuit.

The Rift opens in earnest when Gabrielle sics the Banshees on Xena and later lies to her, saying she has killed the baby. There is a nice nod to the King Arthur legend when the Knights do a double take as Xena casually pulls a sword from a stone to have a look at it and comments, "Nice blade!"

Gabrielle, to Xena

"You said that one day I would have hope again. Here it is. That's what I'm going to call her — Hope."

Disclaimer: Despite witnessing the bizarre and somewhat disturbing birth of Gabrielle's Hope, no farm animals were harmed or traumatized during the production of this motion picture.

THE DEBT, PART I

Story by: Robert Tapert
& R. J. Stewart

Teleplay by: R. J. Stewart

Directed by: Oley Sassone

Guest stars: Jacqueline Kim
(Lao Ma), Marton Csokas (Borias),
Grant McFarland (Ming Tzu), Daniel
Sing (Ming T'ien)

Air date: 3 November 1997

Xena travels to China to assassinate the 'Green Dragon'. Along the way, she remembers her lover Borias, who betrayed her, and her mentor Lao Ma, who saved her life and taught her The Way.

Jacqueline Kim's Lao Ma is both tranquil and powerful, and as impressive as if she'd dominated half a dozen episodes or more, instead of only two. Marton Csokas, in his début as Borias, makes us understand why Xena couldn't leave him alone. And there is a sweeping cavalry battle on a very Mongolian-looking plain.

Ming Tzu
"I have the greatest respect for thieves. Every man born to wealth has a good thief among his ancestors somewhere."

Disclaimer: No Frock Tarts* were killed during the production of this motion picture, although they wish they had been.
*Stage slang for a costumier.

'The Debt, Part I'.

THE DEBT, PART II

Story by: Robert Tapert & R. J. Stewart

Teleplay by: R. J. Stewart

Directed by: Oley Sassone

Guest stars: Jacqueline Kim (Lao Ma), Marton Csokas (Borias), Grant McFarland (Ming Tzu), Daniel Sing (Ming T'ien)

Air date: 10 November 1997

Having betrayed Xena to Ming T'ien, Gabrielle tries to persuade Xena to forgive her and Ming T'ien to spare Xena's life. Meanwhile, in prison, Xena recalls Lao Ma's teachings and her love as she tried to save Xena from her violent ways.

The Rift cracks open still wider, with another lie at the very end of the episode. There's also a good example of just how acomplished the cinematography in the series can be: look out for a beautiful shot of Xena on a porch, composed as artfully as a Chinese painting.

Gabrielle to Xena, who is in the stocks

"*I betrayed you. The pathetic thing is, I thought I was saving you… I know you hate me, Xena. No more than I hate myself.*"
"*Scratch my nose, will you?*"

Disclaimer: Xena and Gabrielle's relationship suffered another blow (although Gabrielle doesn't know it yet) during the production of this motion picture.

THE KING OF ASSASSINS

Written by: Adam Armus & Nora Kay Foster

Directed by: Bruce Campbell

Guest stars: Ted Raimi (Joxer/ Jett), Gina Torres (Cleopatra), Bruce Campbell (Autolycus)

Air date: 17 November 1997

Joxer and Autolycus tag along as Xena tries to prevent the assassination of Cleopatra, but the hired assassin is actually Joxer's look-alike brother Jett, who is secretly in league with Autolycus. Not surprisingly, the usual mayhem and identity confusion ensues.

An episode loaded with terrific quips, silly situations — including a weapons-sniffing Rottweiler and a classic 'mirror' routine — and some nice character stuff between Joxer and his "overachieving" brother. Gina Torres also plays Nebula in *Hercules* and stars in *Cleopatra 2525* and *Firefly*.

Joxer to Autolycus

"*It's me! Joxer!*"
"*How can I be sure?*"
"*I'm hanging from the wall by my underwear.*"
"*Good point.*"

Disclaimer: Due to the infliction of a severe wedgie, Joxer was slightly uncomfortable but not seriously harmed during the production of this motion picture.

WARRIOR... PRIESTESS... TRAMP

Written by: Adam Armus & Nora Kay Foster

Directed by: Robert Ginty

Guest stars: Ted Raimi (Joxer), MacGregor Cameron (Balius)

Air date: 12 January 1998

Meg switches places with Hestian Priestess Leah, in an evil priest's plot to discredit the rival cult of Hestia. While Xena and Gabrielle try to sort out the mess, naïve Leah experiences the world. She tries to persuade Gabrielle to become a virgin, hides out in Meg's whorehouse, where she learns more than she ever wanted to know, and finally poses as Meg to save her Hestian virgins from her rival's murderous scheme.

Lawless adds to her repertoire a third Xena look-alike, the virginal Leah — as well as playing Meg playing Leah, Xena playing Leah, Leah playing Xena and even Leah playing Meg playing Leah — in a virtuoso performance in which every role and every impersonation is distinct. Meg's 'ladies' singing a new version of the Joxer song is a highlight of the episode — finally Joxer has found a place where his prowess is in demand!

Leah to Gabrielle
"Rule One, know thyself. Rule Two..."
"Believe me, if I have to go through the rest of my life without companionship, knowing myself isn't going to be a problem!"

Disclaimer: Despite another look-alike, the gene pool (or rather gene puddle) was not harmed during the production of this motion picture.

'The King of Assassins'.

THE QUILL IS MIGHTIER

Written by: Hilary J. Bader

Directed by: Andrew Merrifield

Guest stars: Ted Raimi (Joxer), Alexandra Tydings (Aphrodite), Kevin Smith (Ares)

Air date: 19 January 1998

Fighting With Fish, Double Bonus Round: Xena wallops the barbarians with an entire cartload of fish, throws a swordfish like a spear and uses an eel as a chakram.

Aphrodite curses Gabrielle's scroll so that everything she writes comes literally true. With a twirl of a quill, Gabrielle has written Joxer and a horde of barbarians in, Xena out with the fishes, and Ares and Aphrodite into powerless mortality. The only way to break the spell is to write the unvarnished truth...

Alison Wall returns as Minya when Gabrielle writes of a leather-clad woman with a whip. The scroll-induced silliness includes the invention of the drink hat and the limerick, nude go-go dancing Gabrielles, directionally challenged barbarians and a Goddess of Love who can't get a date until she gets a bath. It also includes the series' worst pun, "Gabrielle woke up with a jerk", which summons Joxer.

Ares to Gabrielle

"We were starting to warm up to each other there, weren't we? I didn't like it."
"Right back at you!"

Disclaimer: No naked Gabrielles were harmed during the production of this motion picture.

MATERNAL INSTINCTS

Written by: Chris Manheim

Directed by: Mark Beesley

Guest stars: Amy Morrison (Hope), David Taylor (Solan), Danielle Cormack (Ephiny), Jeff Boyd (Kaleipus), Hudson Leick (Callisto)

Air date: 26 January 1998

Nearly Departed: Hope murders Solan and is then poisoned by Gabrielle.

Hope, now a little girl, releases Callisto from her lava prison and reveals herself to Gabrielle. While Gabrielle tries to keep her secret from Xena, Hope and Callisto plot to destroy Xena by killing her son, Solan.

The Rift blows apart with riveting performances all around, especially from Amy Morrison as the sociopathic Hope. Dramatic highlights include Callisto's laughter as she finally gets her revenge, and Gabrielle almost putting a bottle to her lips. Hope's child-name for Callisto, who at one point is stuck full of arrows, is perfect: "the monster lady".

Xena, to Callisto

"You let your pain kill you years ago. I'm gonna live with mine."

Disclaimer: Xena and Gabrielle's relationship was harmed during the production of this motion picture.

THE BITTER SUITE

Lyrics by (in alphabetical order): Joseph LoDuca, Pamela Phillips Oland, Dennis Spiegel

Written by: Steven L. Sears & Chris Manheim

Directed by: Oley Sassone

Guest stars: Ted Raimi (Joxer), Kevin Smith (Ares), Hudson Leick (Callisto)

Air date: 2 February 1998

Eagle Eye: Watch for a pouch with an eye and ringlets in Ares' hair.

'The Bitter Suite'.

When Xena and Gabrielle try to kill each other, they fall into the dreamland of Illusia, where they have to sing their way through their hatred and pain, guided by dream doubles of Joxer, Callisto, Ares and Lila.

Xena's first musical episode wowed fans with its gorgeous tarot card-inspired costumes (especially Callisto's jester) and surreal sets, and emotionally powerful music and lyrics. *Xena*'s chakram turns into the Wheel of Fate in the land where "lies may be truth and truth may be lies". The infamous 'Gab drag' is one of the series' most shocking and brutal sequences, while Ares' tango with Xena is one of the most sensual.

Gabrielle
"The Elysian Fields. Only heroes wind up here. Dead heroes. Dead naked heroes!"

Disclaimer: The musical genre was not harmed during the production of this motion picture. In fact, the producers sincerely hope you were A-MUSE-D by this episode.

ONE AGAINST AN ARMY

Written by: Gene O'Neill
& Noreen Tobin
Directed by: Paul Lynch
Air date: 9 February 1998

In the path of an invading Persian army, Xena and Gabrielle take refuge in an old barn, where Xena decides to use an old cache of weapons to delay the enemy. Then Gabrielle gets shot by a poisoned arrow, and Xena has to keep Gabrielle alive while she fights off the attacking troops.

The first episode after the healing of the Rift provides some effective relationship moments, as well as a long battle sequence which plenty of great stunts in a closed space, but which still begs the question, just how many heavily armed soldiers can Xena really fight? Xena mentions the sites of two real battles in the Persian Wars (fifth century BC): the Battle of Thermopylae and the Battle of Marathon (which gave the modern race its name).

Gabrielle to Xena

"A long time ago, I accepted the consequences of our life together, that it might one day come to this. It has. I'm not afraid."
"You've always said that I was the brave one. Look at you now!"

Disclaimer: Gabrielle's ankle was harmed during the production of this motion picture.

FORGIVEN

Written by: R. J. Stewart
Directed by: Garth Maxwell
Guest star: Shiri Appleby (Tara)
Air date: 16 February 1998

A bratty, violent teenage girl tries to win Xena's approval by beating up Gabrielle and then leading Xena to a stolen sacred urn. Along the way, she learns to be less bratty and even to be a team player, as the three warriors take on a ruin full of urn-snatching, girlfriend-exploiting bandits.

Xena is unusually gentle with Tara — if anyone else beat Gabrielle black and blue, she would just throw them right through a wall! Shiri Appleby is better known as Liz Parker in *Roswell*. The three heroines play charades and Catch the Urn. In a grace note to her quest for atonement, Xena declines the forgiveness bestowed by the urn's blessing.

Xena to Gabrielle, about Tara

"She reminds me a little bit of me."
"Oh, no! I knew you were evil, but you were obnoxious, too?"

Disclaimer: No street-talking, cat-fighting, bar-room-brawling juvenile delinquents were harmed during the production of this motion picture.

KING CON

Written by: Chris Manheim
Directed by: Janet Greek
Guest stars: Ted Raimi (Joxer),
Patrick Fabian (Rafe), Cameron
Rhodes (Eldon)
Air date: 23 February 1998

When Joxer gets beaten nearly to death at the orders of a casino owner, Xena and Gabrielle team up with two con men to take the owner for all he's worth. However, things start to get complicated when con man Rafe bets his partner Eldon that he can get Xena to kiss him, and downright convoluted when Xena begins to fall for Rafe, while Eldon seems to have second thoughts about his loyalties.

The Sting comes to Ancient Greece, with more double crosses than a gambler has aces. The savage beating inflicted on Joxer is disproportionately grim compared to the lightness of the rest of the episode. There is only one puzzle left unanswered at the end: how did Joxer get smart enough (or lucky enough) to win that much money to begin with?

Gabrielle, to the unconscious Joxer

"Xena and I, we care about you. I know it's hard to tell sometimes. You're like family to us. Don't leave us, okay?"

Disclaimer: No con men were conned during the production of this motion picture.

WHEN IN ROME

Written by: Steven L. Sears
Directed by: John Laing
Guest stars: Karl Urban (Caesar),
Matthew Chamberlain (Crassus),
Jeremy Callaghan (Pompey)
Air date: 3 March 1998

Xena kidnaps Caesar's ally Crassus, to force Caesar to release the captive Gaulish chieftain Vercinix, whose public execution will bolster Caesar's power. When Xena rescues Vercinix and puts Crassus in his prison cell, Gabrielle and Caesar both have to decide whether to save Crassus, or let him be executed in Vercinix's place.

Jeremy Callaghan's Pompey the Magnus is a worthy rival for Caesar. And Caesar is right, Xena looks fantastic in the costume department's wonderful Roman finery. Gabrielle finds herself in the position of judge, jury and executioner, and doesn't much like how she handles the role.

Caesar to an uninterested Xena

"It's never just business between us, Xena. It's hatred, war, conflict… and it's love."
"I gotta go to the bathroom. Are we done yet?"

Disclaimer: Caesar's Palace was not harmed during the production of this motion picture. However, Crassus and the gladiators went down for the count.

FORGET ME NOT

Written by: Hilary J. Bader
Directed by: Charlie Haskell
Guest stars: Ted Raimi (Joxer),
Kevin Smith (Ares)
Air date: 9 March 1998

Tormented by memories of Hope and the Rift, Gabrielle visits the temple of Mnemosyne, Goddess of Memory. Sent on a dream journey, Gabrielle has a choice: to endure the pain, or to let it go, and with it all memories of happiness as well. Meanwhile her amnesiac body is in the care of Joxer, who tries to convince her that he's her hero.

Yet another clip show that's so central to a character's development that we forget it's 'just' a clip show. Ares, who initially seems a surprising choice for Gabrielle's dream guide, is ultimately revealed as the only possible choice. Joxer has a good time rewriting Gabrielle's scrolls, and then an epiphany when he learns he can't bring himself to take advantage of her.

High Priestess to Joxer
"If you love her, allow her the chance to lose the pain she carries. It's in her memory."
"Well, I can make her forget. I'm a very forgettable person!"

Disclaimer: Xena and Joxer were not forgotten during the production of this motion picture.

FINS, FEMMES AND GEMS

Story by: Rob Tapert &
Adam Armus & Nora Kay Foster
Teleplay by: Adam Armus
& Nora Kay Foster
Directed by: Josh Becker
Guest stars: Ted Raimi (Joxer),
Alexandra Tydings (Aphrodite)
Air date: 13 April 1998

Fighting About Fish: Xena catch fish. Attis, King of Trout, set fish free. Xena wring Attis' neck.

Aphrodite puts an obsession charm on Xena, Gabrielle and Joxer, so they won't interfere with her plans to steal the North Star for her own constellation. As a result, Xena goes nutty on fishing, Gabrielle goes nutty on herself and Joxer goes ape.

'Attis the Ape Man', aka Joxer, follows in the footsteps (or should that be vine-swings?) of Tarzan and George of the Jungle, and according to Raimi, it's really him hitting that tree: the stunt was done by filming him being pulled away from the tree, then reversing the film.

Maecanus to Aphrodite
"Tie your gem on my arrow so my shaft can bring you satisfaction."
"You don't have the thrust. Besides, my guy in Parnassus has better equipment, and he knows when to shoot."

Disclaimer: Joxer's dignity was slightly harmed during the production of this motion picture. However, Gabrielle's pink nightie was restored to its original condition.

TSUNAMI

Written by: Chris Manheim
Directed by: John Laing
Guest star: Bruce Campbell (Autolycus)
Air date: 20 April 1998

Background: This was the first time Angela Dotchin had worked with Bruce Campbell, later her co-star in *Jack of All Trades.*

When a tsunami strikes, Xena, Gabrielle and Autolycus are trapped inside the hull of a merchant ship along with two convicts, the ship's wealthy owner and his wife. As she hatches a desperate escape plan, Xena demonstrates amazing scientific knowledge of deep-water currents and pressure.

Compare this episode's tsunami with the one in 'Lost Mariner' to see how far computer effects advanced in just a year. During production a water tank used in shooting the episode gave way, causing a small tsunami on the set (the tank wasn't in use at the time).

Fortune Teller to Gabrielle

"There's danger! Great danger! And death!"
"Did you hear that? She just described every day of our lives."

Disclaimer:

No cast or crew were singing 'Tanks for the Memories' during the production of this motion picture. However, the phrase "strike the set" was given new meaning.

'Fins, Femmes and Gems'.

VANISHING ACT

Written by: Terence Winter
Directed by: Andrew Merrifield
Guest stars: Bruce Campbell
(Autolycus), John Brazier (Tarsus)
Air date: 27 April 1998

Eagle Eye: Watch for a very big pile of locks.

Xena and Autolycus team up again to recover stolen goods, this time a golden statue. Xena and Gabrielle pose as rival dealers with very phoney accents, with Autolycus as a hunchback servant.

Lawless does her New York accent, while Bruce Campbell does 'Igor the Hunchback Henchman'. Who knew the Ancient Greeks could scuba dive?

Autolycus, to Xena

"What have I done for you lately, huh? Nothing... besides letting you live inside my body while I risked my life to steal back your shapely corpse, all the while having to endure Gabrielle whining and crying twenty-four hours a day about how much she misses Xena."

Disclaimer: Upon the completion of the filming of this episode, Autolycus' scuba gear was placed on display at the Athens' Diving Institute for the education and enjoyment of future generations.

SACRIFICE, PART I

Written by: Steven L. Sears
Directed by: David Warry-Smith
Guest Stars: Kevin Smith (Ares),
Jodie Rimmer (Seraphin), Stephen Ure
(Werfner), Hudson Leick (Callisto)
Air date: 4 May 1998

Callisto teams up with Dahak's priests to bring Hope back into the world. Ares decides he's better off with Dahak than against him, and tells Gabrielle that if Xena kills Hope, the Fates will cut off her life thread.

Renee O'Connor gets her shot at doubling up roles, by playing the adult Hope. That slimy membrane on Hope is made of Elmer's Glue and plastic wrap, which took fifteen minutes to put on and a very hot shower to take off, with an hour of shooting in between. "I felt like the wall, with everyone putting wallpaper on me," says O'Connor.

Callisto, to Xena

"Not happy to see me, are you? Neither am I, really. But I've got a plan to solve both of our problems. But I tell you about it, and the first thing you know, you'll be trying to stop me. You just trust me. You're gonna love it... well, at least half of it."

Disclaimer: No pulsing cocoons were harmed during the production of this motion picture. What you witnessed was purely a re-enactment.

SACRIFICE, PART II

Written by: Paul Robert Coyle
Directed by: Rick Jacobson
Guest stars: Ted Raimi (Joxer),
Kevin Smith (Ares), Jodie Rimmer
(Seraphin), Stephen Ure (Werfner),
Hudson Leick (Callisto)
Air date: 11 May 1998

While Ares and Hope get cosy and Dahak's followers plan a huge blood sacrifice that will let Dahak into the world, Callisto switches sides and Xena tries to get the Hind's Blood Dagger so she can kill Hope.

A heart-stopping finish to the Hope storyline, with so much action and character development packed in that it feels like watching a feature film. As *Xena's* first big season-ending cliff-hanger, it caused a sensation among fans, and took three episodes to resolve.

Nearly Departed: Hope and Gabrielle fall into a chasm of fire. Xena kills Callisto with the Hind's Blood Dagger.

Xena to Callisto

"Let me guess. Things didn't work out with Hope quite the way you expected."
"No, actually, the sight of her and Ares rolling around like weasels made me sick! Yes, Gabrielle, it seems your daughter is in heat."

Disclaimer: Gabrielle finally went off the deep end during the production of this motion picture.

'Sacrifice, Part I'.

JUDGMENT DAY

Written by: Robert Bielak
Directed by: Gus Trikons
Guest stars: Sam Jenkins (Serena), Kevin Smith (Ares), Renee O'Connor (Gabrielle), Lucy Lawless (Xena)
Air date: 24 February 1997

H aving forced Hercules to give up his powers so he can marry Serena, the last Golden Hind, Ares orders Strife to murder Serena and frame Hercules, so that even Herc believes he might be guilty. Xena and Gabrielle eventually trick Ares and Strife into revealing their part in the crime.

This is the third of a trilogy of episodes concerning Hercules' romance with the Golden Hind (played by Sorbo's wife, Sam Jenkins). Joel Tobeck, débuting as Strife, gleefully steals every scene he's in. The trilogy was also Kevin Smith's first *Hercules* appearance as Ares, a role he created in *Xena*.

Strife to Ares
"Maybe if I was — God of Skirmishes? That was a joke. Dig?"
"Dig Hercules' grave. And learn how to talk so I can understand you."

Disclaimer: No Family Values were harmed during the production of this Blood Lite motion picture.

STRANGER IN A STRANGE WORLD

Written by: Paul Robert Coyle
Directed by: Michael Levine
Guest stars: Ted Raimi (Joxer), Alexandra Tydings (Aphrodite), Kevin Smith (Ares), Renee O'Connor (the Executioner), Lucy Lawless (Xena)
Air date: 27 October 1997

I olaus gets pulled into a parallel world, where Hercules is the tyrannical Sovereign, Ares is the God of Love, Joxer is a hero and Xena is the Sovereign's kinky mistress. While Hercules copes with Iolaus' jester double in his world, Iolaus tries to find a way to stop the Sovereign from poisoning Zeus and marrying a very straight laced Aphrodite, Queen of the Gods.

Kevin Smith does the God of Love as a Vegas Elvis, while Xena, in a svelte haircut, plays acrobatic love games with the Sovereign, gets into a cake fight with Aphrodite and throws a mean shoe. O'Connor's role as the spinning Executioner is so slight as to be almost a cameo. The alternate jester Iolaus will later replace the 'real' Iolaus, who is killed by Gilgamesh.

Iolaus, dodging the rough play of the Sovereign and Xena
"Their foreplay is going to get me killed!"

Disclaimer: No Heart-throwing, Love-spewing, Smooth-talking Ares impersonators were harmed during the production of this motion picture.

ARMAGEDDON NOW, PART II

Teleplay by: Gene F. O'Neill & Noreen V. Tobin

Story by: Paul Robert Coyle

Directed by: Mark Beesley

Guest stars: Kevin Smith (Ares), Hudson Leick (Callisto), Renee O'Connor (Gabrielle), Lucy Lawless (Xena)

Air date: 16 February 1998

After Hope sends Callisto back in time to kill Alcmene so that Hercules is never born, Iolaus must travel through a war-torn alternate timeline, trying to set things right. Along the way, he reaches Callisto's village on the day Xena's army kills her family and, years later, encounters Xena, Destroyer of Nations and ruler of the entire world, and Gabrielle, a convicted rebel who Xena orders crucified.

A chilling look at what Xena might have become if she had followed Alti instead of Hercules. Still, she looks stunning in that plumed crown! This two-parter also reveals that Hope has survived Gabrielle's poison.

Xena to Local Leader, who has come to pay tribute

"So good of you to come. [Kicks him over backwards.] You'll have to work on your grovelling."

Disclaimer: Although Alcmene's barn was blown to smithereens, remarkably she and Iolaus were not harmed during the production of this motion picture.

'Stranger in a Strange World'.

ADVENTURES IN THE SIN TRADE, PART I

Teleplay by: R. J. Stewart
Story by: Rob Tapert & R. J. Stewart
Directed by: T. J. Scott
Guest stars: Marton Csokas (Borias), Claire Stansfield (Alti), Sheeri Rappaport (Otere), Vicky Pratt (Cyane)
Air date: 28 September 1998

While searching for Gabrielle in the Amazon Land of the Dead, Xena learns that an old ally, the shamaness Alti, has enslaved the souls of an entire tribe of Amazons. Xena postpones her search to teach the surviving young Amazons how to fight back.

Much of this episode was filmed around North Island's Lake Taupo (the same region that provided locations for 'The Debt'), in wild winter weather. The production base camp was blown away on one occasion, and the day after shooting finished, a flood washed out the road.

Background: In preparation for her first stint as director, Renee O'Connor shadowed director T. J. Scott during production.

Xena
"I hate the dead! You can't take vengeance on them."

Disclaimer: No Dead Amazons lost their lives during the production of this motion picture.

ADVENTURES IN THE SIN TRADE, PART II

Teleplay by: R. J. Stewart
Story by: Rob Tapert & R. J. Stewart
Directed by: T. J. Scott
Guest stars: Marton Csokas (Borias), Claire Stansfield (Alti), Sheeri Rappaport (Otere), Vicky Pratt (Cyane)
Air date: 5 October 1998

While Xena teaches the young Amazons the shamanistic powers they'll need to defeat Alti, the Warrior Princess recalls the past: her alliance with Alti, and her betrayal and massacre of the leaders of Cyane's tribe. Alti meanwhile torments Xena with visions...

This episode introduces the vision of crucifixion that drives this season's story arc. The treetop fights were the first major aerial stunt fights done in the series. Claire Stansfield recalled that filming the sequence was scary, but exhilarating!

Nearly Departed: Alti's body dies when Xena's spirit body, aided by the Amazons' spirits, kills Alti's spirit body.

Cyane, to Xena
"You're a murderer because you still think and act like one. Join us. We can teach you a new way, a new code to live by."

Disclaimer: Xena's search for Gabrielle was not harmed during the production of this motion picture.

A FAMILY AFFAIR

Teleplay by: Chris Manheim

Story by: Liz Friedman & Chris Manheim

Directed by: Doug Lefler

Guest star: Ted Raimi (Joxer)

Air date: 12 October 1998

Xena and Joxer return to Poteidaia to reunite with Gabrielle, but Hope has taken her mother's place in the family, and holds Lila and her parents hostage while she nurtures her child, the monstrous Destroyer. Xena and Gabrielle bait a trap, and the mortally wounded Destroyer, mistaking Hope for Gabrielle, kills her.

The Hope storyline finally wraps with Renee O'Connor's brilliant dual performance as both Gabrielle and Hope, the mother from Hell, who's so scary even the Destroyer is afraid of her. High praise to director Scott and Mark Vinello (the guy inside the Destroyer suit), who make the monster pathetic in its longing for its mother's love, and there is a horrific embrace between Gabrielle and her 'grandson'.

Joxer, gagged and hung up for a Destroyer snack, yells out a string of incomprehensible desperate shouts, ending with a very distinct *"Oh, sh*t!"*

Disclaimer: No Spike-Skinned, Beast-Like, Incredibly Hungry Offspring who can't stand the sun were harmed during the production of this motion picture.

'A Family Affair'.

IN SICKNESS AND IN HELL

Written by: Adam Armus & Nora Kay Foster

Directed by: Josh Becker

Guest star: Ted Raimi (Joxer)

Air date: 19 October 1998

Leapin' lice, foot rot and the trots cause severe harm to Joxer's efforts to convince a village that Xena and Gabrielle can save them from a Scythian warlord, to Xena and Gabrielle's relationship, and to Xena's attempts to rescue Argo from the warlord. Joxer eventually saves the day by giving the whole Scythian army food poisoning.

Fans either love or hate this episode for its gross-out humour and for making our heroines look thoroughly disgusting. Too many outrageous gags to list them all, but the highs (or the pits — your choice) include the dung mud plaster, the Attack of the Killer Bunny (an homage to *Monty Python and the Holy Grail*) and the teeny weeny screams of the doomed lice.

Xena to Gabrielle
"Don't make me hurt you, Scabrielle!"
"All right, EcXema! What are you going to do?"

Disclaimer: No Leapin' Lice were beaten, whipped, smashed or scratched during the production of this motion picture.

A GOOD DAY

Written by: Steven L. Sears

Directed by: Rick Jacobson

Guest stars: Karl Urban (Caesar), Stephen Lovatt (Phlanagus), Jeremy Callaghan (Pompey)

Air date: 26 October 1998

When Caesar and Pompey bring their civil war to Greece for a long campaign, Xena allies with a Greek mercenary and the country people to trick the Romans into a decisive battle that will destroy their armies and leave Greece relatively unscathed.

Another solid dramatisation of the personal costs of war. Watch for two memorably piercing reactions: Xena's face as she watches the villagers burn their own homes, and Caesar's shrug when he sees the battlefield, extending to the horizon and covered with thousands of dead. Stephen Lovatt also plays Hades in *Xena's* fifth season.

Pompey to Xena, as she arrives holding two Roman helmets
"Just a precaution. There were only two guards."
"I know. Otherwise I would have had more helmets."

Disclaimer: No Permanent Battle Scars were inflicted during the production of this motion picture.

A TALE OF TWO MUSES

Written by: Gillian Horvath
Directed by: Michael Hurst
Guest stars: Shiri Appleby (Tara),
Bruce Campbell (Autolycus)
Air date: 2 November 1998

In a town ruled by a puritanical magistrate, Xena and Gabrielle find their former protégée Tara about to be whipped for breaking a law against dancing. Gabrielle resists the urge to dance all the time, while Xena enlists Autolycus to pose as a famous preacher to overthrow the magistrate with some toe-tapping fun.

An homage, believe it or not, to the 1984 film *Footloose*. Autolycus seems a strange choice for an ally this time, until you see his impression of an evangelist preacher. Praise Calliope! Listen for a flush toilet: these people have very advanced plumbing, especially for an ancient desert town.

Autolycus (as Philipon the Reformer) to Istafan

"It's an abomination! Don't tell me you don't see it. Look at the firmness of those rounded peaks! The cleft in that valley."
"And the tower thrusting skyward! Philipon's right! It's obscene!"

Disclaimer: No Self-Righteous Magistrates intent on suppressing the basic human right of freedom of expression were harmed during the production of this motion picture.

'A Tale of Two Muses'.

LOCKED UP AND TIED DOWN

Teleplay by: Hilary Bader
Story by: Rob Tapert & Josh Becker
Directed by: Rick Jacobson
Guest stars: Katrina Browne (Thalassa), William Kircher (Captain), Tanea Heke (Ersina)
Air date: 9 November 1998

Incidentally: How did they talk Lucy Lawless into letting them cover her with live rats again, after her experience in 'Death in Chains'?

Justice finally catches up with Xena when she's arrested for an old murder and condemned to life in Shark Island Prison. While Xena believes that prison will help her atone for her crimes, Gabrielle gets a job as the prison's healer so she can come to the rescue. Then they discover that the murder victim survived and is now the prison warden.

In this episode, it's the turn of prison movies to get the *Xena* treatment, with the usual brutal guards, inmate bullies and some really gruesome crabs.

Ersina to Xena

"You never had to pay for your crimes.
That's always bothered me."
"Then we have something in common.
It's always bothered me, too."

Disclaimer: No Rabid Flesh-Eating Crabs were harmed during the production of this motion picture.

CRUSADER

Written by: R. J. Stewart
Directed by: Paul Lynch
Guest star: Kathryn Morris (Najara)
Air date: 16 November 1998

Fearful of the crucifixion vision, Xena tries to leave Gabrielle in the care of the warrior Najara, who goes around defending the innocent, fighting the bad guys and exhorting everyone to "turn to the light". Then Xena learns that Najara executes any prisoners who don't convert to her way.

After the broad satire of 'A Tale of Two Muses' comes this much more subtle depiction of religious zeal and the thin line between faith and fanaticism. Najara beats Xena unconscious in single combat, without tricks, traps or supernatural powers. No one else has ever done that! Najara's Djinn are the genies of Arabian mythology, perhaps a reflection of the episode's location in Phoenicia, which is now Lebanon.

Xena, spitting out a tooth

"I got my butt whipped, didn't I? Well it serves me right for trusting somebody who talks about being good all the time!"

Disclaimer: Xena's Best Chewing Tooth was not harmed during the production of this motion picture.

PAST IMPERFECT

Written by: Steven L. Sears

Directed by: Garth Maxwell

Guest stars: Marton Csokas
(Borias), Catherine Boniface (Satrina),
Paul Gittins (Kaleipus),
Mark Ferguson (Dagnine)

Air date: 4 January 1999

Xena's past and future meet during a siege, as she tries to protect Gabrielle from her own fears about Alti's vision, and recalls the birth of Solan and her final break with Borias. Then she learns that the slave woman who helped her give birth also murdered Borias and is now the warlord leading the attack.

The flashbacks in this episode dramatise in full events first mentioned briefly in 'Orphan of War'. They also bring to fulfilment Alti's curse that Xena's child will never know the love of his parents. We always suspected that Borias genuinely loved Xena — how might her life have been different if he had succeeded in taking her away?

Borias to Xena

"Don't do this. We lost our love. Don't make me an enemy."
"You became an enemy the moment you thought there was love."

'Crusader'.

Disclaimer: Borias' goose was cooked during the production of this motion picture.

THE KEY TO THE KINGDOM

Written by: Eric Morris
Directed by: Bruce Campbell
Guest stars: Ted Raimi (Joxer),
Bruce Campbell (Autolycus)
Air date: 11 January 1999

Autolycus, Joxer and Meg team up to raid a castle for a key — or is it a baby? Meg wants to adopt the baby, Autolycus wants to use the key to get some treasure, and the baby and his nurse want the prophecy fulfilled, so he'll become a king again. Is anyone not confused?

Meg gives Autolycus a new nickname, "Mr Stinky", the baby takes a chariot for a joyride and Xena shows up at the last minute to whip the bad guys. We knew she couldn't be far away if Meg was around! Joxer tells Autolycus that Meg is *his* girl, in a foreshadowing of their domestic bliss in 'Looking Death in the Eye'.

Autolycus, checking out the security system for a huge ruby

"Let's see. You touch the chimes, the trap snaps shut. Ohhh! You lose a hand. Incredible! Genius! Foolproof! Two minutes, tops."

Disclaimer: No Priceless Porkers, of either organic or ceramic origin, were harmed during the filming of this motion picture.

DAUGHTER OF POMIRA

Written by: Linda McGibney
Directed by: Patrick Norris
Guest stars: Beth Allen
(Vanessa/Pilee), Craig Ancell (Milo),
Bruce Hopkins (Rahl),
Mandy McMullin (Adiah)
Air date: 18 January 1999

Incidentally: Lakota is also a Plains Indian nation's name for themselves ('the People'), so the phrase could be read, in Lakota and pseudo Latin, as 'People all. Good. Only good.'

Xena rescues a Greek girl who was captured by the Horde as a child. Then she discovers that the child was not a slave but the beloved adopted daughter of the Horde leader, and considers herself to be Pomira (the Horde's true name) not Greek. The Horde transforms from bloodthirsty savages to the noble, nature-loving Pomira who only want to defend the natural world from Greek destructiveness.

Milo's line, "The only good Horde is a dead Horde", paraphrases the notorious "The only good Indian is a dead Indian" slogan of the nineteenth century American Indian wars. The Horde language in the disclaimer quotes Cirvik's words, which Pilee translates as, "No fight. No war. Family."

Gabrielle to Xena

"I did all that? And they call you the hero. Hmm... You wanna switch?"
"Fine. You kick butt. I'll take notes."

Disclaimer: No Blonde-Hair, Blue-Eyed Horde girls or their extended families were harmed during the production of this motion picture. Lakota toti. Bonai. Soli bonai.

IF THE SHOE FITS

Written by: Adam Armus
& Nora Kay Foster

Directed by: Josh Becker

Guest stars: Ted Raimi (Joxer),
Alexandra Tydings (Aphrodite)

Air date: 25 January 1999

When little Princess Alesia runs away from her new stepmother, Xena, Gabrielle, Aphrodite and Joxer try to encourage her to return home by telling her half a dozen fractured versions of Cinderella... er, Tyrella. Meanwhile, Aphrodite's goons try to kidnap the princess so the goddess can adopt her as the Demigoddess of Puppy Love.

American viewers unfamiliar with the traditions of British pantomime may be surprised to see the lead actors let themselves be so deliberately 'uglified' for the fairy tale sequences. Joxer's imaginary dance number with Gabrielle goes from a waltz to *Saturday Night Fever* to 1930s film sweethearts Nelson Eddy and Jeannette McDonald. The Goddess of Love seems a strange choice for the bad guy, but this is actually her fourth turn on *Xena* as an episode's main antagonist.

Xena to Alesia
"Why did you run away?"
"Have you ever heard Joxer tell a story?"

Disclaimer: No Fractured Fables were harmed during the production of this motion picture.

'If the Shoe Fits'.

PARADISE FOUND

Written by: Chris Manheim
Directed by: Rob Tapert
Guest stars: Jeremy Roberts
(Aiden), Mervyn Smith (Garr)
Air date: 1 February 1999

Hot Tub Watch: *Another* hot tub —
this one with floating flowers and candles
— and an unusual bed.

Xena and Gabrielle fall down a deep hole to a beautiful paradise, whose resident guru, Aiden, begins to teach Gabrielle about inner peace and healing. Xena grows more and more jumpy and violent, until she offs a bunch of cute birds and bunnies, while Gabrielle gets so relaxed she's going to turn into a garden sculpture.

Jeremy Roberts' Aiden in his gentle guru phase is a far cry from the actor's usual bad-ass villain roles. Gabrielle's got to be in great physical shape to master all those difficult yoga postures in just a couple of days!

Gabrielle to Xena
"It's beautiful, don't you think?"
"Yeah, in that yucky 'I'm in Paradise' kind of way."

Disclaimer: Paradise was found, but not necessarily embraced, during the production of this motion picture.

DEVI

Written by: Chris Manheim
Directed by: Garth Maxwell
Guest star: Timothy Omundson (Eli)
Air date: 8 February 1999

Costume Change: Gabrielle adopts
the yellow Indian-style outfit she will
wear until her final transformation into
the warrior bard.

In India, Xena and Gabrielle encounter a wandering illusionist named Eli and a demon goddess, Tataka, who possesses Gabrielle's body. The demon heals a few people to present herself as a devi, a divine healer, then uses the adoration of the multitude to try to destroy Xena and Eli — who is the true devi.

The opening montage of Indian scenes showcases the superb set and costume design that creates India for these three episodes. The town exteriors are especially realistic, with their crowded, winding alleys, and archways and walls with peeling paint. This episode also had an unusually large number of extras — about a hundred, many of Indian ancestry — as well as a pack of dogs!

Gabrielle, to Xena
"We're gonna do yoga? You and me? Okay, who are you and what have you done with Xena?"

Disclaimer: In Memory of Women's Best Friends: Bear, Dodger, Kali, Samantha, Taffy, Bear.

BETWEEN THE LINES

Written by: Steven L. Sears
Directed by: Rick Jacobson
Guest stars: Claire Stansfield (Alti), Tharini Mudaliar (Naiyima), Ajay Vasisht (Acklin)
Air date: 15 February 1999

A widow, saved by Xena and Gabrielle from her husband's funeral pyre, uses her spiritual powers to send them on a visit to their next life. There, Xena is the 'Mother of Peace', Gabrielle is a warrior prince and their great enemy is the reincarnated Alti, who plans to steal Xena's power and make herself the Destroyer of Nations.

The second instalment in the story of Alti's feud with Xena is enhanced by outstanding production values. Especially notable are the make-up effects of the Mehndi designs and the beautiful CGI light effects of the Mehndi's energy swirling around the characters. And Xena uses energy chakrams instead of the metal variety.

Alti, to Xena

"Don't worry. You'll die slow. I want to feel every delicious moment of your pain."

Disclaimer: Xena's Chakram got Gabrielle by the short hairs during the production of this motion picture.

'Devi'.

THE WAY

Written by: R. J. Stewart
Directed by: John Fawcett
Guest stars: Timothy Omundson (Eli), Jake McKinnon (Hanuman), Rajneel Singh (Indrajit), Rajiv Varma (Krishna)
Air date: 22 February 1999

Background: See page 35 for a look at the controversy sparked by this episode's portrayal of Krishna.

Eli, now acclaimed as an avatar — a god in human form — is being hunted by Indrajit, the demon king. When Indrajit captures Eli and Gabrielle, Xena and the monkey god Hanuman seek the aid of Krishna to rescue them. Gabrielle chooses to follow Eli's Way of Love and Xena sheds her doubts about her warrior path.

The final episode of the 'Indian trilogy' takes us from the opening 'life of a river' montage, to the grisly sight of Indrajit severing both of Xena's arms. Once again, the make-up, costume and special effects crews surpass themselves with Krishna, the nasty six-armed Indrajit and his wonderful flying carpet, and with Xena's incarnation of the four-armed Kali.

Eli, to Gabrielle

"Not 'the truth' — 'the Truth'. I've seen it. It's as real to me as these trees are to you."

Disclaimer: Any similarities between Hanuman and a major character in the motion picture classic "Planet of the Apes" is purely coincidental.

THE PLAY'S THE THING

Written by: Ashley Gable & Thomas A. Swyden
Directed by: Christopher Graves
Guest stars: Ted Raimi (Joxer), Alison Wall (Minya), Jennifer Ward-Lealand (Zehra), Mark Hadlow (Milo), Peter Muller (Dustinus Hoofmanus), Polly Baigent (Paulina)
Air date: 1 March 1999

Incidentally: If Gabrielle's scroll is so special to her, why was she using it in the bathroom?

In the theatre capital of Greece, Gabrielle gets a chance to stage a play from her own scrolls. Her biggest problems: having Joxer as her producer and finding an actress good enough to play herself. Plus, her backers are a couple of crooks using her as a front to con some warlords out of their money.

Not even the series' major theme of peace versus violence is sacred in *Xena*'s second theatrical episode. It has more in-jokes than Gabrielle has scrolls, from a warlord quoting the main title narration, to Joxer's final threat that he's going to tell his brother. Notice that the bandage on Joxer's thumb gets bigger and bigger throughout the episode…

Minya, to Gabrielle

"I never would have met Paulina if it wasn't for you! You made me realise something deep down about myself that I guess I always knew, but just didn't dare admit. Yes, I'm a — thespian!"

Disclaimer: Although no great literary works of art were harmed or plagiarized, a few thespians stole some scenes during the production of this motion picture.

THE CONVERT

Written by: Chris Manheim
Directed by: Andrew Merrifield
Guest stars: Ted Raimi (Joxer),
Kathryn Morris (Najara), Darryl Brown
(Kryton), Mfundo Morrison (Arman)
Air date: 19 April 1999

When Joxer accidentally kills a warlord, he's tormented by the guilt of his first kill, and decides he has to tell the warlord's son himself. Meanwhile Najara, escaped from prison, claims to have embraced Eli's way of peace, causing all kinds of tension between Xena and Gabrielle over whether she should have a second chance, until she finally reveals her fanaticism once again by attacking them.

Najara's apparent conversion reveals that Eli has begun to preach his message of love in Xena's neighbourhood. The newly pacifist Gabrielle replaces her staff with 'smoke compacts' which puff dust in her enemies' eyes. Take that! The stunt team scores again with the elaborate fight on the vines.

Joxer
"It's a lie... My whole life. I'm not a warrior. What kind of warrior kills somebody and then has nightmares every night?"

Disclaimer: Argo's gastrointestinal condition was cleared up upon completion of this motion picture.

TAKES ONE TO KNOW ONE

Written by: Jeff Vlaming
Directed by: Christopher Graves
Guest stars: Ted Raimi (Joxer),
Meighan Desmond (Discord), Alison
Wall (Minya), Willa O'Neill (Lila),
Darien Takle (Cyrene), Bruce Campbell
(Autolycus)
Air date: 26 April 1999

When a bounty hunter is found murdered at Cyrene's inn, Discord threatens to take all Xena's friends to Tartarus unless they hand over the murderer by dawn. The gang spends the rest of the night reconstructing the crime, only to discover the culprit is Argo.

It's a spoof of the board game Clue, as proven by Joxer's line, "Minya in the bedroom with the knife," and Minya's retort, "Oh, get a clue!" Amid the silliness, there are some nice character moments between Xena and Cyrene, and Joxer and (surprise!) Lila. And watch the comic interplay between Bruce Campbell and Ted Raimi; these two long-time thespian pals could play off each other's cues in their sleep.

Discord to Minya
"But I can't take back a horse! I don't do animals!"
"That's not what I heard!"

Disclaimer: Argo was once again proven innocent during the production of this motion picture.

ENDGAME

Written by: Steven L. Sears

Directed by: Garth Maxwell

Guest stars: Jennifer Sky (Amarice), Danielle Cormack (Ephiny), Karl Urban (Caesar), Jeremy Callaghan (Pompey), David Franklin (Brutus)

Air date: 3 May 1999

When Ephiny is killed in battle by Brutus, Xena and Gabrielle learn that the Amazons are caught up in the Roman civil war. Xena rescues Amazon prisoners from Pompey, and once again lures Caesar and Pompey into battling each other. Meanwhile, Gabrielle and Brutus try to broker a peace between Caesar and the Amazons, before Brutus finally discovers just how vast and ruthless Caesar's ambition is.

The irrepressible Pompey buys it in this episode. Jennifer Sky's Amarice was intended to be an ongoing character, until she won the lead role in *Cleopatra 2525*. David Franklin, making his first appearance as Brutus, also plays the power-hungry Braca on *Farscape*.

Amarice, to Xena

"I was thinking about what you said Xena, about not finding my answers at the end of a sword, and it seemed to make sense. Then I started thinking about old Pompey, and it seems to me he found an answer at the end of yours."

Disclaimer: Pompey's reign came to a head during the production of this motion picture.

THE IDES OF MARCH

Written by: R. J. Stewart

Directed by: Ken Girotti

Guest stars: Timothy Omundson (Eli), Jennifer Sky (Amarice), Karl Urban (Caesar), David Franklin (Brutus), Hudson Leick (Callisto)

Air date: 10 May 1999

Determined to clear Xena from his path to the Imperium, and with some unexpected help from the demonic Callisto, Caesar sets a trap with Gabrielle as the bait. While Xena and Gabrielle try to escape the doom they see coming, Brutus finally turns against Caesar.

That snowy vision of crucifixion, first seen in 'Adventures in the Sin Trade', is finally fulfilled in the riveting sequence which intercuts the crucifixion with Caesar's assassination. Girotti and editor Robert Field edited the sequence on — cue *Twilight Zone* music — Good Friday, during a thunderstorm.

Nearly Departed: Caesar gets his "Et tu, Brute?" and Xena and Gabrielle die for real again (it's Xena's third death, Gabrielle's fifth). Xena's chakram breaks when it cripples her.

Xena to Brutus

"Was it snowing on Mount Amaro?"
"Yes, it was snowing when I left."

Disclaimer: Xena and Gabrielle were killed during the production of this motion picture.

DÉJÀ VU ALL OVER AGAIN

Written by: R. J. Stewart

Directed by: Renee O'Connor

Guest stars: Ted Raimi (Harry), Kevin Smith (Ares), Robert Trebor (Marco)

Air date: 17 May 1999

Background: This episode was Renee O'Connor's directorial début.

In 1999, *Xena* fan Annie and her boyfriend Harry go to a past life therapist to find out if she's the reincarnation of Xena. Instead they learn that Annie was Joxer, Harry was Xena, Mattie the therapist was Gabrielle and Mattie's partner Marco *is* Ares, still trying to get his Warrior Princess back.

In an unconventional creative decision, *Xena* follows the cliff-hanger of 'The Ides of March' with this silly and entertaining clip show as a season finale. Joan of Arc, Patton, Custer and Pocahontas all sit in Mattie's waiting room.

Mattie to Marco/Ares

"I don't watch that show, a bunch of chop-socky crap. Besides, this was so repulsive, it couldn't have been an episode."

"Aaah, you never know with that show. They're sneaky. They'll try anything. One week they're melodrama, the next week the Three Stooges. And they're way too serialised."

Disclaimer: No Sword-Wielding, Card-Playing, Therapy-Seeking French Freedom Fighters were deflowered during the production of this motion picture. However, rumors of Custer and Pocahontas remain unconfirmed.

'The Ides of March'.

FALLEN ANGEL

Teleplay by: R. J. Stewart

Story by: Rob Tapert & R. J. Stewart

Directed by: John Fawcett

Guest stars: Ted Raimi (Joxer), Timothy Omundson (Eli), Jennifer Sky (Amarice), Charles Mesure (Michael), Hudson Leick (Callisto)

Air date: 27 September 1999

Eagle Eye: Watch for Angel Callisto starting Xena's pregnancy with a touch.

'Fallen Angel'.

Joxer, Eli and Amarice prepare to bury their friends, but a demon attack led by Callisto on the angels guarding the souls of Xena and Gabrielle causes Gabrielle to fall into Hell. Xena joins the archangels to rescue her, but then takes Callisto's place in Hell to save her.

Angels, demons, CGI heavenly realms and miracles could have become pure television hokum, but the powerful script, beautiful costumes and effects, and an array of fine performances make the episode soar.

Demon Gabrielle to Callisto

"*Callisto, when Xena burned your family, did you see them on fire? Did you smell their flesh sizzling? You know what I think? You wanted them to die so you'd have a reason to be a bitch!*"

Disclaimer: Hell hath no fury like a woman scorned.

CHAKRAM

Written by: Chris Manheim

Directed by: Doug Lefler

Guest stars: Ted Raimi (Joxer), Jennifer Sky (Amarice), Timothy Omundson (Eli), Kevin Smith (Ares)

Air date: 4 October 1999

Costume Change: Gabrielle gets into a woven leather halter and skirt, and acquires a pair of deadly sais.

The resurrected Xena can't remember anything about being a warrior, and she's being hunted by Ares and a rival war god who need her to recover the Chakram of Light, which has the power to kill gods. Meanwhile, Joxer asks everyone for advice on how to tell Gabrielle he's in love with her.

Xena's new chakram, a fusion of the Chakram of Light and her old dark chakram, can split in mid-air into two flying yin-yangs of death. Eli makes Ares back down with just a look: love really is the most powerful force on Earth.

Gabrielle, Amarice and Joxer, to Xena

"Xena, it's not your memory. It's like you've lost your…"

"… fire and edge, your…"

"… marbles!"

Disclaimer: Xena's Dark and Violent Past was restored during the production of this motion picture.

SUCCESSION

Written by: Steven L. Sears

Directed by: Rick Jacobson

Guest stars: Jenya Lano (Mavican), Kevin Smith (Ares)

Air date: 11 October 1999

Costume Change: Xena's outfit changes from the standard brown and copper to the blue and silver she wears throughout her pregnancy — before she discovers she's pregnant!

In an attempt to persuade Gabrielle to join him, Ares devises a game using warrior princess wannabe Mavican. He traps Xena and Gabrielle in an alternate dimension where they share one body — alternating night and day. Mavican tries to kill Xena through Gabrielle, but Xena is not allowed to kill Mavican. Gabrielle can kill Mavican, but if she does, Ares will win. In Ares' game, there is one ultimate rule: anyone who asks for help doesn't deserve it.

The artificial battleground, in which the combatants have to make weapons of natural objects, recalls the classic *Star Trek* episode, 'Arena'. This is Ares' second attempt to seduce Gabrielle — it's ironic that he sees her potential as a warrior while Xena is still trying to be protective.

Xena to Gabrielle

"The next seven little bad guys we come across — they're all yours."

"Little! Is that a crack at my height?"

"No, they're just harder for me to reach."

Disclaimer: Ares' Libido was not harmed during the production of this motion picture.

ANIMAL ATTRACTION

Written by: Chris Manheim

Directed by: Rick Jacobson

Guest stars: Ted Raimi (Joxer), Jennifer Sky (Amarice), Mfundo Morrison (Arman), Alison Bruce (Talia)

Air date: 18 October 1999

Gabrielle finally gets her own horse, Xena learns she's pregnant, and Amarice and Arman battle their egos and their hormones. Meanwhile, Xena's old buddy Sheriff Talia has a showdown with a bad hombre who's also her husband.

Every Western movie cliché ever filmed shows up on the streets of old Greece in this *High Noon* send-up: the deputy turning in his badge, the showdown in the street, Gabrielle twirling her sais like pistols, even the bad guy landing in the water trough. Getting into the spirit, for one day during production, the entire crew dressed as cowboys, cowgirls and saloon hussies. In a more comedic tradition, Talia's tight leather breeches kept splitting across the seat when Alison Bruce tried to fight or mount a horse.

Talia, to Xena

"My mother was a midwife, Xena. Wake up and smell the diapers."

Disclaimer: Although the Rabbit Died, no other animals were harmed during the production of this motion picture.

THEM BONES, THEM BONES

Written by: Buddy Williers

Directed by: John Fawcett

Guest stars: Claire Stansfield (Alti), Jennifer Sky (Amarice), Kate Elliot (Yakut)

Air date: 1 November 1999

Background: Buddy Williers is a pseudonym for Steven L. Sears.

Xena learns that Alti's spirit is attacking her baby's soul in the spirit realm, so she, Gabrielle and Amarice travel to the Northern Amazons to seek Yakut's help.

Kate Elliot reprises her role as Yakut from 'Adventures in the Sin Trade' in an episode loaded with reality-stretching camera effects and images. The battle of the skeletons was choreographed with real stunt performers, who were then digitally replaced with the CG skeletons of Xena and Alti.

Xena to Alti

"There aren't many guarantees in life, Alti, but I promise you this: if you harm my child, I will hound you..."
"Well, at least we'll be together again. I so missed these intimate little moments."

Disclaimer: Xena and Alti were Bad To The Bone during the production of this motion picture.

PURITY

Written by: Jeff Vlaming
Directed by: Mark Beesley
Guest stars: Ted Raimi (Joxer),
Marie Matiko (Pao Ssu/K'ao Hsin)
Air date: 8 November 1999

Incidentally: Gunpowder, the 'black powder', was first used in China around 900 AD.

Xena, Joxer and Gabrielle go to Chin to recover Lao Ma's secret book so that its powers can't be used for evil. There they meet Lao Ma's twin daughters, one good, one bad, and discover that naughty Pao Ssu has the secret of the explosive 'black powder'.

Watch for a repeat of the porch tableau from 'The Debt', this time with Xena standing in Lao Ma's place. Joxer's the mystery guy: how did he catch up with Xena and Gabrielle, who were last seen with the Northern Amazons? And when did he become a good cook?

Joxer to Gabrielle
"You know, that's the first time I ever had three feet in my pants."
"You tell anyone, you're dead!"

Disclaimer: To obtain a copy of Joxer's recipe for Moo Shu Sauce and other Chinese delicacies, visit your local bookstore or look for it at the tavern.

BACK IN THE BOTTLE

Teleplay by: Buddy Williers
Story by: Rob Tapert & Steven L. Sears
Directed by: Rick Jacobson
Guest stars: Ted Raimi (Joxer), Marie Matiko (Pao Ssu/K'ao Hsin), Anthony Wong (Lin Qi), George Kee Cheung (Khan), Daniel Sing (Ming T'ien)
Air date: 15 November 1999

The spirits of Pao Ssu and Ming T'ien have joined with the warlord Khan and his army to lay waste to Chin. While Gabrielle, Joxer and the handsome Lin Qi lead refugees to shelter, Xena uses Lao Ma's mental powers to go one against an army.

The impressive pyrotechnics and battle scenes in this episode use a combination of practical, green screen and CGI effects. If Khan looks familiar, it's because actor George Kee Cheung has had roles in scores of films and television series, from *Lethal Weapon 4* to *Seinfeld*.

Xena to a very hungry Gabrielle
"Ever since that fight with Pao Ssu I can't seem to harness the power. What did Lao Ma have that I don't?"
"A full stomach."

Disclaimer: Pao Ssu's Split Personality was not harmed during the production of this motion picture.

LITTLE PROBLEMS

Written by: Gregg Ostrin
Directed by: Allison Liddi
Guest stars: Alexandra Tydings
(Aphrodite), Rose McIver (Daphne),
Colin Moy (Galantis)
Air date: 22 November 1999

Aphrodite accidentally traps Xena in the body of a motherless little girl. While the goddess and Gabrielle try to find a way to put Xena back before sunset, Xena and Daphne have to fight off a warlord's goons, and break Daphne's grief-stricken father out of his emotional armour.

An odd hybrid of a story, mixing the farce of body switching (co-ed oil wrestling!) with the pathos of the bereaved father and child. Despite Aphrodite's reputation, this is the only episode in which she even gets close to having any fun in her chosen field! Colin Moy also portrays Phantes in 'Hooves and Harlots', and the Emperor Augustus in 'Livia'.

Gabrielle to Castor

"You speak our language with such ease!"
"My brother and I pride ourselves on being cunning linguists."

Disclaimer: No Pie Tins were harmed during the making of Tharon's mask.

SEEDS OF FAITH

Written by: George Strayton & Tom
O'Neill
Directed by: Garth Maxwell
Guest stars: Timothy Omundson
(Eli), Hudson Leick (Callisto), Kevin
Smith (Ares)
Air date: 10 January 2000

Fearing that Eli is a threat to the gods, Ares decides to put him out of business — permanently. Gabrielle and Xena vow to defend Eli, but Eli refuses to let them use violence, even to save his life. Then Ares kills Eli, and Xena swears that she will kill the God of War.

Xena's hundredth episode was surrounded by much publicity. It also marked the final appearances of Timothy Omundson and Hudson Leick. We finally learn that Xena's child is the reincarnation of Callisto's purified soul.

Callisto to Eli

"The new world can only be built on the foundations of the old one. The order of the gods must fall, and you, Eli, are the hammer. There is no reason to be afraid. Your faith is stronger than any who have come before you."
"'Til now."

Disclaimer: Thanks to Eli's non-violent ways, many people lost their lives during the production of this motion picture.

LYRE, LYRE, HEARTS ON FIRE

Written by: Adam Armus & Nora Kay Foster

Directed by: Mark Beesley

Guest stars: Ted Raimi (Joxer/Jace), Gillian Iliana Waters (Amoria), Jay Laga'aia (Draco), Darien Takle (Cyrene)

Air date: 17 January 2000

In Melodia, the music capital of Greece, Xena and Gabrielle put on a battle of the bands for possession of a Golden Lyre. Meanwhile, Cyrene tries to find her daughter a man, Joxer seesaws between his crush on a cute Amazon and his embarrassment at his gay brother Jace, and Draco vows that if he can't have Gabrielle, no one will.

In *Xena*'s second musical extravaganza, the cast sings and dances up a storm, especially Ted Raimi as Jace, but though Darien Takle has had a long career in musical theatre, she does almost no singing or dancing. The last shot in the closing credits is an outtake of a very pregnant Lucy Lawless dancing in Gabrielle's go-go outfit.

Joxer to Jace

"*That stupid accent of yours, like you're from Spain or something. You're from Olympic Street in Athens, two blocks from Akbar the Meat Man, just like me.*"
"*Well, not just like you. I don't have a pasta strainer for a shirt.*"

'Seeds of Faith'.

Disclaimer: No Lyres were strung out during the production of this motion picture.

PUNCH LINES

Written by: Chris Manheim

Directed by: Andrew Merrifield

Guest stars: Ted Raimi (Joxer), Alexandra Tydings (Aphrodite)

Air date: 24 January 2000

Eagle Eye: Watch for an Ancient Greek shopping cart and a 'Wet Floor' sign.

A sleepless Gabrielle recounts her day's adventures to Aphrodite... She bet the pregnant and grouchy Xena that she couldn't go a whole day without losing her temper. Then she offended Lachrymose, the God of Despair, and he shrank her to Barbie size and Argo to pony size. She then had to conceal Argo's plight from Xena, until she could make the gloomy god laugh, thereby breaking the spell.

A second, giant-sized supermarket set was built for the tiny Gabrielle scene. The pie fight (with pies made of egg white and potato flakes) is an homage to the 1965 Blake Edwards romp *The Great Race*, and even Joseph LoDuca's music for the scene echoes Henry Mancini's film score.

Joxer, watching Gabrielle run from Lachrymose

"Must be Lachrymose intolerant."

Disclaimer: Gabrielle and Argo were shrunk and Permanently Pressed during the production of this motion picture.

GOD FEARING CHILD

Teleplay by: Roberto Gaston Orci & Alex Kurtzman

Story by: Chris Manheim

Directed by: Phil Sgricca

Guest stars: Charles Keating (Zeus), Kevin Smith (Ares), Meg Foster (Hera), Kevin Sorbo (Hercules)

Air date: 31 January 2000

Eagle Eye: Watch for a stuffed Hydra that squeaks.

The Fates tell Zeus that Xena's child heralds the end of his reign, so he decides to kill the baby. In response, Xena and Gabrielle try to steal Hades' Helmet of Invisibility to conceal Xena from Zeus. Hercules, initially torn between his father and his friend, soon promises to protect Xena and her baby, and finds an unexpected ally: Hera.

In Kevin Sorbo's last appearance as Hercules, the hero reconciles with Hera, and kills Zeus in one of the finest dramatic moments in either series. Ares professes his love for Xena, and Xena's daughter Eve is finally born.

Ares to Xena

"I thought in your present condition you might be a little more gullible."

"I'm pregnant, not brain damaged."

Disclaimer: Zeus Cashed in his Chips during the production of this motion picture.

ETERNAL BONDS

Written by: Chris Manheim

Directed by: Mark Beesley

Guest stars: Ted Raimi (Joxer),
Kevin Smith (Ares)

Air date: 7 February 2000

Catch the Baby, Round Three:
Eve in her furry pouch zooms up and
down on a rope over a high branch, while
Xena battles the soldiers of three gods.

Now that Eve has been born, all the gods hunt Xena to
kill the baby — except Ares, who hunts Xena for the
usual seductive reasons. Amid the fighting, Joxer is
poisoned by a priest's sword, and he and Gabrielle race to a
healing mandrake tree.

Tornadoes, lightning, a visit from three Magi — who turn
out to be the murderous priests of Apollo, Artemis and
Poseidon — and time coming to a halt all figure in the gods'
pursuit of Eve. Joxer and Ares both get rejected. Gabrielle
shows off her skill at handling her horse, and Xena nurses her
baby on camera, as part of Lucy Lawless' strong advocacy of
breastfeeding.

Joxer, to Gabrielle

*"You said that you loved me but only as a friend, right? I know
you do, but Gabrielle, I will always love you more than that,
and that's just something I'll have to live with."*

'God Fearing Child'.

Disclaimer: Ares' virility was harmed during the production of this motion picture.

AMPHIPOLIS UNDER SIEGE

Written by: Chris Black
Directed by: Mark Beesley
Guest stars: Paris Jefferson
(Athena), Darien Takle (Cyrene),
Musetta Vander (Ilainus),
Kevin Smith (Ares)
Air date: 14 February 2000

Incidentally: Greek fire was an incendiary substance used by the Byzantines to set fire to enemy ships.

Athena lays siege to Amphipolis, and offers Xena and the townspeople a choice between their lives and Eve's. While the town unites behind Xena and Cyrene to fight back, Xena hatches a scheme to use Ares and trick the gods into leaving her and her child alone.

It took two costumiers fifteen minutes each day to put Musetta Vander into Ilainus' silver corset.

Cyrene, discovering Xena in the sack with Ares, and Ares
"I suppose it could be worse. I mean, after all, he is a god. Although I would have preferred Apollo, or maybe Hermes…"
"Excuse me — Hermes? With the wings on the feet? Oh, please!"

Disclaimer: Post Production was under siege during the production of this motion picture.

MARRIED WITH FISHSTICKS

Written by: Kevin Maynard
Directed by: Paul Grinder
Guest stars: Ted Raimi
(Joxer/Hagar), Alexandra Tydings
(Aphrodite/Crabella), Meighan
Desmond (Discord/Sturgina)
Air date: 21 February 2000

Gabrielle gets hit on the head and wakes up in a fantasy world, where she's a fishwife (literally!) with amnesia. Her children are brats (and sprats), her supposed husband — whose real wife has left him — has substituted her because he needs a wife to win political office, and her extremely tacky friends are actually trying to steal him from her.

A take-off on the Goldie Hawn/Kurt Russell comedy *Overboard*, overstuffed with slapstick and pop culture references. Discord and Aphrodite carry on their spat from the Hercules episode, 'Love on the Rocks'. Strangely enough, Aphrodite also ends up in the wedding cake again (see 'Stranger in a Strange World').

Discord to Aphrodite
"Well, if it isn't the ever-titillating Aphrodite. I almost didn't recognise you with your legs so close together."
"Discord, are you still looking for someone to shave your back?"

Disclaimer: No Sea Nymphs or other Denizens of the Deep were harmed during the production of this motion picture.

LIFEBLOOD

Teleplay by: R. J. Stewart and George Strayton & Tom O'Neill
Story by: Rob Tapert & R. J. Stewart
Directed by: Michael Hurst
Guest stars: Selma Blair (Utma/Cyane), Monica McSwan (Olan), Danielle Cormack (Samsara), Claudia Black (Karina)
Air date: 13 March 2000

Costume Change: Xena reverts to her iconic brown and copper ensemble.

'Married With Fishsticks'.

Yakut's ghost shows Xena a vision of the Amazons' beginnings, which reveals that the Amazons have strayed from their traditions, into rituals of blood and violence.

The flashback parts of this episode use footage from *Amazon High*, a Renaissance pilot which was cancelled because the leads could not commit to a series. Danielle Cormack and Karl Urban, who have a big brawl here, are paired romantically in the critically praised New Zealand film *The Price of Milk*. Claudia Black is better known as Aeryn Sun in *Farscape*.

Xena
"*I used to think that I had to go through life alone, and anything else was a sign of weakness. So I traded my home and family for violence, blood — so much blood. I never want Eve to know that life. Maybe if she becomes an Amazon she'll always feel a part of something.*"

Disclaimer: Warning: The Surgeon General confirms practising Weird and Grotesque Amazon rituals may be hazardous to your health.

KINDRED SPIRITS

Written by: George Strayton & Tom O'Neill

Directed by: Josh Becker

Guest Star: Ted Raimi (Joxer)

Air date: 20 March 2000

Gabrielle considers becoming the reigning Queen of the Amazons, while Xena slowly goes nuts from too much eager Amazon company — especially a girl who thinks she can replace Gabrielle as sidekick. Meanwhile, Joxer has been caught acting like a man around nubile young Amazons, and faces the penalty of mortal combat.

It's remarkable to see Xena and especially Gabrielle (who was a teenager only yesterday) playing surrogate mothers to these adolescent Amazons. Xena invents the baby swing, and Lucy Lawless and Ted Raimi have a growling good time hamming up a parody of professional wrestling.

Rhea to Xena

"What's it like being with a man?"
"The good news is, it's different every time. The bad news is, it's different every time. You're always hoping for Greek Fire, but sometimes you just get diddly."

Disclaimer: Many Cinnamon Swirls lost their lives in the making of Gabrielle's Headdress.

ANTONY AND CLEOPATRA

Written by: Carl Ellsworth

Directed by: Michael Hurst

Guest stars: Jon Bennett (Antony), David Franklin (Brutus), Mark Warren (Octavius)

Air date: 17 April 2000

Xena takes the place of the murdered Cleopatra to save Egypt from the bloody civil war between Antony, Brutus and Caesar's nephew Octavius. Her plan involves wearing luscious Egyptian wigs, sitting in baths of milk, and getting Antony to fall for her — a strategy that backfires when she falls for him as well.

Lovely Egyptian sets and backdrops add some much-needed visual serenity to an episode that includes lots of nubile queens in the bath, Xena coming on to Antony in nothing but a few golden shackles, and the most gratuitously blood-spattered battle of the series. The sea battle is a nod to *Ben-Hur*.

Gabrielle, to Xena about Antony

"I'm losing sight of your plan, Xena. Are you going to flirt him to death?"

Disclaimer: No Rubberized Snakes intent on destroying the Queen of Egypt were harmed during the production of this motion picture.

LOOKING DEATH IN THE EYE

Written by: Carl Ellsworth
Directed by: Garth Maxwell
Guest stars: Ted Raimi (Joxer),
Paris Jefferson (Athena), Kevin Smith
(Ares)
Air date: 24 April 2000

Nearly Departed: Xena, Gabrielle and
Eve appear to die in a fiery crash staged
to fool the gods.

The Fates decree that Xena must die to end the gods' hunt for Eve and usher in the Twilight of the Gods. Xena devises an elaborate scheme to cheat Fate by capturing Celesta — Death — and using her tears to fake the demise of Eve, Gabrielle and herself in a spectacular wagon crash over a cliff. The plan backfires when Ares entombs the apparently dead Warrior Princess and bard in an ice cave on Mount Aetna.

Old Joxer's flashback, to the fateful day when Xena and Gabrielle disappeared, sets up the twenty-five year jump in the series' chronology. Kevin Smith has one of his finest dramatic moments as the grief-stricken Ares, and Lucy Lawless voices Meg in a brief off-camera cameo. There's an unanswered question: how did Xena find the home of the Fates?

Celesta to Xena
"I only visit those whose rightful time…"
"Who decides when it's the right time? You are at the beck and call of every warlord and murderer."

'Looking Death in the Eye'.

Disclaimer: Death almost died during the production of this motion picture.

LIVIA

Written by: Chris Manheim
Directed by: Rick Jacobson
Guest stars: Ted Raimi (Joxer),
Adrienne Wilkinson (Livia),
William Gregory Lee (Virgil),
Kevin Smith (Ares)
Air date: 1 May 2000

Xena and Gabrielle wake to find that Eve has grown into Livia, Rome's champion and the protégée of Ares. In one steamy encounter, Xena exposes Livia's ambitions to the Emperor Augustus, and shows Livia that Ares, given the slightest 'come hither' from Xena, would dump her in an instant. After Xena publicly defeats her daughter in the arena, Livia swears she'll make her mother wish she'd never been born.

This episode introduces Adrienne Wilkinson and William Gregory Lee in the recurring roles of Xena's grown daughter, Livia, and Joxer's poet son, Virgil. Lawless gets into old age prosthetics and a chubby suit for her final reprise of Meg, now Joxer's wife. Joxer's tavern is decorated with props and costumes from the whole series, including Gabrielle's old costume and staff, and the Xena stage costume from 'The Play's the Thing'.

Xena to Gabrielle
"Meg! It's Meg!"
"No, Xena, you were identical. [Second look] If I were you, I would lay off the starches!"

Disclaimer: Due to an overabundance of Beans and Bard Burgers, Meg's gastrointestinal problems intensified during the production of this motion picture.

'Livia'.

EVE

Written by: George Strayton & Tom O'Neill

Directed by: Mark Beesley

Guest stars: Ted Raimi (Joxer), Adrienne Wilkinson (Livia), William Gregory Lee (Virgil), Kevin Smith (Ares)

Air date: 8 May 2000

Really Departed: Livia murders Joxer when he attempts to rescue his unrequited love, Gabrielle.

L ivia leads her troops on a bloody rampage to punish Xena for humiliating her. After she massacres whole towns and finally murders Joxer, Xena decides her daughter Eve is dead, and that she will have to kill Livia to stop her. Meanwhile, Ares works his tempter's tongue on both of them. In the final mother-daughter duel one can't even be sure which one the God of War is cheering for.

Xena prays for only the third time in the series, this time to Eli, asking him to show her the perfect love that can save her daughter. Livia's conversion recalls that of St Paul described in the Book of Acts: St Paul was on his way to lead persecutions of Christians when he saw a vision in a blinding light.

Woman at a massacre, to Xena

"She killed them all! My husband, my children! I asked her 'Why, why?' She said, 'Ask Xena. Ask my mother.'"

Disclaimer: Joxer's sudden and unexpected death slowed down his rapid aging process during the production of this motion picture.

MOTHERHOOD

Teleplay by: R. J. Stewart

Story by: Rob Tapert

Directed by: Rick Jacobson

Guest stars: Ted Raimi (Joxer), Alexandra Tydings (Aphrodite), Adrienne Wilkinson (Eve), Paris Jefferson (Athena), William Gregory Lee (Virgil), Kevin Smith (Ares)

Air date: 15 May 2000

W hile Eve suffers torments of remorse for her crimes, the gods learn that she is still alive and pursue her again. In response, Eli's god gives Xena the power to kill gods as long as her daughter lives, because Eve will become Eli's Messenger. Athena sends the Furies to torment Gabrielle and drive her to avenge Joxer's death by killing Eve. In the final confrontation, Ares saves Xena — and kills his sister Athena — by giving up his immortality to preserve the lives of Eve and Gabrielle, and with them Xena's god-killing power.

Xena brings on the Twilight of the Gods by killing seven Olympians in a single episode! Gabrielle's attack on Eve was originally much more violent: cut from the final version was Gabrielle stabbing Eve repeatedly, and a battle with the Furies.

Ares, to Xena

"You shot me! I'm the God of War! Nobody shoots the God of War!"

Disclaimer: All the Gods were harmed during the production of this motion picture.

COMING HOME

Written by: Melissa Good

Directed by: Mark Beesley

Guest stars: Kevin Smith (Ares)

Air date: 2 October 2000

Nearly Departed: Xena dies for the fourth time, in a ploy to free Ares from the torment of the Furies.

While Ares tries to make his armies believe he's still a potent God of War, the Furies pose as Xena, Gabrielle and Eve in an attempt to drive Ares mad and trick him into attacking the real Xena and the Amazons.

Xena again demonstrates her advanced medical knowledge by using hypothermia to aid her resuscitation after drowning. She also makes a nearly supernatural chakram kill, hitting all three Furies with a chakram that she threw several minutes before they even appeared in the target zone!

Xena to Ares

"The great God of War can't even hurt a fly!"

"Xena! You came!"

"Lucky for you! That fly nearly had you!"

Disclaimer: Xena and Gabrielle's psyches were harmed during the making of this motion picture.

THE HAUNTING OF AMPHIPOLIS

Teleplay by: Joel Metzger

Story by: Edithe Swenson & Joel Metzger

Directed by: Garth Maxwell

Guest stars: Adrienne Wilkinson (Eve), Darien Takle (Cyrene), Anthony Ray Parker (Mephistopheles)

Air date: 9 October 2000

Xena, Gabrielle and Eve return to Amphipolis to find Cyrene long dead and the village haunted by demonic spirits. They soon discover that Mephistopheles, the King of Hell, has opened a portal because he needs the blood of the Messenger, Eve, to take shape in the material world.

A haunted house episode with all the trappings: cobwebs, creaky doors and mysterious wailings, thunderstorms, worms, showers of blood, ghosts and zombies. The worst "Don't look!" moment — maggots eating Gabrielle's hands to the bone.

Mephistopheles to Xena, as they fight

"I thought you were the god killer, Xena..."

"I'm just a little distracted by your good looks."

Disclaimer: No maggots were harmed during the making of this motion picture, although a few were found stuck to Gabrielle's teeth.

HEART OF DARKNESS

Written by: Emily Skopov
Directed by: Mark Beesley
Guest stars: Adrienne Wilkinson
(Eve), William Gregory Lee (Virgil),
Alex Mendoza (Lucifer)
Air date: 16 October 2000

Incidentally: The Seven Deadly Sins, a medieval conceit, were Pride, Anger, Avarice, Envy, Gluttony, Lust and Sloth.

Because she killed Mephistopheles, Xena must become the new ruler of Hell unless she can find someone to take her place. She chooses the archangel sent to cast her into Hell: a proud young spirit named Lucifer. As Xena tempts him, Eve watches the evil from Hell blackening the hearts of everyone in Amphipolis, and succumbs to her own temptation by taking up the sword again to fight the fallen angels.

This episode's orgy, which may be the steamiest Xena sequence yet, includes a dance between Xena and Gabrielle, and Virgil getting very cosy with the bard, while Xena teaches Lucifer the delights of the flesh.

Lucifer to Xena

"Nice place you got here."
"Well, that's the last time I let an evil demon do the redecorating."

'Heart of Darkness'.

Disclaimer: All Hell broke loose during the filming of this motion picture.

WHO'S GURKHAN?

Teleplay by: R. J. Stewart

Story by: Rob Tapert

Directed by: Michael Hurst

Guest stars: Adrienne Wilkinson (Eve), William Gregory Lee (Virgil), Willa O'Neill (Lila), Calvin Tuteao (Gurkhan), Tandi Wright (Sara)

Air date: 23 October 2000

Xena and her little family travel to North Africa to rescue Gabrielle's niece, who has apparently been enslaved by the warlord Gurkhan. To find the real Gurkhan among his doubles, Xena and Gabrielle have to infiltrate his household as members of his harem.

William Gregory Lee enjoyed playing a little of Joxer's humour in Virgil for this episode. When a slave dealer whips off Xena's clothes to examine the merchandise, the exchange of looks between Virgil and Xena is funnier than a dozen one-liners. This episode also gives Xena her worst beating ever!

Xena to Virgil, about Gabrielle

"I gave her something for her seasickness. She'll be out for a while."

"I get it. You're going to Magadoor without her. She's not going to like that."

"She's going to like being beheaded even less."

Disclaimer: Xena's uncanny ability to recover from devastating wounds was not harmed during the production of this motion picture.

LEGACY

Written by: Melissa Good

Directed by: Chris Martin-Jones

Guest stars: Alison Bruce (Kahina), Rawiri Paratene (Tazere)

Air date: 30 October 2000

Hot Tub Watch: Yet another one — is anyone still counting?

In the Sahara, Xena and Gabrielle agree to help two feuding desert tribes in their war against the Romans. Then Gabrielle kills a chieftain's son by mistake. The tribes condemn her to death and Xena has to betray both sides to the Romans to provide the distraction that will save her friend.

This episode finally brings Gabrielle face to face with the consequences of her decision to become a warrior, as she deals with the guilt of killing an innocent. Alison Bruce had a close call during filming: the outer wrap of her costume ignited on a candle in one scene. Look out for polo played with skulls!

Xena to Gabrielle

"I felt that way once. I felt there was nothing left to live for..."

"What changed it for you?"

"You did."

Disclaimer: Despite severe air turbulence, no sand dunes were harmed during the making of this motion picture, although some experienced bouts of motion sickness.

THE ABYSS

Written by: James Kahn

Directed by: Rick Jacobson

Guest star: William Gregory Lee (Virgil)

Air date: 6 November 2000

Eagle Eye: Watch for a glimpse of Joxer's sword at Virgil's camp, and a human bite mark on Xena's neck.

Cannibals capture Virgil and hunt Xena and Gabrielle, while Gabrielle still suffers from guilt and lost nerve over her killing of Korah in 'Legacy'. Xena lets the cannibals capture the wounded Gabrielle to save her from dying of hypothermia, while Xena builds the worlds biggest water booby trap. She dams a waterfall single-handed, and then unleashes it on the entire cannibal war party.

The cannibals, dressed in wild boar masks and skeleton rib armour, outdo the Horde in scary looks and savage behaviour. Renee O'Connor says that being made up to be a cannibal's dinner was her worst experience during the filming of *Xena*: "It goes against every human instinct imaginable!"

Xena, luring the wild boar-mask-wearing cannibals into her trap
"*Here, piggies!*"

'The Abyss'.

Disclaimer: Virgil's appetite was suppressed during the making of this motion picture.

THE RHEINGOLD

Written by: R. J. Stewart

Directed by: John Fawcett

Guest stars: Brittney Powell (Brunhilda), Renato Bartolomei (Beowulf), Alexander Petersons (Odin)

Air date: 13 November 2000

Gabrielle follows Xena on a quest to the far North, where she meets the warrior Brunhilda, Xena's biggest fan. Brunhilda tells her the thirty-five year old story of Xena, the most feared of Odin's Valkyries. Meanwhile Xena joins forces with the warrior Beowulf to track down Grinhilda, who was once a rival Valkyrie who Xena turned into a monster.

Xena takes on Norse, Germanic and Anglo-Saxon mythology as she battles Odin, the Valkyries and the monster Grindl. The constant sunset skies bring some beauty to the Valkyries' flights, while KNB FX Group triumphs again with the creation of mother and son monsters.

Beowulf to Xena

"The people up here think of you as a demon."
"So they should."

Disclaimer: No flying horses were harmed during the making of this motion picture, although several villagers were bombarded with aerial manure.

'The Rheingold'.

THE RING

Written by: Joel Metzger

Directed by: Rick Jacobson

Guest stars: Brittney Powell
(Brunhilda), Renato Bartolomei
(Beowulf), Alexander Petersons
(Odin), Victoria Hill (Waltraute), Roger
Morrissey (Monster Grinhilda)

Air date: 20 November 2000

Gabrielle and her guide Brunhilda catch up with Xena and Beowulf and they hunt together for Grindl and the evil ring made of the Rheingold Xena stole long ago. While Odin pursues them with his Valkyries to capture the ring for himself, Brunhilda falls in love with Gabrielle and betrays both sides by kidnapping her.

The cold-hearted and ambitious Odin of this story seems a completely different god from the noble Odin of the *Hercules* Norse episodes. The ring's power, which can only be used by those who have renounced love, is a metaphor for the old saying about the corruption of absolute power. Both Beowulf and Brunhilda fall in love with Gabrielle, not Xena — maybe these Nordic types prefer blondes.

Brunhilda to Xena

"Xena, I have waited my entire life to meet you."

"If I knew I had a fan coming, I would have combed my hair."

Disclaimer: Gabrielle's popularity surged during the making of this motion picture.

THE RETURN OF THE VALKYRIE

Written by: Emily Skopov

Directed by: John Fawcett

Guest stars: Brittney Powell
(Brunhilda), Renato Bartolomei
(Beowulf), Alexander Petersons
(Odin), Victoria Hill (Waltraute), Roger
Morrissey (Monster Grinhilda), Dean
O'Gorman (Wiglaf)

Air date: 27 November 2000

A year after Xena put on the ring, Beowulf finds her as the amnesiac bride of King Hrothgar. He rescues her and takes her back to the Norse lands, where only she can defeat the monster Grinhilda and awaken Gabrielle from Brunhilda's magic fire.

Xena and Gabrielle lose yet another year of their lives, this time to the ring's enchantments. Lucy Lawless shows off some sensational snow princess gowns, and gets a ride on a cow. Not surprisingly, the Sleeping Beauty kiss that Xena gives to awaken Gabrielle caused a sensation among subtext fans.

Wiglaf to Xena

"That's what Vikings do! Fighting gives our lives meaning!"

"Fighting gives your lives meaning? Do you have any idea how stupid that is?"

Disclaimer: Any similarity between our story and the classic Children's Fairy Tale is purely coincidental.

OLD ARES HAD A FARM

Written by: R. J. Stewart
Directed by: Charles Siebert
Guest star: Kevin Smith (Ares)
Air date: 15 January 2001

When Ares' warlord enemies put a bounty on his mortal head, Xena and Gabrielle coax him to hide out on an abandoned farm, disguised as a farmer. Getting the former God of War to do a little honest work proves harder than driving off the bounty hunters. But he does finally get to sleep with Xena and Gabrielle.

Lucy Lawless and Renee O'Connor romp about the farm in Daisy Mae dresses, while Kevin Smith flaunts his very manly pecs — making it hard to believe he's lost *all* his powers. The dog's affection for Ares was 'encouraged' by the fact Kevin Smith was smeared with meat jelly!

Xena to Ares, who is on the floor covered with roof debris and a dog
"What are you doing?"
"I'm just lying here, smelling my mortality, every muscle in my body aching. I have grey hair, and the dog has its tongue in my mouth."

Disclaimer: Ares went to the dogs during the making of this motion picture.

DANGEROUS PREY

Written by: Joel Metzger
Directed by: Renee O'Connor
Guest stars: Tsianina Joelson (Varia), Sandy Winton (Prince Morloch)
Air date: 23 January 2001

The hunter Prince Morloch, whose favourite prey is humans, plans to hunt the Amazons to extinction. Then he encounters Xena, and decides she is the most worthy prey he has ever seen. Xena's plans to defeat him are hindered by the angry and reckless young Amazon Varia.

Tsianina Joelson, in her début as future Amazon Queen Varia, gives ample warning of the trouble she'll cause. Special effects provide a nifty new chakram effect zinging around inside a cave and a very realistic forest fire. The stunt team's duel on the tower of stacked logs recalls a classic block stacking game.

Xena to Morloch
"I'm not an Amazon."
"But you're so tall."
"It's the boots."

Disclaimer: Raczar mysteriously disappeared at the completion of production of this motion picture and is rumored to have been living under the guise of 'Prince Vladimar Barbiqueue Raczar of Lower Alhambra.'

THE GOD YOU KNOW

Written by: Emily Skopov
Directed by: Garth Maxwell
Guest stars: Adrienne Wilkinson (Eve), Alexandra Tydings (Aphrodite), Charles Mesure (Michael), Alexis Arquette (Caligula), Kevin Smith (Ares)
Air date: 29 January 2001

The mad emperor Caligula is stealing Aphrodite's immortality to turn himself into a god, and plans to execute Eve and Ares, who tried to stop him. Xena and Gabrielle pose as a Celtic goddess/charioteer and her manager to rescue their friends from the madman, and to get close enough for Xena to kill him.

The amnesiac Aphrodite reveals a very kinky new side as she makes passes at her friend Gabrielle and even her brother Ares. After a dust-up with Michael, Xena loses her power to kill gods. The series' third and final chariot chase takes Xena and Caligula through the streets of Rome and along country roads, but not onto any beaches.

Caligula, about Eve

"Now I remember why I love to kill Elijans. It's the only way to shut them up."

Disclaimer: Gabrielle's undercover disguise was severely harmed during the making of this motion picture.

YOU ARE THERE

Written by: Chris Black
Directed by: John Laing
Guest stars: Michael Hurst (Nigel), Adrienne Wilkinson (Eve), Alexandra Tydings (Aphrodite), Renato Bartolomei (Beowulf), Alexander Petersons (Odin), Alexis Arquette (Caligula), Kevin Smith (Ares)
Air date: 5 February 2001

As Xena tries to capture Valhalla's Golden Apples of Immortality, she and her friends and enemies are stalked by a TV journalist determined to uncover the exclusive story of her plan to make herself a god, and the true nature of her relationship with Gabrielle.

This episode pushes the story format farther than it's ever been pushed. It succeeds because it has a significant plot, plenty of tongue-in-cheek cameos of familiar characters, and Michael Hurst's superb parody of a muck-raking TV journalist.

Charon to Caligula

"Come on, fancypants! I thought you were in a hurry."
"Get your hands off of me! I'm in the middle of an interview, you impudent cur!"
"Yeah, yeah, you may have been a big shot on Earth, but down here you're just dead. Get used to it!"

Disclaimer: The concept of linear time was severely harmed during the making of this motion picture.

PATH OF VENGEANCE

Written by: Joel Metzger
Directed by: Chris Martin-Jones
Guest stars: Adrienne Wilkinson
(Eve), Tsianina Joelson (Varia), Kevin
Smith (Ares)
Air date: 12 February 2001

Varia, the new Amazon Queen, decides to strengthen her tribe by serving the God of War — whose plans for her include a huge conflict with Rome, to restore his own prestige. When Eve arrives as the new Emperor's emissary of peace, Varia condemns her to death for her crimes as Livia. Both Gabrielle and Xena are forced to fight Varia for Eve's life and the soul of the Amazon Nations.

Ares is back on his old form as the seductive God of War, while Eve atones for her crimes, and sets out in search of Eastern wisdom. And for once, the Roman soldiers are the victims, slaughtered by vengeful Amazons. Even after six years, the stunt team can still find new fight venues, this time a scaffold over a sulphur pit.

Varia

"I hereby sentence Livia, killer of the Amazons, to death, so that Eve, the Messenger of Peace, may live."

Disclaimer: The disclaimer for this episode was harmed during the making of this motion picture.

TO HELICON AND BACK

Written by: Liz Friedman &
Vanessa Place
Directed by: Michael Hurst
Guest stars: Tsianina Joelson
(Varia), Craig Parker (Bellerophon)
Air date: 19 February 2001

Incidentally: Bellerophon was the name of the hero who tamed Pegasus.

Another big bad guy targets the Amazons. This one is the son of Artemis, who wants revenge for his immortal mother's death. He captures Varia to lure the Amazons into a doomed attack on his castle. Despite the leadership of Xena and Gabrielle, the Amazons suffer massive casualties. When they retreat Bellerophon makes the fatal mistake of pursuing them to their own fighting ground...

Xena and the Amazons replay *The Longest Day* with their landing on the beach before Bellerophon's castle, while Gabrielle struggles to balance her love of life with the harsh choices needed to keep her troops alive.

Xena to Gabrielle

"You won."
"I don't think I did. With each battle, I lose more of myself."
"War's tough on the soul, Gabrielle."

Disclaimer: No shark bait was harmed during the making of this motion picture.

SEND IN THE CLONES

Written by: Paul Robert Coyle
Directed by: Charlie Haskell
Guest stars: Claire Stansfield
(Alexis Los Alamos/Alti), Alison Wall
(Clea), Ian Hughes (Mac), Polly
Baigent (Polly)
Air date: 23 April 2001

Alti is alive and bad in the 21st Century. She's a genetic scientist who clones Xena and Gabrielle, then suckers a trio of *Xena* fans to help her program the clones. Her nefarious plan: to reveal to the world that Xena was bad to the bone, then use Xena to help her conquer the planet.

Claire Stansfield loved doing her own driving for the muscle car sequence. Polly Baigent had appeared in the show many times before, but not so you'd notice: she was one of Lucy Lawless' doubles. The Xena and Gabrielle clones drive off into the sunset, giving at least one incarnation of our heroes a happy ending.

Clea to Mac, who is cutting the Gabrielle clone's hair
*"Oh no! Her hair! I wanted her to have long hair,
like classic Gabby!"*
"Only in the reruns, babe."

'Send in the Clones'.

Disclaimer: No Xena fans were harmed during the making of this motion picture.

LAST OF THE CENTAURS

Written by: Joel Metzger

Directed by: Garth Maxwell

Guest stars: Marton Csokas
(Belach/Borias), Danielle Cormack
(Ephiny), Hamish Hector-Taylor
(Xenan), Katrina Devine (Nicha)

Air date: 30 April 2001

Ephiny's spirit visits Gabrielle to ask for help in protecting her Centaur son Xenan. The warlord Belach, son of Borias, is slaughtering Centaurs because he believes Xenan has abducted his daughter Nicha. Xena and Gabrielle have to persuade Belach to accept the truth — that Nicha and Xenan have fallen in love, and Nicha is about to give birth to Belach's grandson.

A major piece of Xena's past finally falls into place as we learn how she first met Borias, and seduced him away from his wife to become a warlord in the Far East. The pit full of the bodies of butchered Centaurs is one of the most horrifying images of the series, and is played for all it's worth.

Xena to Borias

"So do you want to live here in squalor or ride to glory with me?"

"How can I say when I've never ridden with you?"

"Giddyap!"

Disclaimer: The Centaur population was severely harmed during the making of this motion picture.

'Last of the Centaurs'.

WHEN FATES COLLIDE

Written by: Katherine Fugate

Directed by: John Fawcett

Guest stars: Ted Raimi (Joxer), Karl Urban (Caesar), David Franklin (Brutus), Claire Stansfield (Alti)

Air date: 7 May 2001

Nearly Departed: Xena and Caesar both die again, the same way each died in 'The Ides of March'. It's Xena's fifth death.

Caesar escapes from Tartarus, captures the Fates, and tries to change his destiny. In his new life, he and Xena are Emperor and Empress of Rome, Gabrielle is a successful playwright, and Alti, High Priestess of Rome, schemes to have it all once again, by seducing Caesar and destroying Xena.

Alti gets to show some skin and sexuality for the first and only time. Ted Raimi's appearance was a fortuitous last-minute inclusion, because Raimi had arrived in New Zealand early for production of 'Soul Possession'.

Xena to Gabrielle

"In the third act you had your hero throw himself over the cliff with no fear of dying, all for her. Do you really believe that kind of love exists?"
"It's what we all dream about isn't it? That someone would look so deeply into our soul that they'd find something worth dying for."

Disclaimer: As the Fates would have it, Caesar was once again harmed during the making of this motion picture.

MANY HAPPY RETURNS

Written by: Liz Friedman & Vanessa Place

Directed by: Mark Beesley

Guest stars: Alexandra Tydings (Aphrodite), Katie Stuart (Genia), Hori Ahipene (Ferragus)

Air date: 14 May 2001

Eagle Eye: Watch for a bad guy handing Xena a bottle just before he keels over.

Travelling to Thebes the day before Gabrielle's birthday, Xena and Gabrielle rescue a virgin from a cult of zealots and enlist Aphrodite's help to teach the innocent to enjoy worldly pleasures. Meanwhile, both the cult's priest and a goofy warlord are after the virgin and the Helmet of Hermes, which gives the wearer the power of flight.

A last treat for the subtext fans, as Xena gives Gabrielle a birthday scroll of Sapphic poetry (with a fragment of a real poem by Sappho) and the two fly off into an ocean sunset — literally, thanks to the Helmet of Hermes.

Genia to Aphrodite

"The Goddess of Love is an evil myth, told to rob women of their virtue and strip men of their pride."
"Well, you got the stripping men part right, honey!"

Disclaimer: No fish guts were harmed during the making of this motion picture.

SOUL POSSESSION

Written by: Melissa Blake

Directed by: Josh Becker

Guest stars: Ted Raimi (Joxer/Harry), Kevin Smith (Ares)

Air date: 4 June 2001

In the past, Xena and Joxer search for Gabrielle after her fall into the lava pit with Hope, while Ares blackmails Xena into marrying him to get Gabrielle back. Xena hides the scroll sealing the marriage in a sea cave — where it's found by archaeologists in the present. Ares invades the press conference announcing the find, to claim Xena's reincarnated soul in the body of Harry.

The final fan tribute in a fandom-heavy season has nods to the Whoosh website, *Xena* scholarship and fan fiction. It also continues the tale of the Xena scrolls and 'Déjà Vu All Over Again' with the present day reincarnations, Harry, Annie and Mattie. Ares' putting Xena's soul back in the body of her look-alike, Annie, makes a married couple of Annie and Mattie.

Ares to Xena

"Can you imagine? Zeus and Hera are going to be your in-laws."

"Just when you thought it couldn't get any worse!"

Disclaimer: Joxer's process of elimination was harmed during the making of this motion picture.

A FRIEND IN NEED, PART I

Teleplay by: R. J. Stewart

Story by: Rob Tapert & R. J. Stewart

Directed by: Rob Tapert

Guest stars: Michelle Ang (Akemi), Mac Jeffery Ong (Kenji), Marton Csokas (Borias), Adrian Brown (Yodoshi), Kazuhiro Muroyama (Harukata)

Air date: 18 June 2001

Xena and Gabrielle travel to Japan to answer a ghost's call for help. Long ago, Xena's friend Akemi murdered her father, who became the Lord of the Dark Land and the eater of souls. Only a powerful ghost can fight him and free the 40,000 souls he has eaten — souls who died because of Xena.

This episode was originally broadcast as a two-hour movie in most American markets. Xena finally teaches Gabrielle the pinch and her warrior listening skills — why has she waited six years?

Akemi, to Xena

"You're a master of war, yet you have no words to speak of love. And then you go and save my life. There's no greater gift of love a teacher can give a student than that."

Disclaimer: Xena and Gabrielle's Flying Circus and Amateur Fire Brigade will be arriving in your town soon.

A FRIEND IN NEED, PART II

Teleplay by: R. J. Stewart

Story by: Rob Tapert & R. J. Stewart

Directed by: Rob Tapert

Guest stars: Michelle Ang (Akemi), Mac Jeffery Ong (Kenji), Marton Csokas (Borias), Adrian Brown (Yodoshi), Kazuhiro Muroyama (Harukata)

Air date: 25 June 2001

Really Departed: Xena insists on staying dead, to avenge the souls of the 40,000 so they can enter a state of grace. We miss you, Xena!

'A Friend in Need, Part II'.

I n a rain of arrows, Xena lets herself be killed so her ghost can fight the Lord of the Dark Land. Meanwhile, Gabrielle goes on a quest to recover her body and take the ashes to Mount Fuji, where a sacred fountain can restore her life.

The stunts and special effects departments have one last fling with the spirit battles between the ghosts of Xena and Higuchi, including turning them into mists and tornadoes of fire. It's still hard to watch Xena's spirit and Gabrielle sitting by that life-giving fountain and letting the sun go down.

Gabrielle, to a Samurai

"You call yourself honourable? You outnumbered her a thousand to one. You're not a samurai, you're a fraud. You couldn't have killed her unless she wanted you to."

Disclaimer: Xena was permanently harmed in the making of this motion picture, but kept her spirits up.

**"I'm looking for my best friend. Maybe you've seen her?
Six feet tall, dark hair, lots of leather.
She fights like the Harpies in a bad mood."**

From the start, Xena's creators intended her to be larger than life — a compelling superhero who happens to be a woman. Smarter, faster, stronger and tougher than even the gods, though she might have flaws, she could never appear weak. "I think with Xena we were even more careful because the show was a pioneer in many ways," says R. J. Stewart. "She was, I'd say, the first female superhero that has a broad following. We needed to combine Xena's dark past with a very believable superhero, and so we really did not want her in any way to seem vulnerable, or 'less' than other superheroes." "We don't write Xena as a woman, we write her as a person," Chris Manheim stressed in an interview during production. "In the Xenaverse, the inhabitants don't blink when they see Xena fighting, even though she's a woman. But that would have been different in real life."

While much of Xena's superhero aura came from the writing, just as much came from the star herself. Lucy Lawless as Xena always made an indelible impression, as Karl Urban recalls of his first Xena episode, 'Altared States': "My most vivid memory is of rehearsing my first scene with Lucy, but I'd never seen her fully made up as Xena. So when we started the rehearsal, I came charging on the set, with a knife to Gabrielle's throat, and I was just blown away to be faced by Lucy and that piercing Clint Eastwood gaze that she does. I was playing the villain, but my immediate instinct was to run away as fast as I could!"

In some ways, Xena is indeed much more like a Clint Eastwood character than she is your typical noble superhero fighting for truth and justice. Ever since she rallied Amphipolis to fight an invading warlord, Xena's life led her down a long, dark road of war, violence, betrayal and ambition. By the time Xena meets Gabrielle, she has already turned the corner and committed herself to the path of justice, but it's a long road back from being the Destroyer of Nations. Both Lawless and the creative staff understood this from the start. "The most attractive thing about the character of Xena is that she's very flawed," says Lawless. "She has a flawed past and she has a temper and always has the devil on her shoulder. To be the best you can doesn't mean you're great, but Xena's doing the best she can. I play her as somebody who struggles to be the best, to give 110 per cent of whatever she has, every day."

Xena knows that atonement is not achieved simply by deciding to reform and use her gifts to be a hero. The very fact that she is still using the abilities that made her the Destroyer of Nations, even in a good cause, has its own

XENA'S PAST

Listed here, arranged to form a rough timeline, are the major episodes concerned with Xena's past. One critical event is missing: exactly when Xena's army caused the deaths of Callisto's parents is never revealed.

'Death Mask' and **'Remember Nothing'**: Though not specifically flashbacks, these episodes recall Xena's relationship with her brothers and her first battle experience, defending Amphipolis from a vicious warlord.

'Destiny': Xena, now a pirate warlord, meets the young Roman Caesar and has a fling with him. When he betrays and crucifies her, she swears that a new Xena has been born, whose only mission is death.

'The Last of the Centaurs': Xena begins her liaison with the warlord Borias by persuading him to abandon his wife and son and join her in forming an army to conquer Asia.

'A Friend in Need, Part I' and **'A Friend in Need, Part II'**: Xena and Borias get involved in the politics of feudal Japan, and Xena causes the destruction of a city and the deaths of many thousands.

'The Debt, Part I' and **'The Debt, Part II'**: When her intemperate violence forces Borias to cast her off, Xena is taken in by the mystical Lao Ma, who teaches her The Way, a path of self-control and constructive power.

'Adventures in the Sin Trade, Part I' and **'Adventures in the Sin Trade, Part II'**: Reconciled with Borias, Xena is seduced by the shamaness Alti, who curses her unborn child and tempts her to become the Destroyer of Nations.

'Past Imperfect': Xena breaks with Borias over her desire to make war on the Centaurs. Her treacherous servant and her lieutenant murder Borias. Xena gives her baby to the Centaur Kaleipus.

'The Rheingold' and **'The Ring'**: Xena rides with the Valkyries of Odin, and meets the hero Beowulf and the monstrous Grindel.

pitfalls. As Gabrielle tells her in 'Paradise Found', "I just wonder if maybe your fighting for good has more to do with the fighting part than the good part." Violence — the power Xena feels when she kicks ass, defeats an enemy, shapes the world with her sword — can be seductive. Conversely, because she chose to live and acknowledged her crimes, Xena always carries the terrible burden of remorse for the harm she's done to people like Borias, Solan, Callisto and Cyane's Amazons. This is why, in 'Maternal Instincts', even with her son's murder fresh in her heart, she can say to Callisto, "You let your pain kill you years ago. I'm gonna live with mine."

Xena's conflicts with people like Ares, Caesar, Callisto and Alti are as much a result of her constant struggle to overcome her bloody past as they are acts of heroism. Xena's enemies spread the destructive violence that she once lived — they are what she was, and she has to stop them. But her battle is always more than just stopping the bad guy, whether it's Ares' latest scheme to

win his Warrior Princess, or Callisto's vengeful cruelty. In fighting them, she has to use all the warrior skills of her mind and body, without letting her heart be corrupted by hatred. It's a line she walks right to the edge in episodes like 'The Price', 'Seeds of Faith' and 'Heart of Darkness'.

An important aspect of being the hero is never losing sight of what's essential. Xena always seems to be able to keep her focus, even when the gods are trying to drive her crazy, as they do in 'Fins, Femmes and Gems' and 'The Furies'. When Xena is going mad under the Furies' curse, she carefully ties Gabrielle to a tree; even though crazed and delusional, she still knows that she has to protect Gabrielle from her madness. When she considers throwing herself off a cliff, she's not trying to escape her own torment, but once again, to protect others. As she tells her mother: "I am a lunatic with lethal combat skills. If I stay around here much longer, some innocent people are going to get killed. I'm doing them a favour."

Xena's clarity of focus makes the infamous 'Gab drag scene' in 'The Bitter Suite' all the more shocking. This is not Xena under the influence of a spell, or amnesia, or any similar story cliché that television writers use to turn their heroes against those they love. This is Xena, entirely in her right mind, trying to kill her best friend in the most brutal way possible, because Gabrielle has lied to her, betrayed her and, finally, caused the death of her beloved son. The old Xena would never have given up her revenge, even for a lesser injury. But after years of a friendship that has grown into love, Xena understands that what she has lost during her rift with Gabrielle is far more precious than revenge — so she gives up her hatred, and forgives both Gabrielle and herself.

Gabrielle's quest for meaning after Hope's death leads Xena to examine her own life path once again. In 'Between the Lines' she experiences a future incarnation as a pacifist leader, the 'Mother of Peace', and it makes her wonder whether being a warrior really is the right way for her to live. It's ironic that Xena, who has never had any use for gods, receives her definitive answer to this question from a god in 'The Way'. Crucially though, Krishna is nothing like the self-centred Olympians, instead, he almost radiates joy. "You must not be hesitant to fight in a just cause. It is better to die following your own way than to live following someone else's," Krishna tells Xena. "When you ride into combat, act without attachment, and carry with you the confidence that you are fulfilling your calling in this life. Then you will know the Way."

Though Krishna settles Xena's biggest question, Lucy Lawless' pregnancy had its inevitable dramatic impact on Xena's life. During the fourth season, Renee O'Connor shared her insights into how Xena's pregnancy changed the Warrior Princess: "I think if anything it provides a relationship where Xena can be more dependent on a person than she has ever been in her life, because she has a sidekick who can hold her own and help out in situations. She's never had that before. It does make Xena more vulnerable, though. She now has a daughter and a friend who she cares about. The more people that she invests in emotionally, the more vulnerable she is as a warrior."

On 16 October 1999 Lawless gave birth to Julius Robert Bay Tapert. At about the same time in the chronology of the show — mid-way through season five — Xena gives birth to her daughter Eve, an event which triggers the Xenaverse-changing Twilight of the Gods. Eve's arrival also causes profound changes in Xena's personal life. Having given up her first child, Solan, to protect him from who she was then (as much as to protect him from her enemies), the reformed Xena is determined to raise Eve as well as she can, and Gabrielle is determined to help her. The challenges Xena faces would seem overwhelming to a lesser mortal, and even the Warrior Princess finds them pretty daunting. It's bad enough that she has to battle the whole pantheon of Greek gods to keep her daughter safe, but on top of that, she also has to rethink

her way of life yet again. When she wipes a splash of blood off of Eve's face after the battles in 'Eternal Bonds', she understandably wonders whether it's right to expose a child to so much violence.

When Xena, Eve and Gabrielle visit the Amazons in 'Kindred Spirits', Xena is torn. She knows that the Amazon village would be a wonderful place to raise her daughter, providing both safety from the gods, and a large and loving extended family. Yet Xena has no purpose for herself here, no role in this peaceful tribe, and nothing to occupy her but taking care of Eve, cleaning the cabin and watching Gabrielle being queen.

It could have been interesting, on a personal level, to see how Xena resolved the conflict between her calling as a warrior and the nurturing life of a mother, but such a story would probably not make exciting drama. Instead, fate intervenes in the form of a twenty-five year sleep. When Xena and Gabrielle awake, Eve has grown up, and the stage is set for the defeat of the Olympian gods in their war with Xena. "We're on the brink of the death of the gods and the notion of monotheism, and how Xena is a player in that," says Lawless, assessing the situation at this turning point. "She has a child to consider, who becomes an interesting force in the show in her own right. We'll

be losing some of the old foes, basically, but we'll make sure that the characters are still in danger. Also, the friendship between Xena and Gabrielle remains strong, though it does change."

As Xena faces the changed world, a final battle with the gods and the salvation of her now adult daughter, she gains new wisdom and patience — the last thing we might expect of the Warrior Princess. Compared to Gabrielle's drastic growth over the course of the series, Xena's development after her initial reformation may appear deceptively insignificant. She presents the same surface personality — taciturn, strong-willed, quick to act or react — but in fact the Warrior Princess does mature considerably between the first and final seasons.

This can be seen very clearly in 'Path of Vengeance', when Eve has been condemned to death by the Amazons. The Xena of a couple of years before would have charged right in with sword and chakram to save her daughter. This time, as hard as it is for her to do so, she holds back, and gives Gabrielle the chance to follow every avenue of Amazon law. Only when all those avenues are exhausted, and when Gabrielle herself tells Xena to go ahead, does Xena resort to battle.

'Path of Vengeance' also reveals how much Xena's perception of Gabrielle has evolved. At the beginning of season five, in 'Succession', Gabrielle has to insist that Xena let her share the fighting. And in everything that concerns the baby Eve's safety or the grown-up Livia's salvation, though Gabrielle gives unswerving support, it is Xena who leads. In 'Path of Vengeance' though, Xena lets Gabrielle take the lead in the protection of her daughter. By doing so she is recognising not only Gabrielle's status as an Amazon queen, but the possibility that Gabrielle may actually have a better way than she does to rescue Eve. Xena finally recognises Gabrielle as an equal.

Another mark of Xena's growth is that even late in the series, Lawless could still make discoveries about her character, as Xena made discoveries about

LETHAL WEAPON

Prop designer Roger Murray's most famous creation for *Xena: Warrior Princess* was Xena's trademark weapon, the chakram.

The requirement was for Xena to have a throwing weapon that would return to her hand. So an ancient Indian weapon design, the circular chakram (from the Sanskrit for 'wheel'), was combined with the most distinctive property of the Australian aboriginal boomerang, before the final addition of a little Warrior Princess magic — since no real boomerang would return to its thrower after ten or twenty ricochets! The original template of the chakram took Murray about eight hours, including the patterns incised around the circle on both sides. Silicon moulds were made from that original, to produce foam copies of the chakram in hard, medium and soft urethane foams around a core of sprung steel, to provide strength and weight. Copies were also made from a hard resin, for effects with sparks or the chakram slicing into an object. Some of these 'stunt' chakrams were made with a rig inside so they could be attached to a wire for flying. Finally, there were the painted aluminium chakrams, used in close-ups. At any given time, the main and second unit would each have on hand a full selection of chakrams made from all the different materials. The props department was constantly making new chakrams as well, especially the soft foam ones, which might only hold up for two or three episodes. The aluminium chakrams lasted for years, because of their more durable construction and because they were only held, never thrown.

Xena's new chakram, used in the fifth and sixth seasons, took the visual symbolism of the circle a bit further by incorporating a yin-yang design in the bar across the centre. This design reflected Xena's nature as a balance of good and evil, and also, of course, allowed for some neat new chakram effects when the weapon split in two to fly in different directions before rejoining and returning to Xena's hand!

herself. One moment of insight came in a conversation with Caligula in 'The God You Know'. "We ad-libbed a line at the end of the scene in which Xena tells him that she understands him — and she truly does. It was a revelation for Xena in terms of her growing understanding of this person," Lawless recalls. "It was also the first time in a long while that I had experienced a character development for her... my character learned something about herself, and it happened on screen."

Xena understands Caligula because, as she says of him after his death, "He was damaged. He wasn't evil." Damaged, as she, in her innocence, was damaged by Caesar. Perhaps Caligula was no worse than Xena was in her darkest days, but unlike him, she had enough time to find her redemption. The Warrior Princess' search for redemption means always choosing to do the right thing, paying the price for her sins, trying to put right whatever she finds that's wrong and helping others to avoid her mistakes. In *Xena*, we see that redemption — forgiveness itself — is not a moment when you repent and become a new person, it's a journey that lasts a lifetime. ⚔

GABRIELLE

"Well listen to my story about Gabrielle, a cute little gal that's lookin' really swell: perfect hair, such a lovely lass, nice round breasts and a firm young..."

The 'sidekick' character is supposed to remain secondary and inferior to the hero. She's the comic relief, the sometimes useful assistant and, most important, the person who makes the hero look smart and strong by asking for some essential plot point to be explained, and by constantly needing to be rescued. From the moment she walked into Xena's life, Gabrielle has been all those things. She has said herself that she's just the sidekick, while many others have called her, in comic relief vein, the "irritating blonde". But of course, since the day she first jumped up behind Xena on Argo, Gabrielle has grown into far more than an "overachieving sidekick".

Unlike Xena, whose life before 'Sins of the Past' merits a whole series of backstory episodes, Gabrielle's life was uneventful, even boring, until Xena came along. As she begins her adventures with Xena, Gabrielle's education in life is all ahead of her. Her story, throughout the series, is a story of growth. "Because I'm older than Gabrielle, she goes through a lot of things in life just after I've experienced them," Renee O'Connor reflected, while looking back late in the series. "When I first started the show, Gabrielle was going through adolescence. I had already been through that, so it was kind of frustrating for me, having to be patient with the mistakes she made and her growing pains. I suppose as my life has changed, I've fed that into Gabrielle. During most of the seasons up until the fourth, I felt I had to hold back and sort of let Gabrielle take over."

The first three seasons see Gabrielle emerging from her adolescence. From at first trying to be exactly like Xena, she learns to follow her own heart more and to make her own choices, such as deciding to become the Queen of the Amazons when she believes Xena is dead. Gabrielle also encounters evil for the first time when Callisto kills her bridegroom Perdicas, and she has to make the terrible choice of whether to take her revenge or spare the murderess. Yet Callisto's evil pales next to Gabrielle's experience with Dahak, which causes the loss of her blood innocence, her rift with Xena and her attempts first to save her evil daughter Hope, then to destroy her.

No matter what happens to her, Gabrielle retains a special quality of innocence. It's not *naïveté*. Having seen the heart of evil in others and in herself, she can never be naïve again. It is rather the quality that draws her to Eli's Way of Love: a purity of intent, a selflessness, a devotion to goodness. Even the bad guys recognise this in her. "Renee plays such a kind character," Hudson Leick points out. "I would always be this really overwhelming bad guy.

You can't fight her because she's like, 'I'm love!' That was a little bit more difficult [than playing opposite Lawless' Xena]. It's like being a big bully picking on the smallest kid." However, according to Kevin Smith, Gabrielle's purity was the reason for Ares' interest in her, in 'Seeds of Faith': "Gabrielle's essence is pure, so one of Ares' big things with this episode is trying to subvert her. He figures if he can subvert her — subvert the purest of the pure — then he's got a foot in the door for this big battle."

After all the trauma of the third season, the fourth season sees the bard go in a new direction, as she looks for a way to heal her goodness and innocence. "What I love is that they're still experimenting with the characters," said O'Connor at the time. "We tried the whole idea of Xena trying to fight for good, and now Gabrielle doesn't believe in violence anymore, so they've created a bit of a rift between the characters. Now we're moving away from that and we're going to try to create a loyal friendship where these two people — despite having different ideals — create a balance between them. So Gabrielle will be the intellect and the pacifist, whereas Xena will be the might and the strength behind the pair."

Gabrielle's season of pacifism had important effects on O'Connor's portrayal of her, including one that the athletic actress regretted: "I miss my staff! As part of Gabrielle's growth, she's discarded her staff to move on to this non-violent way.

They've come up with what they call 'weapons of peace' that Gabrielle keeps in her little knapsack. But they're not as physical as the staff was."

The Way of Love also confronted O'Connor with a dramatic challenge often faced by actors who have to play saint-like characters — that of making so much goodness interesting. "As an actor, I find [Gabrielle's pacifism] so idealistic that its almost unreal," she explained. "So I'm trying to find a dichotomy in the character, where maybe she's a little bit more complicated than that. Just the challenge of making her believable is keeping me going."

At the end of season four, Gabrielle dramatically, and bloodily, renounces the Way of Love as she tries to save the crippled Xena from their Roman captors. "I chose the way of friendship," she tells Xena in 'The Ides of March', a choice that opens the way for a new Gabrielle in the remaining seasons. "We all had input into Gabrielle's character for season five," producer and writer Chris Manheim explains. "I see Gabrielle as growing stronger in an outward sense and Xena growing deeper in an inward sense. We also needed Gabrielle to step into a role that was more proactive, because with Lucy (and Xena) being pregnant, she couldn't fight so much or ride."

Xena's pregnancy is a watershed for Gabrielle. Through her protection of Xena and Eve, she completes her transition from sidekick to equal partner. Xena had always recognised Gabrielle's importance in the emotional balance of their relationship, frequently thanking her friend for showing her the way to

stay on the side of good. But only with Xena's pregnancy does Gabrielle begin to assume an equal role in battle — at least, as equal to the Warrior Princess as anyone can be who is not a god! She fights side by side with her friend, no longer needing Xena's protection. Indeed, she is often out in the forefront, taking the lead and protecting Xena, as she does in 'God Fearing Child', when she, not Xena, captures the Helmet of Invisibility.

"Obviously Xena was capable of defending herself and her baby but Gabrielle — who's our little loyal friend — felt she had to get in there and help out as much as she could," said O'Connor of this transformation. "It definitely explored a strengthened side of Gabrielle that she could take on, and have the *desire* to take on, as many people in battle as she had to in order to protect her little family. That's been a first, I'm sure. She stopped asking Xena if she needed any help and just jumped in whenever she could. Actually, I take that back. I don't think Gabrielle's ever really asked if Xena needs help. What's so endearing about her is that she just loves Xena and everything that Xena represents so fully that she will do everything she can to be with her."

Gabrielle understands that she has reached a new stage in her friendship with Xena, one that's more independent, but not more distant. She explains to

QUOTES ON FRIENDSHIP

**Xena and Gabrielle speak of their friendship in many, many episodes.
These are a few of the choicest quotes.**

Gabrielle on her best friend:

"She taught me when to fight and when to talk. She taught me how to know the difference between a friend and an enemy. She taught me what it means to have a best friend." **'The Prodigal'**

"Do you think I could have understood the power of selfless love without our friendship?" **'The Way'**

"You brought out the best in me. Before I met you, no one saw me for who I was. I felt invisible. But you saw all the things that I could be. You saved me, Xena." **'The Ides of March'**

"My path is with Xena, helping her however I can. I'll do whatever I have to do to protect her." **'Chakram'**

Lin Qi: "Ever think about settling down?"
Gabrielle: "You know, sometimes people think that a home is a place. It can be a person." **'Back in the Bottle'**

"You're my whole life, Xena. I won't lose you." **'A Friend in Need, Part II'**

Xena on her best friend:

"You're my source, Gabrielle. When I reach inside myself and do things that I'm not capable of, it's because of you." **'One Against an Army'**

"You are the best thing that ever happened to me. You gave my life meaning and joy. You will be a part of me forever." **'Sacrifice, Part II'**

Young Amazon Woman: "She must be a very good friend."
Xena: "She's the only friend." **'Adventures in the Sin Trade, Part I'**

"I was trapped in a cycle of violence and hatred, and no matter how I tried to break free, something always pulled me back. Until you. You talk about trying to find your way, but to me, you are my way. I'm searching for answers, too. But how we look for them doesn't matter, as long as we look for them together, you and me." **'A Family Affair'**

"The love we have is stronger than Heaven or Hell. It transcends good and evil. It's an end in itself." **'Fallen Angel'**

Amarice in 'Them Bones, Them Bones', "For many years I walked in Xena's shadow, and I wanted to be her. She taught me something: it's warmer standing in the sun."

By this time, no one is calling Gabrielle a "sidekick" anymore — except an overeager young Amazon in 'Kindred Spirits', who's desperately auditioning to become Xena's new "sidekick", now that Gabrielle is going to become queen. Xena never says much, but every time the girl starts gushing about how she can replace Gabrielle, Xena's look alone expresses her thoughts on the subject of

whether Gabrielle's place in her life could be filled by anyone else — let alone a teenager who thinks Gabrielle is no more than a sidekick.

Like any individual, Gabrielle still has ways she needs to grow. She is learning new lessons about the cost of living by the sword, including experiencing the anguish of killing an innocent when she accidentally does so in 'Legacy'. Perhaps the hardest part of her journey is the part we won't see. After Xena's death in 'A Friend in Need, Part II' Gabrielle will have to get used to walking her path without her best friend. While that may be hard and lonely sometimes, Gabrielle has shown that she has the courage and the wisdom to survive and continue bringing good to the world.

She has one other gift to help her on her way. While many paths and choices in Gabrielle's life have been influenced by her relationship with Xena, her dream of being a bard has always been completely her own. Gabrielle starts telling stories in her very first episode — not only the tale of Oedipus, but her fast-talking to the Cyclops and the mob that's about to kill Xena. Xena is quick to recognise this gift, telling Gabrielle in 'Dreamworker' that her tongue is her best defence in any trouble. When she stops writing for a while because of the chaos surrounding Eve's birth, she finds that she feels incomplete. Both old friends like Aphrodite and new friends like Lin Qi urge her to keep using her

gift, for the sake of her own happiness. Though Gabrielle knows many other stories about heroes like Oedipus, living with Xena gives her something special to write about, and ultimately, the scrolls also give Gabrielle a way to find meaning in all the adventures, terrors and tragedies she experiences.

Ultimately, of course, without Gabrielle, we'd have no Xena. As we see in episodes like 'The Xena Scrolls', 'Looking Death in the Eye' and 'Soul Possession', Gabrielle's scrolls are the reason Xena became a legend. They are her tribute to the Warrior Princess, and to a friendship that endures through many lifetimes. ⚔

DO THEY OR DON'T THEY?

In different interviews late in the series production, some of *Xena*'s leading creative lights addressed what fans have come to call 'the subtext'.

Rob Tapert: "I've used the same line a thousand times, which is: Xena and Gabrielle are the best of mates, and whether they have a sexual relationship is kind of their own business. But they certainly love one another. They would die for one another.

"We went out of our way to calm it down. I'm glad that gay people have found something that they like and enjoy and can rally behind. I don't want to [downplay] how important I think that is. Two to eleven year-olds watch this show, whose parents write me and say, 'We don't think it's right that you're telling our seven year-old daughter to have a lesbian relationship.' I understand their concern. I don't want to be the one who says, 'This is what's right.' But I also want to leave the door open for people to say that there's certainly nothing wrong with this... It's a tricky road to walk."

R. J. Stewart: "The people that I deal with at the studio have an expression which they call the 'Ellen effect'. You get a curiosity, and then after that you see people turn off the show in droves. We had a famous episode a long time ago, 'The Quest', which was our highest rated episode, and then there was 'A Day in the Life' which was the girls in a hot tub together playing hide the soap. And after that, our executives put a great deal of pressure on us to stop, to not go down that road because it could only lead to ruin."

Liz Friedman: "The only thing that was important to me when I was involved with the show was not to jump in with both feet and make a statement about it. I think pre-*Will & Grace* and *Ellen*, that was sort of the way television tended to deal with gay relationships.

You'd make the joke or you'd play the real intimacy between two women, and then say, 'But they're straight, okay?' To me it was much more subversive, and also something we could actually achieve, just by not having them ever say one way or the other."

Renee O'Connor: "At first we were surprised by the recognition and support we got from the gay community. Then we decided to absolutely nurture it. We have fun playing with the subtext on the show. Then it became almost a stereotype that Lucy and I dealt with. I'm sure no gay couple would want to be stereotyped as a gay couple — they're two human beings first. In that respect, Lucy and I decided to pull back on the whole thing and nurture the friendship between these two characters.

"It ruins the show if we say yea or nay. Also, that's what's exciting about it as well: everyone can watch the show and see an aspect of themselves in the characters. If we were to say 'Yes there is subtext,' or 'No there isn't,' it might alienate people and that just seems unfair.

"The most important aspect of the show is that Xena has a best friend — who happens to be a woman — who she relies on more than any other person in the world, and they have a loving friendship. To me, that's more important than whether or not they are having sex."

Lucy Lawless: "We wanted it to be about love. It's never been grubby and we didn't want to present it that way. Whether you want to believe that they're gay or straight is irrelevant to the fact that these two love and care for each other."

JOXER

"Joxer the Mighty at your service. I'm fierce and I have a lust for blood. My nickname is 'Bloody Joxer'."

H e's too clumsy to ride a horse, or even walk under a tree without bumping his head. He likes girls a lot, but they almost never like him. He can drive a sage crazy with his incessant inane, boastful chatter. And if he gets into a fight, it's an even chance whether he'll get more bruises from the bad guys, or from accidentally hitting himself with his own sword. He's the worst warrior who ever escaped having his head sliced off in battle by tripping over his own feet. He's also the funniest. Basically, Joxer the Mighty is the perfect comic foil for the Warrior Princess.

Ted Raimi began his professional career with a bit part in *The Evil Dead*, and can often be spotted in small roles in his brother's films (his brother being of course *Xena* executive producer Sam Raimi). However, before playing Joxer, Ted Raimi was best known as Communications Officer Tim O'Neill in *seaQuest DSV*.

Surprisingly, despite Raimi's close relationship with his brother, he wasn't the original choice to play Joxer. The role, intended to provide *Xena* with the same sort of comic relief that Salmoneus provides in *Hercules*, was initially developed for Wallace Shawn (Vizzini in *The Princess Bride* and the Grand Nagus Zek on *Star Trek: Deep Space Nine*). But Ted Raimi happened to meet Rob Tapert in Los Angeles while the dorky warrior was in development, Raimi was between jobs, and Tapert offered him the part. Quickly recognising Raimi's chemistry with the series' leads, *Xena*'s creative staff wrote him in as a semi-regular player. He has subsequently appeared as Joxer, or some incarnation of him, in forty-one episodes of *Xena* — more than any other actor except Lucy Lawless and Renee O'Connor.

To Raimi's delight, the writers and directors also recognised his comic talent, and soon began to allow him to invent some of the comedy. "I've had writers actually write in: 'Ted will do something funny here.' That's my favourite part of the day!" says Raimi. "There are directors who are extremely creative. If you get good ones on your side, who like to work with you and enjoy watching the character, then you're in a good place."

First on the list of *Xena* directors on Raimi's side is Josh Becker, who helmed many of Joxer's best episodes. Becker, who grew up in the same Detroit neighbourhood as Raimi, gives an example (from the filming of 'Kindred Spirits') of how far Raimi's comic talent can take a scene: "The one piece of direction I was able to give Ted, and that he was able to wring twenty laughs out of, was where he's caught spying on the naked Amazons and is stuck in the

middle of the village in stocks for almost the whole show. I said, 'Ted, Joxer has only two modes: he's either apologetic for what he did or he's hitting on the girls...' and Ted was great. He knew where to find the laugh in every single moment."

Raimi knows one reason why he and Becker worked so well together. "I adhere to Josh Becker's philosophy that if you're going to be silly about it, be *really* silly about it. Don't go halfway," he says, recalling the shooting of 'Fins, Femmes and Gems'. "If you've got a monkey man running around and all that crap, you might as well go the whole hog. Josh let me create a lot of that dialogue, like when I'm up in the tree: 'Lambs form protective positions. Billy goats, elephants, destroy him!'"

Raimi's best collaboration with Becker is also Joxer's finest hour — the comic masterpiece 'For Him the Bell Tolls', in which, under Aphrodite's spell, every time a bell rings Joxer transforms into the next Errol Flynn, before turning back into 'Jerkster'. The premise came from a conversation between Raimi and R. J. Stewart about their favourite movie, the Danny Kaye classic *The Court Jester*. Fans ask Raimi about that episode more than any other, and no wonder. It is the perfect showcase for Raimi's talent and his flawless comic timing.

However, it's not always safe to assume that Ted Raimi's name in *Xena*'s credits is a guarantee of straightforward comedy; Joxer can sometimes reveal unexpected dramatic depths as well. 'A Comedy of Eros', one of the series' more supremely silly episodes, gives us an hour of solid laughs as Xena, Gabrielle, Joxer and Draco all run after each other because of Cupid's arrows.

Until the end of the plot that is, when Cupid tries to remove the spell from Joxer, but he can't — Joxer's love for Gabrielle is real. An oblivious Gabrielle makes fun of the notion that she and Joxer could ever be lovers, and the pain on Joxer's face turns the last moment of this light episode into pathos.

This 'romantic' aspect of Joxer's story might never have developed without Raimi's undeniable appeal. Wallace Shawn playing unrequited love for Renee O'Connor would have been funny, but would it have been poignant? Despite Joxer's dorkiness, Raimi gives him a charm that makes it possible for us to take his love seriously, and even to wish sometimes that Gabrielle could see past Joxer's dopey hat to his gentle heart.

"Salmoneus and Autolycus are both aware of their faults: Salmoneus knows that he's greedy and Autolycus knows he's a thief. Joxer, conversely, does not know he's an incompetent warrior. He believes he's a very competent warrior," observes Raimi, speculating on why Joxer, unlike his *Hercules* counterparts, has developed beyond mere comedy into a dramatic and ultimately tragic character. "Very few of us have probed deep enough that we know our own faults. Joxer, like most of us, is unaware of his, which is why we have sympathy for him."

A particularly challenging aspect of Joxer's dramatic scenes was trying to be serious while wearing what Raimi describes as "a clown suit". "What I love and hate about the show," he says, "is that hat. I've always thought it was funny for about two minutes on camera and then it's not funny anymore, so I always would try and take it off, but the writers think it's so clever and cute that they'd want me in that thing the whole episode. So there's always a fight between me and the costume department; I'd try and take it off and they'd try and keep it on." When Raimi wrapped the fifth season, his colleagues, led by Renee O'Connor, gave him the best parting gift they could think of: "Renee took a picture of everyone in the crew wearing that hat. They put it in a book for me so I wouldn't feel like I was the only one suffering with it on. It was the funniest thing I've ever seen. Lucy's wearing it, Renee's wearing it, Kevin Smith wears it… It's great!"

The story of Joxer's unrequited love for Gabrielle does inevitably have its funny moments, such as the sight of 'Attis the Ape Man' swinging through the trees with his jungle queen in 'Fins, Femmes and Gems', or the three naked, dancing Gabrielles who Joxer conjures in 'The Quill is Mightier'. Yet the overall impact is to pull the character in a more serious direction, and most of Raimi's best dramatic moments as Joxer have been related to this love. One can't forget the anguish on Joxer's face as he lowers Gabrielle's body from her cross in 'Fallen Angel', or the bittersweet moment in 'Eternal Bonds' when the gravely ill Joxer comes to terms with the fact that Gabrielle will never love him as he loves her. And no one could have dreamed, when we first saw Gabrielle beat the stuffing out of the dorky warrior in 'Callisto', that Joxer of all people would be given one of the most moving death scenes in the entire series. In 'Eve', the sweet but ever klutzy old man gives his life trying to protect Gabrielle from Livia. He dies as he lived, always in the wrong place at the wrong time, but without a thought for himself and, as Xena once said, with "the heart of a lion". ⑄

EPISODES FEATURING TED RAIMI AS JOXER (UNLESS NOTED)

Season 1: Callisto

Season 2: Girls Just Wanna Have Fun; The Return of Callisto; Warrior... Princess... Tramp; Intimate Stranger; Ten Little Warlords; The Xena Scrolls (Jacques S'Er/Jack Kleinman/Ted Raimi); For Him the Bell Tolls; A Comedy of Eros

Season 3: Been There, Done That; King of Assassins (Joxer/Jett); The Quill is Mightier; The Bitter Suite; King Con; Forget Me Not; Fins, Femmes and Gems; Sacrifice, Part II

Season 4: A Family Affair; In Sickness and In Hell; Key to the Kingdom; If the Shoe Fits (Joxer/Tyro/Messenger); The Play's the Thing; The Convert; Takes One to Know One; Déjà Vu All Over Again (Harry)

Season 5: Fallen Angel; Chakram; Animal Attraction; Purity; Back in the Bottle; Lyre, Lyre, Hearts On Fire (Joxer/Jace); Punch Lines; Eternal Bonds; Married With Fishsticks (Joxer/Hagar); Kindred Spirits; Looking Death in the Eye; Livia; Eve; Motherhood

Season 6: When Fates Collide (Joxer the prison guard); Soul Possession (Joxer/Harry)

EVEN XENA DOESN'T HAVE A SONG

The full lyrics of Joxer's song from 'For Him the Bell Tolls' (variants of the song are also sung in 'A Comedy of Eros', 'Warrior... Princess... Tramp', 'The Bitter Suite' and 'King of Assassins'):

Joxer's episode version:	End credits version:
Joxer the Mighty	Blood! Valour! And victory! Ha-HA!
Roams through the countryside	Joxer the Mighty
He never needs a place to hide	He's very tidy
With Gabby as his sidekick	Everyone admires him
Fighting with her little stick	He's so handsome it's a sin
Righting wrongs and singing songs	When things get grim
Being mighty all day long	He'll take it on the chin
He's Joxer — he's Joxer the Mighty!	If you're in jeopardy
Oh, he's Joxer the Mighty	Caused by the enemy
He's really tidy	Don't call the cavalry
Everybody likes him	There's a better remedy
'Cause he has a funny grin	(Although he doesn't work for free!)
Joxer —	He's every man's trusty,
Joxer the Mighty!	He's every woman's fantasy,
	Plus he's good company
	Look out! He's Joxer —
	Joxer the Mighty!
	Joxer — Joxer the Mighty!

ARES

"Life isn't worth living. It's to be taken and beaten and wrestled and formed in your image."

From the moment Ares appears in 'The Reckoning', trying to draw Xena back into his service, the God of War has been an essential adversary and foil to the Warrior Princess. He is the incarnation of her dark side, the seductive voice that calls her to return to the ways of violence which she has left behind. In the person of Kevin Smith, that voice often seems irresistible.

Smith, a native of New Zealand's South Island, was cast as Ares soon after playing Iphicles in *Hercules: The Legendary Journeys,* and portrayed the god in thirty episodes of *Xena,* as well as in many episodes of *Hercules* and *Young Hercules.* His continued interest in the long-running role is understandable in light of the wide range of stories that Ares plays a part in — anything from being a tempter in episodes like 'Chakram' and 'Succession', to a tragic lover in 'Looking Death in the Eye' and 'Motherhood'.

In interviews for the *Xena* magazine during the last two seasons of the show, Smith reflected on the many aspects of the role: "I've always felt really lucky with Ares; I've been able to cover all the genres with him. He's a villain, so there's that, and there are episodes where I've played him as a romantic lead opposite Lucy, and I've had times — like in 'Old Ares Had a Farm' — where he's been the comic relief. The beauty about Ares is that I've been able to do a little bit of everything."

Early on, Smith feared that Ares might become no more than a two-dimensional witty villain. "When we first started Ares, it was cool to have a bad guy who was roguish and charming and kills people with a chuckle," he admitted. But Smith recognised that this approach had its disadvantages: "For a while I think Ares kind of lost his teeth, because he was always the one-liner, quip guy. In the early days I'd lightened up a few lines and it came off, so they started writing for that. I was playing a lot of it for laughs. I'm such a slut that way. I can't help it! If there's a laugh to be had, I really have to fight not to do it, and sometimes I lose the battle…"

But Smith was ultimately able to use this humour to make Ares more complex and vulnerable, adding layers that could be peeled off in later episodes. "You look at the funny kids at school, and it's often to hide a vulnerability. Laughter can diffuse situations, and if [Ares] is having second thoughts, the laughter will hide that," Smith observed. "As a functioning, high profile God of War-man about town — second thoughts, doubts, moral qualms… you just couldn't function with those things. That's why I think there

was a lot of the laughter, the charm, the throwaway quips. That came about to hide the fact that he was ever having any doubts about what he was doing.

"All said and done, Ares is a soldier, albeit taken to the nth degree. [In the fifth season] we see that it is his brief as the God of War, and he's really doing his job, but every now and then, you'll see he's increasingly aware of the consequences of his own actions, that there is a cost."

Ares' breakout episode is 'Ten Little Warlords', in which the God of War loses his powers. "That was the first time we got to see the embryonic stages of the Ares we see now," said Smith. "Him losing his powers, we get a glimpse of the humanity… and I think that was where the present day Ares was born." The episode also generates sympathy for Ares because it's the first time he gets to play the hero. For once, he and Xena are working on the same side trying to stop Sisyphus from taking his place, and he's actually more concerned that the power of the God of War fall into responsible hands, than he is for his own immortality.

Smith and the creative staff of *Xena* worked hard to maintain the audience's sympathy no matter what Ares did, as Smith described while looking back on one of Ares' darkest moments, his murder of Eli in 'Seeds of Faith': "It was like a little test: if I can have any kind of sympathy after I've effectively killed Jesus, it's a biggie. That's a long way to come back from. But it was something which I think we could realistically shoot for, because that happens quite early on in that episode, and then he goes to Gabrielle. And I thought, 'My god, he's getting away with it! Here he is, he's just run through the saviour, and now he's actually turning Gabrielle around!' I just dug that, the fact that he's so on his game that he could do something like that."

Smith recognised that one thing is key to maintaining empathy between the *Xena* audience and the God of War: "He's done terrible, terrible things. The only way this works is if you believe he truly loves Xena. Rather than simply wanting to get an acquisition back that slipped through his fingers, he does actually deeply love her. And I think that was the challenge, to say, 'How can someone who is capable of such love be capable of such appalling acts as well?'"

Smith especially enjoyed the part Ares played in the Twilight of the Gods storyline at the end of the fifth season, and how this affected his character. "Here's a man who's lived for thousands of years, suddenly to be confronted with the very real prospect of his mortality, and going through that journey has been kind of cool," he said. "I think Ares has always been a total pragmatist, and he sees the inevitability of change. The other gods have rallied against it; he'll move and shift to do whatever it takes to survive. Even if Olympus falls, he wants to survive as a mortal. Quite apart from his love for Xena — having a child with her — it's all about surviving the fall of Olympus."

Watching Ares, one never knows which way he will jump, or whose side he is on in the contest between Xena and his own family of gods. According to Smith, this uncertainty is exactly as it should be: "I don't believe television should necessarily be a passive experience, and one of the best ways to guarantee continued involvement is if you just keep a little question in the back of [the audience's] mind the whole time. So ambiguity is something which the directors, Rob Tapert the producer, and myself and the writers have tried to keep, [to keep the audience] guessing as to his real motives."

Despite appreciating the importance of ambiguity to the role, Smith was quite clear about what he wanted for Ares in that scenario, and admitted, "My own preference is that he means to do the right thing by Xena and the child." That wish was fulfilled in the last moments of 'Motherhood', when Ares proved, in the most surprising action of his life, that his love for Xena was genuine. He gave up his own immortality to revive Gabrielle and Livia, and thereby saved Xena's life.

THE TONGUE IS MIGHTIER

Ares wields words as easily as swords. Here are a few choice quotations:

"I don't want to see you throw yourself off some cliff, if for no other reason than it's such a tastelessly melodramatic way out of this life." **'The Furies'**

"Nothing more need be said. Ding dong, the bitch is dead!" **'The Bitter Suite'**

"I handled you all wrong. I know that. She knew what you needed: unconditional, unselfish love. And I couldn't give that to you. But I appreciated you in ways she never could — your rage, your violence, your beauty. When you sacrificed yourself for others, you were hers. But when you kicked ass, you were mine." **'Looking Death in the Eye'**

"Mortality stinks! Not to mention hurts." **'Coming Home'**

Xena: "I despise you! You've been tormenting me for years!"
"That? That was just foreplay!" **'Soul Possession'**

Smith enjoyed his final appearance as Ares in 'Soul Possession', and felt that neither the modern setting, nor the modern clothes were out of place for the ancient God of War. "War is just as at home now as it was back then. In my head, Ares has always been a contemporary character," Smith explained. "I've never really thought of him as being in any particular time frame. Perhaps, as I said, that's just because of the timelessness of his job. These swanky danky Armani gigs are no different for me than being in the leathers, because I think if Ares was in our world and he had to dress himself, this is what he'd wear."

In one of his last *Xena* interviews, Smith looked back fondly on his time playing the God of War, observing, "I've done some of the best work I've ever done on this show, because it has given me so many gifts as an actor. I'm going to miss that. Ares has been the most fun ongoing role; basically six years of being a naughty kid!"

Kevin Smith passed away on 16 February 2002, from injuries suffered in a fall while he was in China to shoot a film. His passing was mourned by the entire New Zealand film community, as well as the worldwide family of *Xena* and *Hercules* fans. The immortal Ares endures as an indelible part of his film legacy. ✖

EPISODES FEATURING KEVIN SMITH AS ARES

Season 1: The Reckoning; Ties that Bind

Season 2: Intimate Stranger; Ten Little Warlords; The Xena Scrolls

Season 3: The Furies; The Dirty Half Dozen; The Deliverer; The Quill is Mightier; The Bitter Suite; Forget Me Not; Sacrifice, Part I; Sacrifice, Part II

Season 4: Déjà Vu All Over Again

Season 5: Chakram; Succession; Seeds of Faith; God Fearing Child; Eternal Bonds; Amphipolis Under Siege; Looking Death in the Eye; Livia; Eve; Motherhood

Season 6: Coming Home; Old Ares Had a Farm; The God You Know; You are There; Path of Vengeance; Soul Possession

"In a way, I'm disappointed, Xena. There was a part of me that hoped that you would win and put out the rage in my heart. Sometimes it scares even me. Then I get over it."

C allisto is the anti-Xena. Created by R. J. Stewart to show what Xena might have been if she had not found redemption, she outdoes even the darkest side of Xena in her cruelty, ferocity and the excesses of her violence. At the same time, in the dainty person of Hudson Leick she reminds us that Callisto was once an innocent young girl who never imagined she could become a warrior or a murderer.

Leick fell in love with acting at a very early age, but worked as a model before deciding to study the art professionally (spending two years at New York's prestigious Neighborhood Playhouse). In addition to playing Callisto, she has appeared in movies (*Chill Factor*) as well as in television guest roles (*Melrose Place, Touched By an Angel*).

Leick's *Xena* audition is something of a legend. Fed up with the impersonal treatment of actors in these situations, she marched in and — instead of waiting to be told what to do — went up to every person in the room (including casting director Beth Hymson-Ayer and producers Liz Friedman and R. J. Stewart), shook their hands and asked, "What's your name and what do you do?" Friedman later recalled that her intense eye contact was a bit spooky. Stewart concluded that an actor who could scare the producers at an audition would be just right for Callisto. As for Leick, she has said that the role initially appealed to her because it represented a chance to visit New Zealand.

However, Leick soon developed as much of an appreciation for her role as she did for the geography. "I think in all human beings there is this kind of rage," she says, when asked what makes Callisto both scary and fascinating. "She's funny about it. She's spoilt and bratty, and I think she acts in a way that other people would like to act, but it's politically incorrect. I think people can relate to her being a victim, because Callisto really is a victim. I don't mean that in a positive way. But she needs to get over herself!"

Callisto's fundamental vulnerability is another important aspect of her character. Unlike Xena, who at every stage of her life has managed to put her losses behind her and focus on something new, Callisto has never left behind that moment when her parents were killed before her eyes by Xena's army. Underneath all her cruelty and ferocity is a teenage girl who can't bear the terrible grief and fear she experienced as a result of that act. When she makes Xena stand in a town market and publicly confess to the murder of Callisto's parents, she expects that confession to hurt Xena. Instead, it hurts her. So much anguish shows on her face that even Gabrielle, who has excellent

reasons to hate her, asks if she is all right.

Instead of letting herself feel grief and thereby heal, Callisto has made an armour of hatred to keep the pain from touching her. And of course, the greatest hatred is reserved for the person she blames the most: Xena. "I think I was obsessed, speaking as the character. I was obsessed with Xena," says Leick of the Warrior Princess' role in Callisto's psyche, "and that's why there were those moments when I could have killed her and I didn't. Because without her, I'd be lost. I'd be truly lost. She gives me a focus to hang all that hatred on while she's there. And hate and love are very close. There's a great deal of emotional energy poured into that. What would she do without that? Where would she go? What would become of her?"

Callisto has decided that everything that's wrong in her life is Xena's fault. Every time she expresses her rage and pain by killing someone, she justifies her atrocities by telling herself that it's really Xena who bears the guilt, not herself, because Xena made her into a monster. It is not until they're both in Tartarus that Xena manages to force Callisto to face up to her choices, as they meet the spirits of her dead mother and dozens of her victims. "Every time you killed, you were killing me," her mother's spirit tells her. "How many of your victims had faces, Callisto? How many had families, sons and daughters who loved their parents?" Xena asks. "How many were just like your mother when they died at your hand?" Callisto's response is desperately defiant: "No! No, you can't make me feel guilty," she screams. But she can't shut out the moans and screams of the dead, and she flees.

Becoming an immortal, and even a god, is not enough to free Callisto from the prison of hatred she has made for herself. At first, she clings to the belief that the only thing that can free her is to make Xena suffer what she suffered. "When Hope kills Xena's child, I think Callisto wanted her to feel the pain, and when she actually hears Xena's anguished cries, it's what she's really craved. It's like, 'Now it's you — now *you* feel it!'" Leick explains. "But then it's over and it doesn't feed her. It's like any human being: you want the revenge. You think, 'I'm going to get them, and it's going to be really sweet, and then it's going to be all better,' but it's not. When you harm another human being, it

doesn't make you feel better. It makes you feel worse. It doesn't fill the void in the soul which you think it's going to."

Callisto expresses her subsequent despair when, in 'Maternal Instincts', Xena comes hunting her soon after Solan's murder. "You don't seem to get it do you? You've won," she tells Xena. "All these years I've spent living to destroy you, thinking that if only I could give you the same pain that you gave me I'd be rid of it, and life could go on. And then I do, and nothing changes. I don't feel better. Just empty. So you let me go, Xena. You can't win this battle, and you've already won the war."

When Callisto returns to Xena's world in 'Sacrifice', she has only one thing on her mind — putting herself out of her misery. She wants Hope to give her oblivion: "No immortality, no Tartarus, no nothing. I want it all to end." But what she gets, when Xena finally kills her, is not oblivion, but Hell itself. She becomes a demon in the deepest levels of Hell, where her only value to that realm's ruler lies in the fact that she might be useful in bringing her archenemy, Xena, under his dominion.

However, Callisto's exit from *Xena* is as unpredictable as her character. She does finally succeed in sending Xena to Hell, but not through any of the schemes she is involved in during 'The Ides of March' or 'Endgame'. Instead, Xena — in the most profound act of compassion — gives her mortal enemy her own inner light, thereby damning herself and taking Callisto's place in Hell, while restoring to Callisto the innocence she had before her parents' deaths. The angel Callisto finally ends her long feud with the Warrior Princess when she gives Eli the power to revive Xena and Gabrielle, and finds the peace that she has longed for. ⚔

EPISODES FEATURING HUDSON LEICK AS CALLISTO (UNLESS NOTED)

Season 1: Callisto
Season 2: The Return of Callisto; Intimate Stranger (Callisto/Xena); Ten Little Warlords (Xena)
Season 3: Maternal Instincts; The Bitter Suite; Sacrifice, Part I; Sacrifice, Part II
Season 4: The Ides of March
Season 5: Fallen Angel; Seeds of Faith

APHRODITE

"Honey, don't let the blonde hair fool you!"

"People tell me over and over again that they love how funny Aphrodite is," says Alexandra Tydings of her Olympian alter ego. "She's so much fun, and she's also so surprising. She rarely behaves in the way you'd expect the Goddess of Love to. I also think another thing people really love about Aphrodite is that she doesn't prevent herself from doing whatever she wants. She's almost like pure id; she really doesn't have a lot of restraint. And she also gets what she wants a lot of the time. I think the audience enjoy that because they can imagine themselves being so uninhibited and having so much fun and power." Uninhibited fun is exactly what you would expect of a woman whose preferred attire is a sheer pink negligee that leaves little of her curvaceous figure to the imagination, and whose temple features a wall decoration that makes Gabrielle comment, "I didn't know that was possible…"

Tydings — whose slender form and fine straight hair are so unlike Aphrodite that, out of costume, she could pass unnoticed even in a crowd of *Xena* fans — studied film and media at Brown University, then moved to Hollywood. She appeared in various series such as *Vanishing Son*, *Party of Five* and *The Red Shoe Diaries*, before being cast as Aphrodite for 'The Apple', a second season episode of *Hercules: The Legendary Journeys*. Ironically, she took the role against her management's advice, because she wanted to visit New Zealand. "My manager at the time really didn't want me to do *Hercules*. I had just done this movie [*The Sunchaser*] with Woody Harrelson which everyone thought was going to be this huge success — which it wasn't — and I was auditioning for all these big movie roles. So my manager and agent were being very protective of my career and what I did, because they really wanted to create a film career for me. But once I heard *Hercules* was shooting in New Zealand, I didn't really care!"

To play the role, Tydings initially had to re-adjust her concept of the Greek Goddess of Love: "My ideas about Aphrodite were much more romantic than the script's idea of Aphrodite. In the script, she seems like a complete bitch! She's funny, she's silly and she's not usually vindictive, but sometimes she is, and that really wasn't my idea of who Aphrodite was. But I started reading the myths and I discovered Aphrodite was actually quite vindictive at times. She was really, really mean to a few mortal women here and there, and the first script showed that."

Vindictive is the operative word for Aphrodite's actions in her first *Xena* episode, 'For Him the Bell Tolls'. She is determined to break up a royal

marriage that will end a war, only because the newly allied kingdoms plan to demolish some of her temples. As her son Cupid explains to Gabrielle, "When the Goddess of Love decides to do something petty and spiteful, she can be a tad difficult to reason with."

Her notorious self-conceit is on display too, as she brags to Cupid that she can make a romantic "boy toy" out of any man, no matter how unromantic he seems. Next thing we know, Joxer is acting like Errol Flynn, heads and hearts are at stake, and war is brewing on all fronts. To persuade Aphrodite to break the spell, Gabrielle has to make a full-frontal attack on the goddess' self-interest by threatening to have Joxer demonstrate his extremely destructive fighting technique in every one of her temples.

Since her first appearance, Aphrodite has often been teamed with Gabrielle, in episodes including 'The Quill is Mightier', 'Little Problems' and 'Punch Lines'. While this pairing was sometimes a script necessity — 'For Him the Bell Tolls' was one of the episodes created to cover Lucy Lawless' injury in the second season, and 'Little Problems' was scripted to allow for her shorter shooting hours during her pregnancy — the bard and the goddess are a good team. Gabrielle, being a bit self-obsessed herself at times, understands perfectly what makes Aphrodite tick, enabling her to undo the trouble Aphrodite has

caused in 'For Him the Bell Tolls' and 'Little Problems'. In return, Aphrodite has plenty of fun with Gabrielle's pet obsessions, such as when she enchants the bard's scrolls in 'The Quill is Mightier' and bestows an overdose of her own self-conceit on her in 'Fins, Femmes, and Gems'. As *Xena* progressed, the writers deliberately continued to build on their relationship. In 'Punch Lines', Aphrodite switches careers from matchmaker (or should that be troublemaker?) to psychologist, when she counsels Gabrielle about the ancient world's earliest recorded case of writer's block. The Goddess of Love (Yourself) whips out a smart looking pair of specs and actually helps her friend find a cure by rediscovering her inner child.

The friendship between Gabrielle and Aphrodite becomes critical in 'Motherhood', when the goddess — faced with her sister Athena's 'if you're not with me, you're against me' attitude — must chose between helping the mortal bard or her Olympian family, during Xena's battle against the gods. Aphrodite approaches Athena and asks that Gabrielle, at least, be spared the gods' wrath in the battle to come. When the Goddess of War and Wisdom rejects her request, Aphrodite is forced to act alone, sneaking into the house behind Athena's back, to try to help the critically injured Gabrielle. In fact, on her first day on set for that episode, Tydings arrived while they were shooting the subsequent scene, in which Xena pulls the injured Gabrielle and Eve out of the house. "They come dragging out of this house, and there's all this blood. I was really touched and moved and saddened by it," Tydings remembers.

Aphrodite's actions are all the more remarkable because she is in mourning for her beloved Hephaestus, who died at Xena's hands. It is difficult to imagine anyone being able to set an injury like that aside. Yet, when it matters, the usually self-centred Goddess of Love shows an unselfish, compassionate side we rarely see. At Xena's request, she carries Xena, Gabrielle and Eve to Olympus, giving Xena her only chance to defeat the gods and save her family. "That was my first really serious *Xena* episode," Tydings recalls. "I

was kind of floored by it, actually, because Aphrodite usually just does comedies. I had been in a few fight scenes, but nothing really serious."

Aphrodite's reward for not participating in the attacks on Eve is that she is one of the few Olympians to survive the Twilight of the Gods. But life afterwards proves to be far from simple. While Aphrodite remains a goddess, her brother and counterpart Ares, though still alive, sacrificed his powers to save Xena. Without a God of War to balance her, the Goddess of Love is vulnerable, and she is seduced by the power-hungry Emperor Caligula, who begins to steal her immortality. Under Caligula's influence, Aphrodite is not just an air-head, she's virtually amnesiac. She also seems to be infected with Caligula's lasciviousness: she tries to kiss Gabrielle, and she embraces her brother Ares in a way that makes the

practically unshockable God of War recoil in embarrassment, gasping, "Bad touching!" Xena, the former slayer of gods, is left to rescue the last Olympian goddess from Caligula and restore her immortality.

Aphrodite's fans were delighted to see the Goddess of Love restored to her bubbly immortal self in her final episode, 'Many Happy Returns'. It's our reward, and hers, for all that she's been through. Reflecting on those years, Tydings, the actress who brought Aphrodite so memorably to life, had this to say: "I've had a ton of great episodes! The writers have constantly challenged us to do different things, which has been wonderful." ✄

EPISODES FEATURING ALEXANDRA TYDINGS AS APHRODITE (UNLESS NOTED)

Season 2: For Him the Bell Tolls

Season 3: The Quill is Mightier; Fins, Femmes and Gems

Season 4: If the Shoe Fits

Season 5: Little Problems; Punch Lines; Married with Fishsticks (Aphrodite/Crabella); Motherhood

Season 6: The God You Know; Many Happy Returns

"I want to tap into the heart of darkness, the sheer naked will behind all craving, hatred and violence."

The script for 'Adventures in the Sin Trade' describes Alti as "a gnarled, ugly woman with gleaming eyes that are so bewitching they seem to be windows into some horrible abyss…" but there is nothing gnarled or ugly about Claire Stansfield — except the voice she puts on for Alti. However, at six feet one inch tall, the American actress is accustomed to being cast as warrior women and Amazon types (though her second most famous genre role is the 'Jersey Devil' in the eponymous early episode of *The X-Files*). Stansfield's first contact with Pacific Renaissance was an audition for the part of Morrigan in *Hercules*. She knew at the time that she didn't look or sound Irish enough for that role, but her audition did impress the producers, and within a couple of weeks she was offered the part of Alti, the power-hungry Siberian shamaness.

Alti comes into Xena's life soon after she has left Lao Ma and reconciled with Borias. The young Warrior Princess is looking for direction, and is tempted by the idea of becoming an Amazon and being part of their code of honour and discipline. Alti uses everything she's got — her arcane knowledge, her shamanistic powers and all the force of her personality — to seduce Xena into following her. What Alti offers is exactly the opposite of The Way that Lao Ma tried to teach Xena. "Your friend Lao Ma, her powers come from denial, self-sacrifice, from the light," Alti tells Xena in 'Adventures in the Sin Trade'. "That's not for people like you and me. I want to tap into the heart of darkness, the sheer, naked will behind all craving, hatred and violence. I'll become the face of death itself, capable of destroying not only a person's body, but their soul. Help me, and I'll make you the Destroyer of Nations."

Why does Alti want Xena so much? Like Lao Ma, she sees Xena's great potential for good or evil. She needs to harness Xena's huge capacity for violence in order to gain the kind of power she wants. It is for the same reason that she curses the unborn child of Xena and Borias. "She knew that the light from a child's face would turn me away from her darkness. She couldn't afford that," Xena explains. Alone, Alti could not kill the leaders of the Amazons, so she seduces Xena into killing them for her and then enslaves their souls to feed her dark powers.

The intensity of evil Stansfield portrays in Alti sometimes spooks even those close to her, but Stansfield doesn't tap into some inner demon to play the role. "I don't play the evil. I play the moments of excitement," she says. "I'm not playing that I'm enjoying somebody's pain, I'm just feeling the pure joy she gets in every moment of power, and wherever that power comes from, that's her

world. So I would just really work on the feelings that you get when you're really happy or excited about something and filled with the joy of it, that you just want to throw your head back and laugh because it's just so great. And that makes it even more evil that she's just loving it so much."

After being defeated by the Warrior Princess in 'Adventures in the Sin Trade', Alti's interest in Xena becomes a personal karmic grudge that stretches across many lifetimes. When Xena encounters her again in 'Between the Lines', Alti has been reincarnated as an Indian warlord who is searching for Xena's reincarnation so that she can destroy her enemy's soul and consume its power. By then, Alti's ability to inflict psychic torture has grown exponentially. "She has this power where she can put this grip on you, and she's able to make them look at their past and their future," Stansfield explains. "Renee and Lucy are so tormented by this that my character gets off on seeing their struggle and their pain. When I make Renee see her death, and I make her relive horrible things, I'm really just in the moment. Renee goes for it, she's sobbing and

crying. And I really have to play that I *love* that. Alti just thinks that's a hoot. The more she's got somebody afraid, the better. She thrives on that fear."

Stansfield recalls that even her make-up artist for 'Between the Lines' was impressed by the effect Alti has on Xena and Gabrielle, telling her, "'Claire, you have destroyed those two! Look at them over there. Nobody's ever done that before.' Xena and Gabrielle are crying, their legs are broken, they're bleeding... That was kind of a kick for me to know that for Alti, this was the most powerful she would ever be."

As a warlord, Alti also gets involved in some heavy fighting, which Stansfield found as exhilarating as her alter ego is supposed to. "Sword fighting was something I'd never done and always wanted to do, and I was petrified of it! Then I did it and I really got into it," Stansfield admits. "Ten guys are coming at you screaming, and you've got this choreographed sequence, and they're going to react to whatever you do. You've got to do it full force. And the director [T. J. Scott] kept saying, 'Claire, Alti loves this stuff, so when you stab somebody, you've got to [be] just laughing and screaming.' So forget being afraid and trying to remember your choreography, and forget this 200 pound Maori guy screaming, running at you — is he going to stop? All that is just out the window. You've got to just be Alti and go for it!"

Alti's obsession with Xena is such that when her deceased spirit needs to steal a soul so she can return to the material plane in 'Them Bones, Them Bones', the soul she picks is that of Xena's unborn child. For Alti, it's revenge; but for Stansfield, it was unsettling to play someone preying on a baby, especially a good friend's baby. "Because Lucy was pregnant, it made it really uncomfortable when she was having problems giving birth to the little sort of alien," she remembers. "It was a little disturbing, because she really *was* pregnant, and God forbid if anything were to happen. So it was a little strange having Xena be pregnant and having her worry that there might be something wrong with her baby. It was a little bit too close to home."

Even two millennia later, when she returns in 'Send in the Clones' as the evil scientist Alexis Los Alamos, the reincarnation of Alti is still obsessed with Xena. "In the real world they made a television series about Xena and Gabrielle, and now everyone loves her, and Alti is pissed! A couple of guys came along and made them heroes," says Stansfield, summing up Alti's perspective. "Alti has decided that she wants to let everyone know that that's

not really the truth, so she's bringing back Xena. Of course she has to bring back Gabrielle too, to mess with her. That's how she's going to show everyone that [Xena] is actually quite evil. And then Xena and Alti will rule the modern world. She believes in her heart that Xena is truly like her, an evil and power-lusting badass!"

For her final appearance in 'When Fates Collide', Alti is teamed with another major *Xena* villain, Julius Caesar, in an alternate timeline that she never actually lived. It's the first time that Alti shows any skin, or any interest at all in sex, as she is Caesar's mistress, while Xena is his wife. But she's still the same old Alti. "Alti is absolutely power driven. Even though she loves Caesar and hates Xena, ultimately she wants Rome, which at that time was the world. She wants to rule the world," Stansfield observes. "In her reality, she needs to get rid of Xena and then ultimately Caesar." Of course, as in all her lives, Alti has the same old luck. When it comes to Xena, she just can't win. ▩

EPISODES FEATURING CLAIRE STANSFIELD AS ALTI OR HER REINCARNATIONS

Season 4: Adventures in the Sin Trade, Part I; Adventures in the Sin Trade, Part II; Between the Lines
Season 5: Them Bones, Them Bones
Season 6: Send in the Clones; When Fates Collide

CAESAR

"Each event in our life is part of a great plan.
There are no accidents, only destiny."

O f all the major characters in *Xena* and *Hercules*, only Julius Caesar was once an actual living, breathing person. Karl Urban, the rising New Zealand actor who plays Caesar in *Xena*, studied the historical figure in preparation for the fictional role. "I don't think the Caesar portrayed in *Xena* is supposed to be a carbon copy of the actual man," he observes. "From what I've read — and I have read a lot about Julius Caesar — I think he is more of an amalgamation of a lot of people and characters from that time. He's kind of there to represent the arrogance and power of the Roman Empire."

Urban has received international attention for his starring role (opposite Danielle Cormack) in the New Zealand film *The Price of Milk*, and more recently as Eomer in *The Lord of the Rings*. But it was his roles in *Xena* and *Hercules* that first gained him recognition outside his homeland. Before Caesar, Urban played two other characters in the *Xena*verse. He was first cast as Maell in 'Altared States', which led to him being offered the part of Cupid in the *Hercules* episode 'Green-Eyed Monster'. While he was shooting that story, Rob Tapert invited him to audition for Caesar. He went straight from a long day on the set to the audition, and still impressed the producers enough to win the role.

When Caesar first appears in 'Destiny', he is a young Roman patrician who is so arrogant that he's not even afraid when Xena and her pirates capture him. He allows Xena to seduce him — in a memorable scene involving a very small red dress — but uses that seduction to capture *her*, and order her execution. "When Caesar first lays his eyes on Xena, he's intrigued," says Urban. "He's not frightened of anything, because he knows his destiny and he knows he's untouchable. And obviously he feels an intense attraction, which leads them to become lovers. But in that first episode, Caesar uses Xena. He betrays her and ultimately she means nothing to him." Caesar never realises that his betrayal has made Xena into a bloodthirsty warlord, nor would he care. He only cares that his victory over the pirates has advanced his political power, putting him one step closer to his goal.

By the time Xena comes back into his life in 'The Deliverer', Caesar has become the most powerful man in the Roman Republic. He has forged a political alliance with two other powerful Romans, Crassus and Pompey, and has the military might to attempt an invasion of distant Britannia. But Xena helps Boadicea to thwart his plans, and manages to destroy his precarious Triumvirate by forcing him to execute Crassus.

Despite this interference, Caesar does not immediately consider Xena to be a threat to his ambitions. "It's not really until the later episode, 'When in Rome', that Xena starts to become a bit more of an element in Caesar's life," Urban explains. "He is simply mystified that someone he thought he had executed can come boldly marching into his inner sanctum. It's at that point that he realises Xena is a major player, and he then tries to turn that to his advantage."

Caesar remains fascinated by Xena. The sight of her in Roman finery in 'When in Rome' leads him to make a pass at her — partly, no doubt, for strategic reasons, but partly because he feels a genuine sexual attraction. Unlike her continuing attraction to Ares though, Xena's feelings for Caesar did not survive his first betrayal, and her only interest is in winning the release of his prisoner, Vercinix.

In the Xenaverse, Caesar's historical place as one of the greatest generals who ever lived serves to confirm that Xena has become the world's greatest warrior. No matter what Caesar does, Xena finds a way to outfight him, both in hand-to-hand combat and in grand military strategy. She defeats every move he makes — even the plans meant specifically to outwit her. Finally, in 'A Good Day', she leaves both his and Pompey's armies in ruins, effectively halting their civil war for control of Rome. Despite this, Caesar remains undeterred. "This is only a minor setback, Xena," he murmurs to the empty air. "You can't change my destiny."

Caesar's power struggle with Pompey — who is almost his equal in charm, ambition and military ability — adds a more petty human element to Caesar's lofty plans: he wants to destroy Pompey primarily because the other Roman is so much like him that Rome isn't big enough for both of them. In their scenes together, Karl Urban and Jeremy Callaghan, portraying two men who are practically defined by their rivalry, strike real sparks off each other. This rivalry is so intense that once Caesar and Pompey start fighting in 'A Good Day', even the woods bursting into flames around them isn't enough to make them stop!

Defeating Pompey and making himself master of Rome still doesn't provide Caesar with the means to bring Xena down single-handedly. He needs the supernatural help of her most intimate enemy, Callisto. With Xena finally out of the way, Caesar feels confident that he can move to claim his empire. He never learns that Xena and Gabrielle played their role in his downfall even before they were captured…

The real Julius Caesar was not only a great military strategist but also a charismatic leader, beloved by all his soldiers. Brutus' initial trust in his general shows that, at some point at least, Xena's Caesar has some of the same leadership quality. Initially, no matter how much Xena and Gabrielle try to convince Brutus that Caesar's ambitions are selfish, Brutus won't hear a word against him. "Your vision of Caesar is blinded by hatred," he tells the two women in 'Endgame'. "He is the only hope to restore the democracy of the Republic." Eventually, Gabrielle does raise doubts in Brutus' mind, while

Xena gives him hard information about all Caesar's self-serving plans. She tells Brutus that Caesar intends to make himself Emperor of Rome and assassinate anyone, including Brutus, who might oppose him. Though Brutus doesn't want to believe her, Caesar's own actions finally convince him: Caesar rejects the Amazon peace treaty, which Brutus believed might benefit Rome, and after promising Brutus that Gabrielle and Eli will only be held hostage, he orders their execution.

David Franklin, who plays *Xena's* Brutus, reveals the impact of those actions on Caesar's faithful lieutenant: "Brutus was betrayed. He thought he was working for the common good. To reach that point and then realise that everything he'd done had been for Caesar's benefit, and not for the good of Rome... I think that murderous rage was justifiable!"

Despite the historical finality of 'The Ides of March', Caesar does get one last chance to fulfil his destiny, when his spirit weaves him a second life in 'When Fates Collide'. Yet once again, his vices and ambitions carry their own punishment: instead of being murdered by Brutus and the Senators, he is murdered by his lover, Alti, whose hunger for power exceeds even his own. Caesar's great destiny turns out to be sheer murder.

"Caesar was the first archenemy I'd ever played and it was just a lot of fun," says Urban, summing up his time playing Caesar. "Playing a villain is great, because they get to do and say a lot of things that are forbidden in ordinary life. It was fun to be so maniacal and arrogant. It's also been great to see the response from viewers. From what feedback I've received, Caesar is a character a lot of people love, but also someone a lot of people love to hate. He definitely seems to have made a strong impact, which is terrific." ☒

EPISODES FEATURING KARL URBAN AS CAESAR

Season 2: Destiny
Season 3: The Deliverer; When In Rome
Season 4: A Good Day; Endgame; The Ides of March
Season 6: When Fates Collide

"You don't often let people see who you really are... I was in there. I know. Despite all your bluster and bravado, Autolycus, you're a nice person."

When Autolycus swaggers into an episode of *Xena*, he brings with him plenty of swashbuckling adventure, comedy and razor-sharp repartee. The King of Thieves is as quick with a fast retort as he is with a skeleton key, but it's his charm, and the ongoing inner conflict between his 'profession' and his conscience, that endear him to us the most.

Bruce Campbell always had an inside track on the role, having begun his career by teaming up with Sam Raimi and Rob Tapert to make *The Evil Dead*. He had already directed a first season episode of *Hercules* when he learned of a one-time guest role in *Xena's* sister show. "Rob called me and said, 'I've got a part for you that's perfect!' And I just went, 'Yeah, yeah, I've heard that before,'" Campbell remembers. "But then I read it and thought, 'Yeah, he's right. It's perfect.' So I agreed to do it."

Campbell's suave charm fitted right in to the world of *Xena* and *Hercules*, and soon he, and Autolycus, gained a more important role: "My function was to add some spice to the main course, and to provide back-up when Kevin was not up to speed or if Lucy was injured. I would just fill in until they got back

on their feet." Handsome enough to be a hero and athletic enough to command the screen in any number of stunt fights, Campbell made a perfect substitute when Lucy Lawless was injured during the second season. The event also provided viewers with the opportunity to watch Autolycus bicker with his own body when Xena's spirit borrows it in 'The Quest'.

As undisputed King of Thieves, Autolycus takes his greatest pride not in his ill-gotten gains, but in his skill. Being chained up with 200 locks in 'Vanishing Act' isn't a punishment, it's a test, and he enjoys seeing how fast he can get all those locks open. He also takes pride in following a certain code, which includes robbing from the rich (especially if they provide a challenge), but doesn't include bloodshed. In 'Takes One to Know One', he is

offended that any of his friends would suspect him of murder: "Come on, Gabrielle, you know my rap sheet. Do you recall seeing 'ruthless murderer' anywhere on it?"

Autolycus also fancies himself in one non-professional area — charming the ladies (as he would put it). And many of them enjoy being charmed, most notably Cleopatra in 'King of Assassins'. Autolycus tries his charms on Xena several times before accepting that she's not going to succumb. Though a career criminal, he doesn't have the dangerous quality that Xena is attracted to. As she admits in 'The Quest', "Despite all your bluster and bravado, Autolycus, you're a nice person. I knew I could trust you."

In fact, career criminal or not, Autolycus really is a softy, who somehow always ends up on the side of the good guys. "I think people will always have a little place in their hearts for scoundrels," says Campbell. "Autolycus doesn't have to do the right thing, but at the end of the day, the audience knows that he *will* do the right thing... I don't think I've ever stolen anything that I didn't give back or forfeit!" ⬛

EPISODES FEATURING BRUCE CAMPBELL AS AUTOLYCUS

Season 1: The Royal Couple of Thieves
Season 2: The Quest
Season 3: King of Assassins; Tsunami; Vanishing Act
Season 4: Key to the Kingdom; Takes One to Know One

"Trust Salmoneus. He only has the customer's interest at heart. Ask anybody. Later."

The salesman of the ancient world holds an important place in *Xena* history. He witnesses Xena's conversion, and is the first to urge that she join forces with Hercules to fight a greater evil, in the *Hercules* episode 'The Gauntlet'. First, though, he had to talk Xena out of killing him. Luckily for Salmoneus, the Warrior Princess, like most people, found him amusing — especially in drag.

There is however more to Salmoneus than merely being amusing. He is without doubt the most versatile entrepreneur Ancient Greece has yet seen. He has sold kitchenware, Black Wolf merchandise, shoddy armour and seltzer, been a celebrity biographer and emceed a major beauty pageant. And that's just in his adventures with Xena.

Robert Trebor, an experienced stage and screen actor, first came to the attention of *Xena*'s producers when he was cast as the slave Waylin in *Hercules and the Lost Kingdom*. They liked his performance so much that Salmoneus was created especially for him. The original two *Hercules* episodes planned for the character eventually increased to more than twenty appearances in both series.

Comic foils can deteriorate into mere vehicles for repeated gags and one-liners, but Trebor takes care to give Salmoneus a heart underneath that veneer of hucksterism. "Salmoneus was originally written strictly as a comic sidekick.

He was extremely greedy and would do anything for a dinar, although he would grudgingly do the right thing in the end. My contribution was to round him out so that he wasn't just lecherous and greedy, but a full human being," says Trebor, explaining Salmoneus' development. "If you're playing an ongoing character [it's] a richer experience if the audience cares about what's happening to the person. Salmoneus is still there to get the laughs, but it's good to reveal more character and show the humanity underneath." Of course, a huckster with a heart also provides more opportunity for conflict, whether dramatic or comic. Much as he

would like to let greed and self-interest be his guides, Salmoneus' better nature usually won't let him — often much to his dismay.

His three *Xena* appearances give Salmoneus the chance for some fine comedy — as a reluctant jailbird in 'The Black Wolf', a seltzer magnate in 'The Greater Good' and a razzle-dazzle showman in 'Here She Comes... Miss Amphipolis' — but the last episode also reveals his fundamental benevolence. His primary motivation in running the Miss Known World Pageant is not the money and the publicity, but making sure the pageant serves its purpose by preventing a war. Of course, as the organiser, Salmoneus just happens to have chosen the best possible venue to showcase his own talents too. He's an admirable emcee, completely at home surrounded by the glamour and the beautiful women.

Undoubtedly, Salmoneus' finest dramatic moment comes in 'The Greater Good', when he discovers that Xena has apparently died of a poison dart. There's not a laugh in sight as the comic salesman sits beside his friend's body, mourning her untimely death. Fortunately, Xena's death is even more temporary than most deaths in this universe, and the salesman of the ancient world soon recovers his smile. ℥

EPISODES FEATURING
ROBERT TREBOR AS SALMONEUS
Hercules: The Legendary Journeys (Xena episodes): The Gauntlet; Unchained Heart
Season 1: The Black Wolf; The Greater Good
Season 2: Here She Comes... Miss Amphipolis

"I would kill to protect you, Xena. Any mother who loves her child would."

W here does the Warrior Princess get her inner warrior? From her loving mum, of course. In her very first scene, Xena's mother Cyrene shows her own warrior spirit when she walks up to Xena (who towers over her) and takes her sword away. She may be the only person in the world whom Xena would allow to do that!

New Zealander Darien Takle brings to Cyrene all the authority and moral fibre of an actress who, in a decades-long career on stage and screen, has played every great female role from Edith Piaf and Eva Peron to the cream of Shakespeare's women characters. Cyrene frequently needs every bit of this authority to stand up to her warlord daughter and defy the gods themselves. In her darkest episode, she even faces the possibility that Xena will kill her at the behest of the Furies. Cyrene has the courage to face this, just as she had the courage many years before to do the unthinkable: killing her husband Atrius because it was the only way to stop him from sacrificing their little girl, Xena, to Ares.

Before each of her episodes, Takle spent a little time coming up with some back story for Cyrene, to give her performance a little context. She found it

easy to determine what kind of role Cyrene plays in Amphipolis: "I think she's a bit of a spokeswoman. People come to her and tell her what's going on. I think because she's Xena's mum they expect her to be a bit of a warrior herself."

Cyrene shows her leadership qualities in 'Amphipolis Under Siege', when Athena's army besieges the village. Athena appears in a village meeting and confronts Xena, asking whether she wants to destroy her neighbours' faith in the gods for the sake of one child. Cyrene, with her granddaughter Eve in her arms, demands, "Hasn't this village given up enough of its children? I've already lost a son, and a grandson I've never even met. Well, I won't give up this child, not even for the gods themselves." In response, the goddess asks the other villagers if they are so eager to die, but even before she has finished, Cyrene starts to sing a song of defiance and hope, and the whole village joins in, proclaiming their unity.

Amid all these serious moments, Takle worked to give Cyrene a sense of humour as well. "[I made a choice] to lighten her up, to actually make her funny, to be a bit ditzy," she explains. "I think that's where Xena gets her sense of humour and probably her independence and feisty character, because mum's small but feisty. There was one thing that I did which Lucy loved, and we kept it in. In 'Takes One to Know One', where she reaches to get a bit of fruit, I smack her hand — which is what mothers do. I love doing that sort of thing, giving it a bit of fun. That's the sort of relationship that they've got now, and probably always had except when Xena was being a bad girl…"

Looking back over her years as Cyrene, Takle recalls, "I auditioned to play Hercules' mother once a long time ago, but I ended up playing Xena's mother. I was very happy about that, it's been a very happy time." ⬛

EPISODES FEATURING DARIEN TAKLE AS CYRENE

Season 1: Sins of the Past
Season 2: The Furies
Season 4: Takes One to Know One
Season 5: Lyre, Lyre, Hearts on Fire; Amphipolis Under Siege
Season 6: The Haunting of Amphipolis

"When you need to make a decision as an Amazon, think of Ephiny. Do what she would do."

Though she has appeared in only seven episodes, the Amazon Ephiny looms large in *Xena* mythology. This is largely due to the compelling screen presence of Danielle Cormack. An award-winning actress in New Zealand, Cormack has begun to attract international recognition for her work in films, including *The Price of Milk*, in which she co-starred with Karl Urban.

Cormack's Ephiny, when we first meet her in 'Hooves and Harlots', is the toughest of tough girls. She is eager to deal retribution to the Centaur accused of killing her friend Princess Terreis, and she's outraged that a little village nobody like Gabrielle has succeeded Terreis as an Amazon princess. She demonstrates her hardness when she introduces Gabrielle to Amazon weapons. The peace-loving Gabrielle chooses a staff, because it seems less violent than a blade. After her first lessons, she comments that using the staff is "kind of fun". "Fun?" asks Ephiny, taking the staff and proceeding to give a detailed demonstration of how Amazons use it to cripple and kill their enemies, the Centaurs. "Still think it's fun?" she concludes. Cormack remembers that first episode well: "It was sometimes confusing and sometimes exhilarating to run around in these tiny costumes, screaming and fighting all the bad guys! It's a heightened reality… a different level of performance [than a contemporary piece]. There's always the danger of going over the top."

Ephiny develops a softer side in later episodes, which had always been the

intention. "Her natural progression from being an evil little witch who was just the control freak… that was just what the writers wanted to do," says Cormack. "They wanted to evolve the character, and she became more maternal, she began to understand her flaws, which I think is generally something that happens when you grow up." Ephiny certainly shows her maternal side in 'Is There a Doctor in the House?' when she gives birth to a Centaur's child. It comes to the fore again later in 'Maternal Instincts' when she protects her son and other children from Callisto, and finally in 'The Last of the Centaurs', when her spirit returns to protect her unborn grandchild.

Though her character develops, Ephiny never loses her Amazon warrior strength and sense of

honour. In 'The Quest' and 'A Necessary Evil', she opposes the ambitious Velasca, who wants power for herself, and is not concerned about serving her people. Ephiny is only interested in making sure that her tribe has a good and compassionate ruler, and accepts the role of Queen for the good of the tribe, not out of personal ambition.

Ephiny dies an Amazon warrior's death in her shortest screen appearance. She is killed in battle by Brutus in the first three minutes of 'Endgame'. When the episode was in development, producer Eric Gruendemann asked Cormack's opinion on whether Ephiny should die, and Cormack voted wholeheartedly in favour. "Even though I know there are people out there that have booed and hissed at the whole storyline of Ephiny getting killed off, I think it's interesting to create great drama, and especially by killing off a character that is actually good," says Cormack. "I see some of the responses to Ephiny's death, and I think it's perfect that these people feel this way, that they feel so passionate about it, because I like extreme responses. It's great for the character. I'm not scared to go there with characters." 卐

EPISODES FEATURING
DANIELLE CORMACK AS EPHINY

Season 1: Hooves and Harlots; Is There a Doctor in the House?

Season 2: The Quest; A Necessary Evil

Season 3: Maternal Instincts; The Bitter Suite

Season 4: Endgame

Season 6: The Last of the Centaurs

"Selfless pure love is the only expression of divine perfection we have in this world."

Timothy Omundson had auditioned for two previous roles in *Hercules* and *Xena* before he learned from his friend Ted Raimi that the producers were casting the part of a holy man. "The funny thing is that they wanted anyone but a Caucasian for the role," Omundson recalls, "and look who ended up with it! I think the producers had been seeing actors for the part for quite a few weeks, and weren't able to find him. I'm not sure what I did right, but the next thing I know, I'm on a plane to New Zealand."

What Omundson did right was to bring out the humanity in his portrayal of the compassionate prophet Eli. "Eli was discovering who he was; his human side, warts and all. And I decided that Eli should be a prophet discovering what he was and not particularly liking it, but at the same time also realising his potential," Omundson says. "The hardest thing about the character was always

playing him on the same beat, as Eli is not the most glamorous of roles. I wanted to make him exciting for the audience, so I tried to find flashes of humanity." To build his portrayal of Eli, Omundson drew on the lives and teachings of Ghandi, Martin Luther King Jr and Jesus, focusing especially on theories that Jesus lived and studied in the East during the 'lost years' of his teens and twenties, which are not mentioned in the New Testament.

Instead of condemning those who can't follow his Way of Love, Eli warns people that it is the hardest path of all, and he is full of fears and doubts about himself and his mission. "I used to envy you when I thought you were a devi," he tells Gabrielle. "And now I have this power to heal people and cast out demons and give people hope, and it terrifies me."

As well as suffering self-doubt, Eli doubts his god at moments of crisis. When Amarice accuses him of causing the deaths of Gabrielle and Xena, because his message of peace made Gabrielle weak, he sits alone in the cold twilight and voices a prayer of grief and rage: "My friends died because of my teachings. The Way of Love wasn't the way for Gabrielle. I was too proud to see that. What good is this gift if I can't at least protect those I love? Why did you ever give this to me? What am I supposed to do?" This prayer is answered when the powers of heaven, through Callisto, allow Eli to resurrect Xena and Gabrielle.

In 'Seeds of Faith', Eli comes into his own as the prophet who sees his destiny clearly, even though the consequences frighten him. When Callisto tells him he is to be martyred, he asks if there is any other way, and sits alone crying silently at the answer. But he doesn't turn back. His death at the hands of Ares does more than give courage to his followers, it gives Xena the wisdom not to avenge him by shedding more blood.

Though 'Seeds of Faith' was Omundson's last *Xena* episode, Eli's spirit endures in the *Xena*verse, as his followers form a new religious cult in the service of the God of Love that will eventually be led by Xena's daughter Eve.

EPISODES FEATURING
TIMOTHY OMUNDSON AS ELI
Season 4: Devi; The Way; The Ides of March
Season 5: Fallen Angel; Chakram; Seeds of Faith

EVE/LIVIA

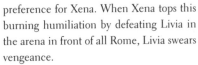

"A lifetime serving Rome doesn't change the fact that she's your daughter, Xena. When she looks inside herself, she'll see you there. She'll be Eve again."

For Adrienne Wilkinson, playing Eve/Livia was a chance to try many new things — including going on the ocean, being dragged behind a four-wheeler and playing with a very large spider — but it was the Livia aspect of the character that intrigued her. "Regardless of what your character's personality is like, regardless of how objectively you feel about them, you've got to love a character — and I loved her," says Wilkinson. "I thought she was a total spoiled brat, but she was intelligent and conniving, and obviously very fierce and the most amazing warrior. I could comprehend the manipulativeness of her plans, especially because I'd never gotten to play a character like that. There's absolute freedom in playing someone who isn't sorry for anything they're doing. That freedom is overpowering."

Livia will manipulate anyone or destroy anything for the power she craves, and woe betide anyone who gets in the way of her ambitions. Even while she's betrothed to the Emperor Augustus, who can give her the power to rule Rome, she's having an affair with Ares, whose promises of power encompass the whole world. It's bad enough that Xena destroys her hopes for imperial power by revealing to Augustus her secret liaison with Ares. Far worse is Ares' obvious

preference for Xena. When Xena tops this burning humiliation by defeating Livia in the arena in front of all Rome, Livia swears vengeance.

From then on, she goes on a bloody rampage, venting her humiliation on the world — like the wounded child that she is inside. Of course, if she can hurt anyone close to Xena in the process, so much the better. She massacres whole towns, persecutes the Elijans, captures Gabrielle and, finally and worst of all in our eyes, she kills the harmless, aged Joxer when he dares to get in her way.

This final murder hangs over the early days of Livia's transformation into Eve. "With Eve, it's been far more realistic. It's just not as much fun, because Eve is very righteous," says Wilkinson, contrasting

playing the amoral Livia with playing Eve after her repentance. "She's so desperately trying to repent of her past that she's too shy to get involved in the battles. Plus she's nervous whenever she deals with something that's evil."

Eve has to overcome that nervousness in 'The Haunting of Amphipolis' and 'Heart of Darkness', when she confronts the powers of Hell with the force of her prayers and her faith. Through this frightening and exhausting experience, Eve makes mistakes, but finds in herself new kinds of strength.

When Eve returns in 'The God You Know', she has come into her own as a prophet. She is ready to defy Caligula and face martyrdom, and she is furious with her mother for taking that choice away from her. She is also ready to accept the Amazons' trial and punishment as part of her atonement — perhaps a little too ready, as Xena proves by forcing her and the Amazons to acknowledge Ares' role in her evil deeds. When last seen Eve is headed east, in the footsteps of Eli and Xena, to learn more about The Way. ✖

EPISODES FEATURING ADRIENNE WILKINSON AS (THE ADULT) EVE

Season 5: Livia; Eve; Motherhood
Season 6: Coming Home; The Haunting of Amphipolis; Heart of Darkness; Who's Gurkhan?; The God You Know; You Are There; Path of Vengeance

BORIAS

"Borias was very wise. He found his way long before I did."

hen the warlord Borias fell under Xena's spell, he left his wife and
son, not to mention his entire army, to start anew with her in the
heart of Asia. Xena's association with Borias brought many
important people into her life, including Alti, Lao Ma and their son Solan.

New Zealander Marton Csokas, who gives Borias his fire, has played many
roles on screen and stage, including appearing in *Farscape*, *Star Wars: Episode
II* and *The Lord of the Rings*. "I don't see Borias as being bad," says Csokas. "I
see him as a person who is loyal to his principles, with war being a part of his
world. His fundamental motivation was derived from survival, principles of
war, family and even love, and the maintaining of a life beyond just running
around and killing people. So, in that way, he has quite an honest profession."

Borias knew Xena during the most destructive phase of her life, and
though drawn to her by her passion and fierce determination, time and again
he had to restrain her violent impulses. When she ruined his efforts to form an
alliance with the powerful Chinese houses of Ming and Lao, he banished her,
and when she abducted Ming Tzu's son, he betrayed her. Yet, only a few weeks
later, he was willing to reconcile with her.

In 'Adventures in the Sin Trade, Part II', Cyane
counsels Xena to let Borias go: "He's trying to
change, Xena. Let him. If you two stay together,
you'll just end up killing him." Borias was indeed
changing, as the prospect of fatherhood lead him to
seek peace, and to protect the child Otere from both
Xena and Alti. Unfortunately, while Borias cultivated
peace with the Amazons, Xena formed her
murderous partnership with Alti. Borias' hopes for
peace and a family life with Xena and their unborn
child were crushed not just by Alti's curse, but by
Xena's dark impulses and her revulsion at the very
thought of such emotional ties.

Borias' final break from Xena came when she
tried to make war on the Centaurs. He begged her to
leave the Centaurs alone and — just as important to
him — not to make herself his enemy. Though she
turned on him, Borias couldn't turn his back on her,
because of their child, and because of his love for

her. "Before Alti, before all this, we had love, Xena," he tells her. "Maybe we confused it with power but it was there, is still there. For the sake of our son and us, I'm taking you away." He tried to rescue her from her camp and was killed as he first set eyes on his new-born son.

Borias' legacy lives on, not only in the way the Centaurs honour his memory, but in Xena herself. "He showed me the hatred I had for myself. He showed me the love that someone could have for a child," she recalls, many years later in 'Past Imperfect'. Because of him, she gave up Solan to someone who could rear him properly, and because of him, she took the first steps away from being the Destroyer of Nations. ▒

EPISODES FEATURING MARTON CSOKAS AS BORIAS

Season 3: The Debt, Part I; The Debt, Part II
Season 4: Adventures in the Sin Trade, Part I; Adventures in the Sin Trade, Part II; Past Imperfect
Season 6: The Last of the Centaurs; A Friend in Need, Part I; A Friend in Need, Part II

"And I thought the Greek immortals were freaks!"
"Yes, but they're our freaks!"

Second only to Ares in the hunky warlord department, **Draco** holds a special place as *Xena's* first villain. Unlike many of the dumb and despicable followers of Ares, Draco actually has a few virtues, including intelligence, exceptional battle skills, good looks and a sense of honour. Draco's attraction to Xena goes overboard under Cupid's spell, but alas, even being in love with Gabrielle isn't enough to reform him in the end. Jay Laga'aia took pains to make Draco more complex than the usual bad guy: "I wanted Draco to have the face of Tom Cruise and the mask of Hannibal Lecter, a combination that makes him like honey on steel — it was sweet, but if you licked it you would cut your tongue!" **Episodes Featuring Jay Laga'aia as Draco:** *Season 1:* Sins of the Past. *Season 2:* A Comedy of Eros. *Season 5:* Lyre, Lyre, Hearts on Fire.

Gabrielle's little sister **Lila** is a stay-at-home, not an adventurer. She struggles with resentment for Gabrielle leaving her, and with some jealousy of Xena, but soon comes to terms with Gabrielle's new life and even helps her to

Jay Laga'aia as Draco.

recognise how much she has grown. Though she's not a warrior, she has her own kind of courage, in helping Gabrielle and the town fight a warlord, and in standing up for her friends against Discord. During the twenty-five years of Gabrielle's absence, Lila endured more tragedy by losing the rest of her family: her daughter was captured by slavers, and her mother, father and husband died trying to rescue her. **Episodes Featuring Willa O'Neill as Lila:** *Season 1:* Sins of the Past; The Prodigal. *Season 3:* The Bitter Suite. *Season 4:* A Family Affair. *Season 6:* Who's Gurkhan?

As the first person to show Xena her potential as a force for good, **Lao Ma** casts a long shadow over the Warrior Princess' life. Her rival, Ming Tzu, observes that Lao Ma is "hard and soft at the same time."

Jennifer Sky as Amarice.

Gentle in her teaching of Xena and her desire for peace, she is also ruthless enough to keep her tyrannical husband alive but in a coma, so that she can wield his political power. The memory of Lao Ma's teachings helps Xena to make the transition to good, and Lao Ma's children draw Xena back to China twice more: once to kill her son, and once to recover her book and meet her twin daughters. In *Xena* mythology, Lao Ma is the writer of the book associated with the name of her husband, Lao Tzu, making her the founder of Taoism in the *Xena*verse. **Episodes Featuring Jacqueline Kim as Lao Ma:** *Season 3:* The Debt, Part I; The Debt, Part II.

Minya is the world's first Xena fangirl, and she will do anything for her hero — except let Xena have her boyfriend! She finds that leather and whips suit her well. Though she'll never be a Warrior Princess, she proves to be a good friend, when she risks her own safety to distract a dangerous bounty hunter from Lila. Allison Wall auditioned for Minya because of previous work with Michael Hurst, who directed 'A Day in the Life'. **Episodes Featuring Allison Wall as Minya:** *Season 2:* A Day in the Life. *Season 3:* The Quill is Mightier. *Season 4:* The Play's the Thing; Takes One to Know One.

Teenage Amazon wannabe **Amarice** starts out reckless, impulsive and way too quick with her sword. Gradually, through the influence of Xena, Gabrielle and even Eli, she learns not to make snap judgements about people or

situations. Her hardest moment comes when her friends discover that her claim of Amazon origins is a complete lie. Amarice was introduced as a recurring character who might draw in younger viewers, but her adventures in the *Xenaverse* were cut short when Jennifer Sky was cast as Cleopatra in Renaissance's science fiction series, *Cleopatra 2525*. **Episodes Featuring Jennifer Sky as Amarice:** *Season 4:* Endgame; The Ides of March. *Season 5:* Fallen Angel; Chakram; Animal Attraction; Them Bones, Them Bones.

Though he appears in earlier episodes with a line or two, **Brutus** only becomes an important player in 'Endgame'. When Caesar's loyal lieutenant finally sees that Caesar is neither a hero nor a servant of Rome, but a man obsessed with power, he leads Caesar's assassination in 'The Ides of March'. His own obsession with power leads to his bloody demise in battle with Xena. **Episodes Featuring Brutus, Played By Grant Triplow:** *Season 2:* Destiny. *Season 3:* When in Rome. **Played By Darren Young:** *Season 4:* A Good Day. **Played By David Franklin:** *Season 4:* Endgame; The Ides of March. *Season 5:* Antony and Cleopatra. *Season 6:* When Fates Collide.

Charles Mesure as Michael.

Like Xena, **Michael**, the archangel leader of the forces of Heaven, has light and dark sides. He's all light, courage and even love in 'Fallen Angel' when he battles for the rescue of Xena and Gabrielle, and joins Callisto in

rejoicing at their resurrection. He's all cunning, threat and darkness when he manipulates Xena and Eve into destroying Caligula in 'The God You Know'. **Episodes Featuring Charles Mesure as Michael:** *Season 5:* Fallen Angel. *Season 6:* The Haunting of Amphipolis; Heart of Darkness; The God You Know; You Are There.

Joxer's son **Virgil** trained as a blacksmith, but wants to be a bard. His courage and kindness surely come from his father, but his intelligence and skill with weapons must come from somewhere else! Like his dad, he has some special feelings for Gabrielle, especially in 'Heart of Darkness'. The producers had planned to include Virgil in several more season six episodes, but William Gregory Lee's ongoing role as Zack in *Dark Angel* conflicted with the *Xena* shooting schedule,

and he was never able to return. **Episodes Featuring William Gregory Lee as Virgil:** *Season 5:* Livia; Eve; Motherhood. *Season 6:* The Haunting of Amphipolis; Heart of Darkness; Who's Gurkhan?; The Abyss.

THE OLYMPIAN GODS

With the notable exceptions of Ares and Aphrodite, the Olympians play only minor roles in *Xena*, most of the time. Relatives of **Zeus** and **Hera**, they're a quarrelsome, sometimes cutthroat family. But family nonetheless, and when threatened with their demise (in the Twilight of the Gods storyline) they all stand together. Except, of course, for the aforementioned Ares and Aphrodite. Despite their capriciousness, all the gods believe in the order of the universe and in following the rules. Even Discord, though she constantly changes the rules of her little game of Clue ('Takes One to Know One'), still acknowledges that rules are important.

William Gregory Lee as Virgil.

Poseidon, God of the Sea and brother of Zeus, is mostly known for cursing people, in particular Ulysses in the episode of the same name and Cecrops in 'Lost Mariner'. He is perhaps most notable in the *Xena*verse for being the only one of the main Olympians not played by an actor — instead his majestic, watery appearance was created by Flat Earth, the *Xena* special effects team. He dies, without speaking, at the hands of Xena in 'Motherhood'. **Episodes Featuring Charles Siebert as the Voice of Poseidon:** *Season 2:* Ulysses; Lost Mariner.

Hades, King of the Dead, looks regally impressive in his black armour and war chariot, but at bottom, he's more an administrator — an overworked administrator — than a king, who complains about how much work Xena created during her dark warrior stage. Xena has a closer relationship with Hades than with most of the gods, and helps him on two occasions. Yet when push comes to shove, he's just as willing as the rest to fight Xena. **Episodes Featuring Hades, Played By Erik Thompson:** *Season 1:* Death in Chains; Mortal Beloved. *Season 2:* Intimate Stranger. *Season 4:* Adventures in the Sin

Paris Jefferson as Athena.

Trade, Part I. **Played By Stephen Lovatt:** *Season 5:* God Fearing Child; Looking Death in the Eye; Motherhood.

Athena, Goddess of Wisdom and War, represents disciplined force used to uphold authority and order, rather than the chaotic aspects of war represented by Ares and, as such, she *ought* to be the god closest to the heart of Xena. Her army consists of regiments of the most disciplined and respected troops in the ancient world. She believes that the twilight of the Olympian gods will be a disaster for humanity as well as her family, and once she sets her will on something, she will not be turned. Her determination to destroy Xena's child leads her and most of the other Olympians to their deaths. **Episodes Featuring Paris Jefferson as Athena:** *Season 5:* Amphipolis Under Siege; Looking Death in the Eye; Motherhood.

Cupid, God of Love and son of Aphrodite, is a specialist in happy-ever-after pairings — unlike his mother, who seems more interested in hormones. 'Make love not war' might be his motto in 'For Him the Bell Tolls', when he tries to keep his mother from splitting up the lovers whose marriage will end a war. Cupid seems to have very little interest in larger affairs, and he plays no part at all in the twilight of the gods, so he's probably still out there shooting his golden arrows. **Episodes Featuring Karl Urban as Cupid:** *Season 2:* For Him the Bell Tolls; A Comedy of Eros.

Discord, 'goddess of skank' (unofficially, of course), has a long-standing rivalry with Aphrodite, but despite her ambitions to become Ares' second in command, she can't even whip the Goddess of Love in a fireball fight, or stop Aphrodite from washing out her potty mouth with soap. Filling in as Hera's Goddess of Retribution in 'Takes One to Know One', she comes to a fight with Xena backed by her boy toys instead of real warriors, and is sent home empty handed when the 'murderer' she seeks proves to be a horse. She has the dubious distinction of being the first goddess to die at Xena's hands. **Episodes Featuring Meighan Desmond as Discord:** *Season 3:* The Deliverer. *Season 4:* Takes One to Know One. *Season 5:* Married with Fishsticks; Motherhood. ☒

EVERY HERO NEEDS A STEED

Despite a bit of early confusion in the scripts about her gender, **Argo** quickly became *Xena*'s most important non-speaking character. The sight of Xena galloping along on her beautiful palomino is an essential part of the visual appeal of the show. Argo also adds another positive dimension to Xena's character — only someone who's good at heart could care so deeply for her horse. Argo figures in Gabrielle's early adjustment to life with the Warrior Princess, as bard and steed don't really get along until they have to work together in 'The Greater Good'. Argo even has a few adventures of her own: being attacked by Callisto in 'Intimate Stranger', kidnapped by a warlord in 'In Sickness and In Hell' and being the culprit in a murder in 'Takes One to Know One'.

Argo was played by a mare named Tilly and, like her co-star Lucy Lawless, also had her own doubles. Tilly was always paired with Lawless in shots where the actors' faces (and the horse's face) would be visible. Lawless and Tilly had an excellent relationship. According to horse wrangler Sandy Raynor, "Lucy loves Tilly, and Tilly's very good with Lucy."

Tilly's stunt double, Barbie, was responsible for most tricks, such as kicking and rearing. For a scene in which she was required to kick out, it took three weeks to train Barbie so that she would only kick when given a very specific sequence of commands. "You don't want her going around kicking everything!" Raynor points out. "So you have to train her that there's only one type of whip — you know, to tap the ground behind her — that it's a particular colour and there's a particular word that you use, and that only when you do all of those particular things together is she being asked to kick." Tilly also had a body double, Mac, who worked with the second unit, appearing as Argo in long shots.

Once the look of Argo had been decided upon, all three horses were selected primarily because they had the kind of personality needed for filming work: co-operating well with people, and being able to stay calm amid the noise and bustle of the set.

Xena and Argo have stuck together 'In Sickness and In Hell.

The number of look-alikes that have turned up in *Xena* over the years has caused some people to observe that Ancient Greece must have had a gene puddle, rather than a gene pool.

L ook-alikes have always been common in television. When the same actor plays two separate but physically identical characters, the resulting identity confusion can fuel either drama or comedy. In *Xena*, the look-alike characters have mainly been a source of fun for the cast and audience, but occasionally they bring a darker, more dramatic tone to the series.

LUCY LAWLESS

Princess **Diana** is Xena's physical twin, but her emotional opposite, having spent her life in a castle being saluted by guards and pampered by her doting father. Though she hasn't the least notion how to ride a war-horse or throw a chakram, she takes pride in always being beautifully coifed and gowned. She can curtsey perfectly, play the harp like an angel and even accessorise a breastplate. Initially, being outside the castle terrifies her, but her first encounter with the poorest of the poor opens her eyes to the responsibilities of power. Once she and Xena have sorted out which prince she should marry,

Lawless as Princess Diana, disguised as Xena.

she's ready to succeed her father as a good queen. **Episodes Featuring Diana:** *Season 1:* Warrior… Princess. *Season 2:* Warrior… Princess… Tramp.

Meg is usually distinguishable from Xena and Diana because she almost always looks like she is having a bad hair day. Then there's her posture. Princess Diana floats gracefully along with ladylike poise and Xena's spine is as stiff as her sword, but Meg slouches like she's looking for a place to kick back and relax. Always in trouble, Meg is easy prey for the con men who try to trade on her resemblance to certain important and powerful women. She's not above trading on that resemblance herself, as she proves when she masquerades as Xena to snatch a royal baby, but she's got a good heart — even if it does have too big a soft spot for any attractive man. She's a good cook, even though she's a bit too fond

of her employers' silver. She also has a head for business, or she wouldn't be able to make a living running an inn of good repute and a house of ill repute. Most important, she has an eye for Joxer, who she seems to match perfectly in intelligence and temperament. Despite his love for Gabrielle, Joxer keeps going back to Meg, and when Gabrielle's gone, Meg and Joxer settle down and raise a family. **Episodes Featuring Meg:** *Season 2:* Warrior... Princess... Tramp. *Season 3:* Warrior... Priestess... Tramp. *Season 4:* Key to the Kingdom. *Season 5: Livia. Season 6: Soul Possession.*

In her virginal temple, the Hestian Priestess **Leah** is even more sheltered than Diana. She's ready to accept martyrdom in the name of her goddess, even though she'd only be martyring herself for a self-serving priest of a rival cult. As ignorant about love as she is about war, Leah laments the impurity of Xena and Gabrielle, and thinks that Gabrielle would make an excellent virgin. Completely devoted to her celibate way of life, she gets quite a shock when she starts looking behind doors in Meg's establishment. But maybe she can save Meg's girls from their sins — by teaching them to sing Hestian hymns. **Episode Featuring Leah:** *Season 3:* Warrior... Priestess... Tramp.

Lawless as the Hestian Priestess Leah.

TED RAIMI

While no one matches Lucy Lawless' score of three look-alikes (plus two reincarnations), Ted Raimi's Joxer comes closest, though unlike Xena, he keeps it in the family. Joxer's brother **Jett**, the favoured son of his family, took after his warlord father and became a ruthless assassin... well, maybe not completely ruthless. Jett, the King of Assassins, like his sometime partner Autolycus, the King of Thieves, has a certain code of honour that seems to exclude indiscriminate bloodshed. After all, a lot of people, including Joxer and Autolycus, get in his way when he plans to assassinate Cleopatra. A truly ruthless assassin would kill these people to get to his target, and certainly wouldn't care about his weakling kid brother, the black sheep of the family. Though Jett bullied his little brother Joxer when they were young, when push comes to shove, Jett won't hurt Joxer, nor will he allow anyone else to hurt him. **Episode Featuring Jett:** *Season 3:* The King of Assassins.

If Joxer is the family black sheep, then his twin brother **Jace** is the purple

Raimi
as Jace.

cow, who abandoned the family tradition of warriors to become a singer. Even
the kindly Joxer wants to pretend Jace doesn't exist, because of his flamboyant
dress, affected accent and fondness for men. Fortunately for the ancient
musical world, Jace doesn't let his family stop him from following his heart.
Though Joxer's rejection hurts him, he knows the problem is Joxer's, not his. A
talented performer who rocks the concert stage of Melodia, Jace is very happy
being who he is, and is completely uninhibited about expressing himself.
Episode Featuring Jace: *Season* 5: Lyre, Lyre, Hearts on Fire.

RENEE O'CONNOR

Though Renee O'Connor's Gabrielle only has one look-alike, she certainly
makes a dramatic impact. **Hope**, the daughter of Dahak, is 'daddy's girl' from
the moment of her birth, committing her first murder on the day she is born.
A few months after Gabrielle poisons her fast-growing demon child, the nasty
goddess is reborn to carry out Dahak's will. Her plans include having a tumble
with Ares, giving birth to a monster son, and sacrificing hundreds of innocents.
They also include trying to convert her mother to her side — even a demon
daughter can't help craving her mother's love. Unfortunately, Hope doesn't
understand enough about love to know that trying to kill all the people her
mother cares about is absolutely the wrong way to win her mother's affections.
Episodes Featuring Hope: *Season* 3: Sacrifice, Part I; Sacrifice, Part II. *Season*
4: A Family Affair.

REINCARNATIONS

Look-alikes also bring some laughs to more modern times. In 1940 Macedonia, three descendants of our heroes excavate a tomb in search of 'The Xena Scrolls'. Tomb raider Janice Covington (Renee O'Connor), timid scholar Melinda Pappas (Lucy Lawless) and Resistance hero wannabe Jacques S'Er (Ted Raimi) find the scrolls, but they also find the tomb holding the God of War. Sixty years later, in 'Déjà Vu All Over Again' and 'Soul Possession', sweethearts Annie (Lucy Lawless) and Harry (Ted Raimi) learn from past life therapist Mattie (Renee O'Connor) that they are the reincarnations of Xena, Gabrielle and Joxer, and that Ares is still after Xena — if he can figure out which body she's in.

Smith as Ares with O'Connor as Mattie.

MARIE MATIKO

Pao Ssu and **K'ao Hsin**, Lao Ma's identical twin daughters, were raised apart from their mother and each other, when Lao Ma hid them to protect them from their vicious brother, Ming T'ien. K'ao Hsin subsequently learned that her mother loved her so much, she gave her to someone else's care, while Pao Ssu decided that her mother didn't love her enough to keep her. K'ao Hsin studies her mother's peaceful ways and tries to master her wisdom. Pao Ssu builds herself an army and seeks the secret of Lao Ma's powers, to make herself the ruler of Chin. **Episodes Featuring Pao Ssu and K'ao Hsin:** *Season 5:* Purity; Back in the Bottle.

MARTON CSOKAS

Borias' look-alike **Belach** is not his brother but his son. Belach grew up haunted by the memory of his father's desertion of him and his mother for the tempestuous Xena. As an adult and a powerful ruler, he'll do anything to prove that he's not a barbarian like his father and to protect his only daughter Nicha. Unfortunately, anything includes massacring all the Centaurs he can find, because he believes they are monsters who have kidnapped Nicha. **Episode Featuring Belach:** *Season 6:* The Last of the Centaurs.

"I'd go to the art department, the costume department... and watch them create a whole new world based on what the writer had written on a piece of paper." — Renee O'Connor

COSTUMES

From the first days of the *Hercules* telefilms, the decree from the producers was clear: "No togas!" This was a rule that delighted Ngila Dickson, head of the costume department from the beginning of *Xena* until the end of season four. Firstly, because togas use up a lot of fabric and are difficult to get to drape correctly; secondly because it gave her the freedom to re-invent the look of the ancient world for the fantastic settings of *Xena* and *Hercules*.

Dickson's creative imagination ranged from the mock medieval splendour of kings to the stripped down leathers and savage masks of the Amazons and the Horde, and the patrician halls of Rome (where togas did in fact appear, along with the magnificent armour of Caesar, Pompey and Brutus). The costume designer also roamed other distant lands, creatively speaking — drawing inspiration from ancient Egypt for Cleopatra in 'King of Assassins', China for the silk brocades of 'The Debt, Part I' and 'The Debt, Part II', India for the turbans and brilliant saris of 'Devi', 'Between the Lines' and 'The Way', and the Native American look of fringed leathers, antlers and furs for the

Hurst directs O'Connor and Lawless in 'Antony and Cleopatra'.

Siberian Amazons in 'Adventures in the Sin Trade, Part I' and 'Adventures in the Sin Trade, Part II'. Peasants and villagers generally wore homespun cloth in tones of earth, blue or grey, while warriors and warlords got the *Mad Max* look of studded leather, usually black. Dickson even made forays into modern times for 'The Xena Scrolls' and 'Déjà Vu All Over Again', and into pure pantomime for 'If the Shoe Fits'.

Danielle Cormack and O'Connor show off Amazon fashions in 'The Quest'.

Her most important costume designs, of course, were those made for Xena and Gabrielle. Xena's original costume for her *Hercules* episodes consisted of many different pieces, and was difficult for Lucy Lawless to work in. So when Dickson redesigned it for the series, she deliberately stripped it down to a simple and very functional design, using leather (a substance as durable as it is appealing to the eye) for the skirted tunic and the backing of all the decorative pieces on Xena's arms and shoulders. The breastplate and the decorations on the armbands, gauntlets and shoulder pieces were designed by Inia, a moko artist of Maori descent. A traditional art form, moko art features designs which incorporate the pattern of a Maori tattoo. Dickson chose to have the pieces of armour made from copper because, despite its high maintenance needs, it would bring remarkable texture and beauty to the look.

Dickson's new design was a stunning success. Indeed, Xena's costume has become a pop culture classic, as familiar as a *Star Trek* uniform or Batman's mask. It didn't just look good; Lawless herself testified to its practicality, in a

chat for E! Online near the end of the series: "My costume is darned comfortable for fighting in! It was specifically designed for that purpose."

While Xena's basic costume remained unchanged for the entire series (with the exception of her pregnancy), Gabrielle's costume evolved constantly as the bard grew up. From a peasant blouse and long skirt, Gabrielle stripped down to a short skirt and surplice after meeting the Amazons. With the start of the second season, she began wearing the green leather lace-up bodice that is her most famous look — adopted partly, according to Dickson, to get more of Renee O'Connor's very fit body on camera! Gabrielle's costume evolved again in the middle of the fourth season, when she started on the Way of Peace and took to Indian-inspired clothes. Finally, at the beginning of the fifth season, her transition to warrior bard was reflected in her sleek woven leather bodice and leather-trimmed skirt. This last costume change for Gabrielle was one of the first projects that fell to Jane Holland, when she succeeded Dickson as head of the costume department. Like Hercules' famous leather trousers, the woven leather of the bodice and skirt was a labour-intensive, painstakingly hand-made project.

Another task Holland had to take on immediately was designing a different Xena costume, to accommodate the pregnancies of the character and the actress. Instead of adapting the classic costume, Holland took the daring step of creating a new look, with new colours. "There's something quite scary about changing Xena's costume when it has been the same since she started," says Holland. "She's always had the brown and copper, that's her signature, and it's

a very bold move to change that." Holland chose a blue leather dress over blue trousers, in a style which would at first conceal the pregnancy, then expand to accommodate it.

Holland also designed a breastplate and a long coat with a fur collar to go over Xena's dress and trousers. "We wanted to keep some idea and reference to Xena as a warrior, so we kept the breastplate concept," Holland explains. "It wasn't a complete copy of what she had before. It's silver as opposed to copper, because we needed a different look. Lucy's got amazing blue eyes — she looks great in blue, so she's in silver and blue and black." The new armour was moulded and electroplated, instead of being beaten out of metal like the original copper. Much detail work also went into other aspects of the costume, as one can see from a glance at the studded and fringed cuffs of her coat. "Xena's first costume had a lot of hand work in it," Holland explains, "and with her big long leather coat, every seam's got quite a complicated weaving pattern. That takes time."

Taking time is a relative term in a craft where much of the work is done by hand. The costume department at Renaissance often employed more than forty workers, with several specialised workshops under its roof. Among the specialists were jewellers, leather-workers and mould-makers who mainly created armour and helmets, which were then painted or electroplated to make them look like metal. The series also employed two off-set boot-makers, and devoted a workroom just to making costumes for Xena.

The output of costumes for any given episode might number in dozens or even scores. To allow for changes when a costume got dirty, wet, torn or otherwise damaged on set, every stunt or body double would have at least two changes of costume, and a lead character would have four. Stunt doubles doing work in harness had to have costumes specially made to accommodate the harness and wires. To ease the load a bit, all the costumes for extras were recycled from elements of costumes from previous episodes, so that they did not have to be made from scratch. Even with all that recycling, the extras section of the costume department was the largest because of the sheer volume demanded (think of some of those huge crowd scenes in 'Devi', for example).

Costume work was never done in isolation. The costume designer always had to co-ordinate first with the director and producers, to get their vision for the episode, and then with the set designers and especially with the make-up department, to make sure that the costumes, make-up and sets all had a unified look that blended together to create a realistic world.

During her two years in charge of Xena's costume department, Holland's output proved as varied as Dickson's, encompassing not only returns to Rome, China and Amazonia, but also expeditions to the Sahara, the land of the Valkyries and Ancient Japan. Her very first episode was the costume-heavy 'Fallen Angel', in which she had to invent looks for a whole pantheon of angels, archangels and demons. Another high point for Holland was designing

PLAYING DRESS-UP

Alexandra Tydings (Aphrodite/Crabella) on becoming a mermaid in 'Married with Fishsticks': "You've got a whole bunch of guys holding you up in the air and you wiggle your legs into this tail. Then they pull you up and slap you down at the side of the pool, and then they flip you over like a fish. They lace up these little shoelaces that are on your butt and strap on this felt, and then they flop you back over again. From that point on, there's no more walking — you're completely dependent on these guys to carry you wherever you need to be. Actually, it's easier to be in the water, because you float, but only if you're lying on your back. With that ridiculously huge wig, when I laid on my back in the water, the wig would get wet and start pulling me underwater from my head backwards!"

Danielle Cormack (Ephiny) on working in the Amazon masks: "They are a nightmare! They're really, really difficult to work with. Every time I've gone back, if there's a window of opportunity not to wear it, I'll take it. Having said that, they do look so effective, and they just add to that whole Amazon thing, the fighting beasts that they can be. It's lovely to have those masks to really drive the message home that these are the masked warriors, and some of the masks are so vicious and evil-looking that they typify the heart of the Amazon, the warrior. [But] they're difficult to lift up and down. You don't want to do a big fight scene with them on because you'd just be stumbling all over the place like a drunkard!"

Meg Foster (Hera) on costume magic: "They brought this extraordinary gown and cape and boots and crown that they had crafted, and your little blue-jeaned self is put into it, and it's magic making! It's not black, it's like between a green and a purple, it's layered and textured, the whole bodice is beaded and laced. It's extraordinary when you see the amount of work. When I first put it on, there was a feeling of almost 'mermaid', because it was so slender and there's a lovely sort of fin that goes from your waist and drapes around just above your knees. And I don't have a cleavage, none whatsoever, but lo and behold, once they'd gotten me into this thing, there it was!"

O'Connor and her 'Married with Fishsticks' co-stars had to be carried around the set in their mermaid tails.

the costumes for 'Lyre, Lyre, Hearts on Fire'. "We were looking for a world that didn't have the realism that we normally have," says Holland of the whimsical episode. "The reality of our *Xena* world is quite organic. We were looking at the musical as being a heightened world, and not just Xena going into another village. So my approach to it was that it was more graphic than organic, and of course there's that flamboyance of a musical in there as well. Really, there was just a bit of madness involved."

MAKE-UP

When an actor says that his make-up took several hours to put on, and another hour to remove, one thinks of the poor performer sitting in his make-up chair for all that time. One never thinks of the make-up artist, who has to arrive just as early for that 3am make-up call and stay just as late at the end of a fourteen-hour shooting day (or perhaps even a bit later, to clean up after the actor is done).

The hair and make-up department for *Xena*, headed by Francia Smeets for most of the show's run, was responsible for elaborate wigs, bloody-looking wounds — and everything in between. Basic make-up for a lead actor could take as little as fifteen minutes for a man, or as long as an hour for most women, or men who needed something special in the way of hair, tattoos, or scars.

While creating make-ups for the regular players could become routine, each new batch of guest stars meant starting from scratch with a very short deadline. "You have a vague idea of the look when you read the script, which would be eight days prior to the shooting date," Smeets explains. "From that point on, you're working toward completing that look. Most of it happens when you first see the person who's playing that character, and often that's just a few days prior to the shoot starting. It's a fairly fast process."

Of course, the make-up artists' work was far from done when the actor left the make-up chair. Throughout the day, they were available close to the set for constant touch-ups, and reapplying anything from lipstick to dirt to blood. The hotter the day, the more make-up work was needed to compensate for heat and sweat. This became even more challenging when an actor was wearing heavy prosthetics, which don't do well in heat. "Ted had this awful make-up on [to age Joxer] and it was hot, so the make-up was melting," recalls Adrienne Wilkinson of the scene in 'Eve' where Livia kills Joxer. "He is supposed to come charging at me, but with the melting make-up he could barely see, so he kept tripping and falling and not even making it to me. We all kept cracking up!"

Sometimes a location would create unique problems. Alison Bruce (Kahina in 'Destiny') recalls that shooting in the sand hills near Dargaville created havoc with the make-up: "The sand was moving all the time and sticking to your face, so for make-up and things it was quite a lot of work, just trying to keep you looking okay, when you've actually got thousands of grains of sand stuck to your face."

For the special needs of the war-torn *Xena*verse, Smeets' make-up

department developed a whole range of different kinds of blood for all different kinds of wounds and battle situations. They could recreate anything from normal blood for a fresh wound or a bloody nose (lots of those!), to congealed blood and scabs. They even developed a durable blood mixed with spirit gum, which was especially useful for extras in large battle scenes, because it would last all day without needing to be re-applied.

The make-up department was also responsible for wigs. Sometimes these were synthetics with plaits or extensions woven in, and sometimes — especially for lead characters and their doubles — they were made with human hair. Extensions to an actor's real hair or to a human hair wig also had to be made with human hair, because a synthetic would not blend well. Fortunately, many

The combined artistry of costumes, make-up and wigs created the Banshees of 'Gabrielle's Hope'.

of these often very expensive wigs could be restyled and recycled for other characters; a wig would only be locked away in storage if the character was likely to return.

Mephistoph- eles (Anthony Ray Parker) gets a touch- up during 'The Haunting of Amphipolis'.

When it came to creating an angel, a monster or a demon, the magic often came from special make-up effects, created by the Los Angeles based KNB FX Group. KNB had been doing work for Renaissance since the *Evil Dead* films, so the company was involved in Renaissance's New Zealand productions right from the first *Hercules* film. While many large beasts and monsters (especially those seen in *Hercules*) were made in Los Angeles and shipped to New Zealand, KNB also had a New Zealand workshop, headed by Melanie Tooker, for creating smaller make-up effects. KNB were behind the make-up for such notable *Xena* villains as Bacchus ('Girls Just Wanna Have Fun') and Mephistopheles ('The Haunting of Amphipolis'). According to Anthony Ray Parker, who played both Bacchus and Mephistopheles, the Bacchus make-up consisted of as many as fifty separate pieces, and took five hours to put on and three hours to take off each day.

One of the high points of KNB's contribution to *Xena* were the creation of the angels and demons for 'Fallen Angel', an episode that Howard Berger, the 'B' in KNB, names as one of his favourites. Xena's demon make-up, in particular, called for special attention. "We tried to create an incredible look for her," recalls KNB's Bruce Spaulding-Fuller. "We wanted to do a traditional red demon, but at the same time not traditional, so we tried to break it up with different colours of red, reflected in the scales. She's got little horns sticking out

of her head, large yellow contact lenses and full bat wings of course, which weigh quite a bit. We wanted to do something that was still recognisable as Lucy. But of course, Xena would have to be the ultimate demon in hell!"

The wings for both the angels and demons were quite heavy, and required a huge effort, not only from KNB's team but from everyone working with them. Though attached to the costumes by hooks on the back, they often required a crew member to walk behind the actor or stunt performer and hold them up. Working with the wings in wire and harness for flying sequences was especially tricky for the stunt team. "Michael and all the other angels had to wear a wing harness, which is a very uncomfortable piece of equipment. Then, underneath that, we had to wear a flying harness, which is also incredibly uncomfortable. So when you put them both together, it could be a very long day!" recalls Charles Mesure (Michael) of the experience. "You've got these big wide wings on your back weighing fifteen kilograms, and you spend half your time trying not to fall over backwards during stunts and fights! You have to look like this cool, angelic warrior guy. So it's incredibly hard work. And after eight hours in the wing and flying harnesses, I would usually have sweated off a couple of kilos. When you see the finished episode, you only get to see us descending into frame for the final drop of two feet or so. You don't see that we're thirty feet off the ground before we start, so half of the effect is lost."

The beautiful shimmer of the angel wings came from hand-dyed goose feathers, and required extra shipments of feathers to keep them in daily repair. The webbed demon wings also needed constant maintenance. "They got beaten up very badly — the stunt player demons just wanted to thrash them around," explains Spaulding-Fuller. "So we worked for about sixteen hours getting through the shots, then for another four hours at night to repair everything."

STUNTS

The name most closely associated with stunts in *Xena* and *Hercules* is Peter Bell, who brought his stunt team to the first *Hercules* telefilm, and stayed on for the next 500 fights — give or take a few. Bell had many years of experience in stunt work, working on such films as *Willow* and *The Bounty*, before joining Renaissance. For *Xena* and *Hercules* together, he employed about thirty full-time 'stuntees', with a total list of nearly ninety people, categorised by their different skills and their level of experience.

An average episode of *Xena* has three major fight sequences, at the beginning, middle and end of the episode, plus a few smaller scraps to keep things lively in between. Bell was responsible for choreographing all of them, then teaching them to the stunt crew and the cast, and finally overseeing the shooting of the fights.

Certain stunt moves in the fights recur enough to become familiar, such as Xena's run on her enemies' chests, or Gabrielle's flip on her staff over a bad

guy's back. Some patterns also recur, like the bad guys running at Xena one or two at a time and getting knocked out, so that new baddies are always rushing in. But you'll never see the same fight repeated in any episode; Bell choreographed each fight individually, to suit the set, the tone of the story and the characters involved. His system is based on a series of zones, drawn at the knee, the stomach, the shoulders and about three feet above the head, and he designed moves to engage the viewer's eye at all four levels.

Landing from a blow, according to Bell, is as critical in 'selling' the fight as

A crane makes a steadier shooting platform than a tree branch.

Leick and Lawless take a wild ride during 'The Return of Callisto'.

the blow itself, because the landing is what makes the viewer feel the pain of the blow. So when Xena wallops a stuntee, most of the time he doesn't just go down — he flips backwards or sideways before thudding to the ground, or flies through the air to crash spectacularly into a piece of the set (market stalls full of goods and shelves full of crockery are two favourite landing zones).

Both Lucy Lawless and Renee O'Connor worked hard to master the stunt fighting skills demanded by their characters. Lawless did kung fu, boxing and weight training, and even learned to do Xena's fire breathing trick. One can see the difference all that practice made, just by comparing Lawless' fight moves in *Hercules* to episodes as early as the first season of *Xena*. When Gabrielle got her staff, O'Connor learned a whole array of staff moves from Bell, and eventually moved on to Gabrielle's deadly pair of sais in the fifth season. She also learned to be comfortable on a horse, which she had found intimidating at the beginning of the show.

Regardless of practice though, both actors were doubled much of the time, as were all featured actors — Lawless had acrobatic doubles, a stunt double

and a horse riding double. This was partly for safety, and partly to speed up the shooting schedule, as most stunt work was filmed by the second unit. Even in fight sequences when you see two lead characters fighting, chances are that much of the time they didn't actually fight each other on the set. For shots where both actors' faces are visible on camera, both would have to do the shot. But for the many over-the-shoulder shots where only one face is visible, the actor whose face is on camera was usually paired with the stunt double of the other character. This saved the actors from having to do all the fighting, and more importantly, made it much less likely that one of the leads would get hurt filming the sequence.

No matter how much care is taken though, bruises and injuries are an inevitable part of shooting an action series. "Fighting other actors is always dangerous, because they don't have the experience of pulling punches. They just either go for it or they're really lame," Lucy Lawless explained. "I guess you'd prefer the actress who goes for it and really starts whacking you with her sword, rather than the one who just looks like a wimp. I never see [Renee] injured, but Renee is so athletic, and I'm not. I'm always getting smacked about and getting torn ligaments. I popped a rib the other week. Those sorts of things are just par for the course."

As for the high-flying flips and leaps, these were nearly always done by doubles. While many of Bell's stuntees were quite capable of flipping over a character or running up the wall on their own, Bell made extensive use of wire and harness, just to enhance these stunts and raise them a bit higher. Zoe Bell (no relation), who doubled Lucy Lawless for the last three seasons, described working in harness: "I have wires that come off my hips to pick points either off

ACTORS ON ACTION

David Franklin (Brutus) on fighting in Roman armour: "I had so much fun doing the fights, but I found it really hard doing it in the armour, because you're very restricted. You want to get a full movement for all that sword action to work really well, to get that style, and it's really hard when you've been turned into Turtle Man! But thankfully, Xena had a fantastic second unit crew which recreated the fights using really good fighters. So when they put it all together, you ended up looking really brilliant."

Kathryn Morris (Najara) on filming the vine fight in 'The Convert': "They built this scaffolding. Everything's all protected so it's just like you're on another storey. It's very safe. The hard bit about the vine part is trying to swing in at the right angle and say your lines and kick the way you should kick, so it will match the shot when she kicks you back. It's all very non-glamorous, it's all very technical. When I was doing the vine fighting I was so bad at it, it just became a big comedy routine — me swinging back and forth like Tarzan. I lost my balance, the thing kept swinging back and forth, and I'm on it, and everybody's waiting and I'm just swinging back and forth going, 'Oh, I missed it. I'm fine, I'm fine!'"

Stansfield gets high on Alti's aerial stunt fights in 'Adventures in the Sin Trade, Part II'.

the set or on the cherry-picker [crane]. The pick points are like pulleys, so my wires are attached to ropes that go through the pulleys. At the other end are the big stunt men, and quite often they'll just pull me, and I'll go flying into the air and do a flip or a back-flip or whatever it is they need me to do. If there's a new stunt, we'll have rehearsals that usually take half a day. But that doesn't mean we're doing it consistently for that half of the day. Most of it will be fiddling with pick points and dealing with where the wires are and how to combine the timing of everything."

Stunt work on *Xena* extended far beyond just brawls and battles on the ground. Often the stuntees would be co-ordinating with the special effects

team, such as when they were shooting battle scenes where people are getting blown into the air by explosions. Occasionally stunts would involve underwater work, like Gabrielle's struggle with the ghouls in 'The Haunting of Amphipolis' (a memorable scene which was tricky to film: the stunt demons were all wearing full latex masks, which made it difficult to spit water out of their mouths). The stuntees also had to stage chariot races several times in *Xena*, with stunt doubles standing in for Xena and Callisto or Xena and Caligula as their chariots galloped madly over the open sands or through the streets of Rome. When it came to thinking up exciting stunts for *Xena*, imagination was the only limit.

SPECIAL EFFECTS

What the average television viewer lumps together as 'special effects' are actually made up of several basic techniques. Practical effects are filmed directly, with action taking place on camera through various kinds of planned trickery: anything from a chakram on a wire flying into a post, to a house bursting into flames. Blue screen effects photograph live action elements of a shot, which will then be inserted into background that has been photographed elsewhere. Computer-generated (or CG) effects are created entirely in a computer, and can be as minor as adding sparks to the clash of two swords in battle, or as major as the design and animation of an entire scene full of fantastic creatures.

All of *Xena*'s computer effects were done in Los Angeles by Flat Earth Productions. Headed by Kevin O'Neill, Flat Earth began as a "garage band" of computer artists working from their home computers, and linked electronically. In the early 90s, PC software that could create complex graphic effects became widely available, allowing O'Neill to dispense with the huge overhead of a central studio, so that he could produce high quality effects at a very competitive price.

Like many other essential parts of the creative team on *Xena*, Flat Earth had started work for Pacific Renaissance with the *Hercules* telefilms. One of their first jobs for *Xena* was the creation of Poseidon. The watery appearance of the God of the Sea was, according to Flat Earth's Kevin O'Neill, originally created for the initial promotion of *Xena*, and was "just a throw-away effect, something we whipped out real quick." Flat Earth subsequently perfected the god's eye-catching look for his appearances in the opening titles and three later episodes.

Perhaps the most effects-heavy episode of *Xena* was 'Fallen Angel', which required legions of flying angels and demons. In addition, the entire background environment, from the skies and clouds of Heaven to the chasms and cliffs of Hell, was created entirely by computer. The episode took a *lot* of planning. "Basically my job is to sit down with the director and work out what they want to do, then work out the best way to do it," explains visual effects

ACTING ON IMAGINATION

Claire Stansfield describes fighting with computer effects for the climax of 'Between the Lines': "It's so bizarre! The fire's going, fans are going, the director's shouting, and I have to pretend these chakrams are coming at me. And there's nothing coming at me, because they're going to fill it in later. The director kept going, 'Wah! Here comes another! Wah!' I was like, struggle, struggle, and react. And then it's painful and I'm pushing it away with all my might, and then one comes at me and I explode. I see it coming and my eyes widen and I have to throw myself back in the air. You just feel like such an idiot sometimes, like, 'Okay, and action!' and Claire is struggling, struggling, struggling... with nothing. And you have no idea [what you've just done]. If anyone could see us, they'd think we'd lost our minds!"

supervisor George Port. "[With 'Fallen Angel'], it was a case of whether we use practical wings from KNB, and going through the shots [in the script] and saying, 'Okay, this shot will be a close-up. That's a second unit shot. That's a blue screen shot with practical wings. This will be a computer-generated Gabrielle flying up to a matte-painted background. This will be the real Xena on a harness being pulled into frame with real wings. This shot will be second unit with an actor with real wings, or possibly an actor with digital wings, coming up into a digital background.'" The result of combining all these techniques was the creation of an amazing world in which to play out the drama of Xena and Gabrielle's salvation.

While fully digital settings are rare, pyrotechnic effects are unusually common in *Xena*, appearing in about a quarter of the episodes. Often, these were handled with a combination of practical and computer-enhanced effects, like the fires that engulf Gabrielle in 'The Deliverer' or the minefield explosions in 'Back in the Bottle'.

However, one of *Xena*'s most remarkable fire sequences was done entirely practically, with real fire, and even with the real Xena, Lucy Lawless. In 'Amphipolis Under Siege', Athena's general, Ilainus, sets off a fireball that blasts through a tunnel as Xena flees before it. As the shot required Xena to run straight toward the camera, it could not be filmed with a stunt double. The fireball was wide enough (eight to ten feet) to fill the tunnel, and carefully controlled by regulating pressurised gas through electronic valves. In setting up for the shot, special effects supervisor Ken Durey tested the fire effect carefully. The mechanism was so precise that the distance the fireball travelled could be controlled to within two feet. He also set up a fan at the head of the tunnel beside the camera to blow cool air toward Lawless as she ran, and blow any gas away behind her. And just to be on the extra-safe side, he planned to have Lawless at least fifteen feet ahead of the flames — more than twice as far as a stunt double would have been. "Stunt people are allowed to get hotter than Lucy," Durey observed. The result was a truly amazing sequence, nevertheless.

Another effect that became an important part of Xena's world was the creation of the Centaurs (first done for *Hercules in the Underworld*), which required a careful combination of practical, blue screen and computer effects. Three sets of film were used for every shot of a Centaur: a blank plate of the background without any actors, a blue screen shot with a trainer leading a horse in the moves the Centaur would make, then another blue screen shot of an actor wearing the Centaur appliance around his waist. The moves of the actor and the horse had to be matched frame by frame, and the actor also had to learn to move the way a horse moves to make the effect believable. In post production, the three sets of film would be composited, which involved adding

Poseidon, Flat Earth's most awe-inspiring creation, was originally just a promotional effect.

the horse and any other actors to the background, then digitally removing the trainer, the lead line and the horse's head, and replacing them with bits of the background and, of course, the top half of the actor playing the Centaur. The process could take weeks — all to give us characters like Kaleipus.

While creations like Centaurs, angels and demons on *Xena* attract the audience's attention to the work of the special effects experts, a large part of it goes completely unnoticed by most viewers. Wires and cables for aerial stunts were not always visible on film, especially on a dark set, but when they were, it was Flat Earth's job to digitally remove them, pixel by pixel, and fill in with colours and textures to match the background. The digital artists could also make a big scene look even bigger, by turning twenty extras into a crowd of two hundred, or digitally enlarging a set, to give it more space and grandeur than was possible in the studio.

Lawless learned how to do her own fire breathing stunts. Don't try this at home!

The knowledgeable eye can, if it wants to, see all these effects being put together, to form stunning sequences like the battle between Xena and the gods on the beach in 'Motherhood'. But then, when you're watching a moment like that, who wants to think about how the magic was made? ⚡

CHAKRAM EFFECTS

The sequence for a simple chakram throw demonstrates the wide variety of film techniques used in creating special effects. The throw starts with a shot of Lucy Lawless holding an aluminium chakram used in all close-ups. Next comes a shot of her throwing a soft foam chakram, which flies out of the shot in true chakram style — and lands harmlessly on a mat off camera. The chakram in flight was created in one of two ways: either a hard foam chakram spinning on a wire rig against a blue screen or, especially in later seasons as computer imagery improved, a CG image added to a shot. A chakram bouncing off a character's body would again be a soft foam chakram, while one lodging in a wall would be done with a resin chakram on a rig. And for that all-important shot of Xena catching her weapon, Lawless would reach her hand out of the shot, a crew member off camera would put the metal chakram into it, and she would snap her hand back into shot — whoosh! A perfect catch! Sometimes the best effects can be the simplest...

Lawless throws the chakram, but it takes a whole crew to make it fly.

TO HINDUSTAN AND BACK

Italy, Egypt, India, China, Scandinavia, Japan — the travels of Xena and Gabrielle have taken them to more far-flung places on Earth than most people will ever visit, even in the jet age.

I
n the historical world, Xena and Gabrielle would rank among history's greatest travellers. They would also rank among the most important figures in mythic history, since they have taken a hand in the myths and legends of every culture they visit. We take you now on a quick tour of the realities that inspired the heroic travels and epic deeds of the Warrior Princess and the battling bard.

THE EASTERN MEDITERRANEAN

Most *Xena* episodes are set during the first century BC, around the Eastern Mediterranean. Travelling around the area would have been relatively easy at that time, as the Mediterranean was a major highway and most peoples who lived along its shores were good mariners.

Travelling around Greece by foot or horse would have seemed time-consuming to us, but there were plenty of roads, as the land had been civilised for hundreds of years. **Poteidaia** and **Amphipolis** are less than 100 km apart on the northern coast — no more than a few days walk for a healthy Warrior Princess. Athens was about 500 km overland from these towns, but there was also a faster sea route.

Homer's **Troy** probably stood at Hissarlik in Turkey, near the mouth of the Dardanelles, where archaeologists have found the remains of a settlement completely destroyed by fire around 1200 BC.

Among the famous Greeks encountered by Xena and Gabrielle, **Homer** was a figure of legend even in antiquity and probably lived in Asia Minor before 700 BC. Much of the cultural detail contained in the great epics attributed to him, the *Iliad* and *Odyssey*, has been confirmed by archaeological study of the second millennium BC Mycenean civilisation.

The great tragic poet **Euripides** (*c*480-405 BC) is thought to have written approximately ninety-two plays, of which nineteen have survived.

Hippocrates (*c*460-*c*370 BC), the 'father of medicine', advocated reason and observation, not superstition, as a basis for medicine, and building health before resorting to drastic treatments. The Hippocratic Oath, still taken by modern medical students, is attributed to him.

THE ROMAN EMPIRE

All of the Mediterranean lands and much of Western Europe were united by Roman rule by the end of the first century BC, the beginning of the Roman

Empire. The accomplishments of the Roman Empire are still evident today in engineering, art, architecture, law, and the Roman alphabet and calendar.

Rome provides the largest number of real persons to the Xenaverse. The most notable is **Caius Julius Caesar** (c100-44 BC), one of the greatest generals in history. He was the central figure of the ruling First Triumvirate until its collapse, and then virtual ruler of Rome for over a decade. Though popular as a leader and orator, he was assassinated because he grew too powerful.

Marcus Licinius Crassus (died 53 BC) provided the financial power behind the First Triumvirate, but he and Pompey hated each other. Crassus was murdered after leading an unsuccessful military campaign against Parthia (now Iran).

Awarded the title 'Magnus' for military victories as a young man, **Pompey** (Cnaeus Pompeius Magnus; 106-48 BC) was Julius Caesar's son-in-law, but turned against Caesar after his wife died. He was assassinated after Caesar defeated him in their civil war.

David Franklin as Xena's third Brutus.

A follower of Pompey during the civil war, **Marcus Junius Brutus** (85-42 BC) was pardoned by Caesar — a mistake, since Brutus was a principle conspirator in Caesar's assassination. Subsequently defeated in battle by Octavius and Antony, he did the honourable Roman thing and committed suicide.

Marc Antony (c83-30 BC) formed the Second Triumvirate with Octavius and another Roman leader, but when he fell in love with Cleopatra and moved to Egypt, he lost his political influence. He and Cleopatra were defeated by Octavius in a famous naval battle, and he committed suicide.

Egypt was already a vassal of Rome when **Cleopatra** (69-30 BC) became queen. Her attempts to increase Egyptian autonomy at the expense of Roman power made Rome fear and hate her. Her relationship with Antony lasted eleven years (including several years of marriage) before their defeat by Octavius and her suicidal encounter with an asp.

Caesar's grand nephew and heir **Octavius** (63 BC-14 AD) became the first Roman Emperor when the Senate conferred on him the titles Augustus and Imperator. He was a good Emperor, encouraging cultural diversity, local autonomy and the arts. His wife was **Livia**, a lady of high patrician family.

The greatest Roman poet and a favourite of Octavius, **Virgil** (Publius Vergilius Maro; 70-19 BC) composed the *Aeneid*, one of the world's great epics. It relates the journey of the Trojan prince Aeneas from the ruins of Troy to the founding of the Roman race.

Nicknamed **Caligula** (literally 'little boot') because of his childhood footwear, Caius Caesar Germanicus (12-41 AD) was a ruthless despot. His cruelties were so extreme that he was widely reputed to be insane. He was assassinated after only five years of rule.

A queen of the Iceni in Britain, **Boadicea** (Boudicca; died 61 AD) led a rebellion against the Roman occupation and won several victories, but when the Romans finally destroyed her army, she committed suicide.

THE MIDDLE EAST

The Middle East has always added its spices to the cultural melting pot of the Mediterranean. Greeks and Persians battled back and forth from the Aegean to the Indus in the fifth and fourth

Jennifer Ward-Lealand as Boadicea.

centuries BC, and the Romans later extended their empire as far as Mesopotamia and the Caucasus.

One of the region's oldest religions, **Zoroastrianism** comes into the *Xena*verse indirectly. In Zoroastrian mythology, **Ari Dahaka** is a demonic three-headed dragon associated with storms, deceit and destruction. He was created by **Ahriman** (Angra Mainyu), god of darkness and personification of all evil, in his war against **Ahura Mazda**, whom Zoroastrians worship as the creator, and the supreme and only true god. Zoroastrianism was founded in Persia by **Zarathustra** (Zoroaster in Greek), probably between 1500 and 1000 BC. Zoroastrians believe that their religion was the first to introduce monotheism and the concepts of individual judgement, Heaven and Hell, and a final Judgement at the end of the world. Many Biblical scholars believe that the **Magi** who visited Jesus at his birth were Zoroastrian priests.

Far more familiar than Zoroastrianism, **Judeo-Christian** history and mythology play an important part in *Xena*. The story of Eli and his persecuted followers, and their faith in a God of Love, has strong and deliberate parallels with the rise of **Christianity**. The spread of Christianity caused the decline of Graeco-Roman paganism, and was accompanied by bloody persecutions at the hands of many authorities (Caligula was one of the more notorious). Though Eve gets official recognition from Caligula's unnamed successor, it took Christians over three centuries to convert the Roman Empire's leadership.

Among the personalities of Judeo-Christian myth and history, **Abraham** is considered the founder of Judaism and the traditional ancestor of both Jews and Arabs through his two sons Isaac and Ishmael. Abraham's sacrifice of his son Isaac is told in Genesis 22. He may represent a historical person, whose migration from Mesopotamia to Palestine probably took place some time

between 2000 and 1500 BC.

Saul (died *c*1012 BC) was made the Hebrews' first King because of his prowess as a warrior. The conflict between the Hebrews and the Philistines began when the Hebrews migrated to Palestine from Egypt in the thirteenth century BC, and continues to this day.

David (reigned *c*1012-*c*972 BC) is the second King of the Hebrews and one of the great heroes of Judeo-Christian tradition. He solidified Hebrew control of much of Palestine and made his capital in Jerusalem. The Psalms are attributed to him and he may even have written some of the earliest ones.

The archangel **Michael**, often called Saint Michael by Christians, is the leader of the heavenly armies. One of the few angels mentioned by name in the Bible, he appears at the Apocalypse described in the Book of Revelation.

O'Connor as Gabrielle with Antony Starr as David.

Rafael (literally 'god heals') is mentioned in the apocryphal Book of Tobit and in the Talmud.

Lucifer is the original 'fallen angel'. In medieval Christian legend, he is the leader of the angels who rebelled against God at the beginning of creation. The greatest and most beautiful of angels, he was thrown down from Heaven for his disobedience, and founded his own kingdom in Hell. He is usually identified with Satan.

Mephistopheles is a late medieval representation of the Devil, who appears as a tempter in the Faust legend.

INDIA

Gabrielle and Xena visit India as if they're just taking a bit of a holiday, but in the real world the journey would have been considerably more arduous. It is nearly 4,000 km in a straight line from Athens to the Indus valley, and such a trip would have taken weeks or months by overland trade routes, crossing the mountains of Iran, Afghanistan and Pakistan to reach India. The journey could also be made by sailing down the Red Sea and across the Arabian Sea, a journey of nearly 7,000 km.

In India, the travellers encounter the oldest of the world's great religions, **Hinduism**, which arose in the Indus valley before 5000 BC. Hindus believe that all religions are reflections of one eternal truth, so all beliefs should be treated with respect. They also embrace the principle of *ahimsa* ('non-injury' or 'non-violence'). An essential doctrine of Hinduism is the law of **Karma**: that all your actions, good and bad, will be repaid to you.

The Hindu trinity is the three major aspects of the divine: **Brahma** the

Creator, **Vishnu** the Preserver and **Shiva** the Destroyer. Hinduism is unique among the major religions in revering the divine being equally as God and as Goddess. **Devi** (literally 'goddess') is the proper name for the Divine Mother, of whom all goddesses are aspects. She can be both the gentle Mother of Life and the fearsome Mother of Death.

Kali, the black-skinned goddess, is one of Shiva's most fearsome aspects. Usually shown with a necklace of severed heads and riding on the corpse of a demon, she is the Destroyer, particularly of ignorance and evil.

Rama is the hero of the greatest Indian epic, Ramayana, which tells of his exile from his father's kingdom and his war with the Demon King Ravan, who kidnaps his wife Sita.

Hanuman, the monkey deity, is Rama's devoted companion and is worshipped as a symbol of loyalty. He finds Sita, and heals Rama and his brother Lakshman when they are shot with poisoned arrows.

Ravan's son **Indrajit** urges his father to make war on Rama rather than negotiate. He flies into battle firing poisoned arrows at his foes, concealed in a magical mist which makes him invisible. He is killed in single combat by Lakshman.

Tataka (Taraka) is a female demon who attacks Rama and his companions, and is killed by arrows from Rama's bow.

Krishna, one of the most revered deities of Hinduism, is the eighth **avatar** (a god who has taken human form) of Vishnu. He is both childlike and heroic, and his flute represents his power to bring the melody of joy to humanity. Krishna and his favourite consort Radha represent the eternal love between god and humanity.

THE FAR EAST

Xena and Gabrielle make three journeys to the Far East in just six years. In the real world, it is well over 10,000 km by sea or by land from Greece to the kingdoms along the Yellow River in **China**. Without mechanised travel, just one round trip could take years.

Xena's most important ally in China is Lao Ma, whose husband is given the name of the founder of Taoism, **Lao Tzu** (d c604 BC). He may have been a Chinese royal librarian who retired from public service to escape the incessant feuds and violence of his time, or he may be a myth, as the name Lao Tze literally means 'old philosopher'. Scholars believe that the book attributed to him, the *Tao Te Ching*, which forms the foundation of **Taoism**, was probably written in the fourth century BC.

The heart of Taoism is **The Way** (*tao*: 'way' or 'path'): the relinquishing of self-centred ambition, fear and desire, and the achievement of a state of being that is in harmony with the forces of life and the universe. A fundamental Taoist principle is the balance and harmony of opposites, which is portrayed in the yin-yang symbol.

The voyage from China across the Yellow Sea to **Japan** is about 1,000 km — comparable to sailing from Greece to North Africa. Though Xena and Gabrielle encounter the **samurai**, this aristocratic warrior class actually arose in Japan's feudal period, around the twelfth century AD. The samurai were governed by a code of honour called **bushido** (the way of the warrior), which emphasised warrior values and complete loyalty to the warrior's lord. A **katana** is a samurai sword worn in a particular way, with the edge up.

SCANDINAVIA

Xena's quest to atone for her past also takes her and Gabrielle to Scandinavia. Overland travel to the far North of Europe would have taken weeks in that era, but still counts as one of their shorter journeys; even the northern reaches of Scandinavia are less than 3,000 km from Greece. Once there, our heroes

encounter characters and legends that actually come from three different mythologies.

Did Grendel really look like this?

Odin (Wotan in German mythology), the king of the Norse Gods, hung himself on the World Tree to gain wisdom, and he was worshiped as God of War, Poetry, Wisdom and Death. His messengers were the two ravens Hugin ('Thought') and Munin ('Memory').

Odin's **Valkyries** were immortal maidens armed with spears and mounted on winged horses who served as his messengers and as the 'choosers of the slain': after a battle, they brought the most heroic slain warriors to **Valhalla** to await the final battle of **Ragnarok.** The most famous Valkyrie was **Brunhilda**, whose story is told in the Norse *Volsungasaga* and the German *Nibelungenlied* (the basis for Wagner's *Ring* operas). She defied Odin and as punishment was put in enchanted sleep on a rock surrounded by fire, until the hero Sigurd (Siegfried in German) passed through the fire and woke her.

The **Rheinmaidens** and the **Rheingold** come from Germanic myths related to the *Nibelungenlied*. A dwarf steals the Rheingold from the gods of the Rhine River, and when the treasure is stolen from him in turn, he curses it. The curse follows everyone who possesses the treasure and the ring made from it, causing endless tragedies.

The warrior **Beowulf** comes from a different tradition. He is the hero of the great Anglo-Saxon epic of the same name. He travels to the hall of King **Hrothgar** and his Queen **Wealhtheow**, and there does battle with the monster **Grendel**, who has been attacking Hrothgar's hall every night. Beowulf kills not only Grendel, but the creature's equally monstrous mother. ⌛

"I am proud to have been a part of the lives of people who have been a force for good in the world. It was an honour playing a role that inspired and encouraged you." — Lucy Lawless

In January 1997, midway through the second season of *Xena: Warrior Princess*, the first official *Xena* and *Hercules* fan convention was held in Burbank, California. By then the show's considerable audience was making its impact on syndicated ratings, and the most devoted viewers were already expressing their enthusiasm on that great playground of fandom, the internet. That first convention, headlined by special guests Lucy Lawless and Kevin Sorbo, was standing room only. It was just the beginning of *Xena* fandom.

For every fan who attended the 1997 Burbank convention, there were probably hundreds — perhaps thousands — who wished they could have been there. The Burbank Airport Hilton could hold about 2,000 fans, but after the annual *Xena* convention filled it to overflowing two years running, event organisers Creation Entertainment decided to move to a larger venue for the third year: the Santa Monica Civic Center, with 3,000 seats. *Xena* fandom was visibly expanding! But even this venue wasn't large enough to accommodate the crowds that came in 1999 to meet their fellow fans and to see Lawless and Sorbo, along with many of their co-stars, in person. In 2000, the event moved once again, this time to the Pasadena Center, a venue which Creation had previously used mainly for their huge *Star Trek* conventions. There the annual *Xena* convention has remained, and there *Xena*'s fans still flock every year, not only to see the stars, but also to see each other and renew friendships made at past conventions or over the internet.

To most *Xena* fans, these friendships are an essential element of fandom, and it's the internet that makes many of them possible. From the earliest days, *Xena* websites, news groups and message boards have proliferated, celebrating every aspect of the show. There are general sites with episode guides, reviews and transcripts, sites devoted to fan fiction and fan art, sites packed with downloadable images from the series and sites focusing on just about every significant guest star on either *Xena* or *Hercules*. While English is the dominant language, there are plenty of others too.

Both the internet and the conventions provided a vital link between those who produced *Xena* and those who watched it. Sometimes that connection was less than positive, as Lucy Lawless commented during the fifth season: "If I was to log on to the internet every day, it would be very hard to believe all the great things they say about me, because they say so much crummy stuff as well, and I find it hurtful sometimes. These are the hardcore

*Xena fans
have their
day in the
lab in 'Send
in the
Clones'.*

fans. They think you're an angel and they think you're Satan at the same time — consequently, we are loved and reviled out of all proportion. It's just easier not to pay attention to it either way."

Yet on balance, *Xena*'s creators seemed to have a largely positive relationship with the fans. At the end of his work on *Xena*, Steven L. Sears commented on the value he had found in his encounters with the fans as a group and as individuals: "I still enjoy going to conventions, even if I'm not speaking. Just to walk around and see what's happening. Most of the fans we have are very intelligent and articulate people. I've had some great discussions with a few of them, and they are always interesting. As far as the critics of the show are concerned, I've had some great discussions with them as well. There are a few who just go out of their way to hate the series and those of us working on it, but that's their problem. Most of the critics are respectful and give me something to think about."

The *Xena* staff had an unusual relationship with the show's most passionate followers, the subtext fans. From their first awareness of the subtext phenomenon, *Xena*'s creative staff began an artful balancing act, playing with the subtext just enough to keep most of its devotees happy, without ever being so explicit as to alienate those who didn't want a subtext (see Do They or Don't They? on page 154).

Xena's first acknowledgement of its fans within an episode was 'Déjà Vu All Over Again' at the end of the fourth season, when Annie (Lucy Lawless) is portrayed as a devoted follower, while her boyfriend and her therapist dismiss the show. But Renaissance Pictures' relationship with *Xena*'s fans

Nigel tries to get the dirt for the fans in 'You Are There'.

really came to the fore during season six. In direct response to letters complaining that the all-important relationship between Xena and Gabrielle had been sidelined during season five, Rob Tapert and the creative staff chose to focus strongly on the relationship in the final season. The result was a year rich in Xena-Gabrielle intimacies such as the enchanted kiss in 'The Return of the Valkyrie', the love-at-first-sight scenario of 'When Fates Collide' and many heart-to-heart talks in episodes like 'The Abyss' and 'To Helicon and Back'. Material like this reinforces a solid friendship for those who want to see strong female bonding between Xena and Gabrielle — and it is also of course pure ambrosia for the subtext fans.

But *Xena*'s producers were far from done with paying tribute to the people who made the show a success. The fans played an important part in several season six episodes. By recruiting fan fiction writer Melissa Good to write two episodes, Tapert made the strongest possible statement of his faith in the fans' ability to 'get' the show, and to make a creative contribution. Fans also appeared as characters in 'Send in the Clones' and 'Soul Possession'. The three in 'Send in the Clones' appear surrounded by *Xena* collectibles, and live any fan's fantasy of meeting not the actors, but the actual characters in the flesh. In 'Soul Possession', two overly enthusiastic aficionados crash a press conference of 'bona fide' Xena scholars. In a tribute to one of *Xena* fandom's largest and most popular websites, a reporter at the event identifies herself as the webmaster of Whoosh.

Like many film and television properties with strong fan followings, *Xena* has generated a wide variety of licensed merchandise of all the usual varieties: photos, posters, videos, soundtracks, comics, novels, action figures,

XENA IN CYBERSPACE

Official Websites:

Creation Entertainment, home of the official Xena Fan Club and Xena conventions:
www.creationent.com

Club Ted, The Official Ted Raimi Fan Club: **www.tedraimifan.com**

Alexandra Tydings' official website: **www.alextydings.com**

Hudson Leick Official Fan Club: **www.hudsonleickfan.com**

Official Claire Stansfield Website: **www.clairestansfield.net**

Bruce Campbell Online, the Official Bruce Campbell Web Site: **www.bruce-campbell.com**

Official Adrienne Wilkinson Fan Club and Site: **www.adriennewilkinson.com**

Beckerfilms, the official website of director Josh Becker: **www.beckerfilms.com**

Fan Websites:

Any search of the World Wide Web will turn up scores of Xena fan websites. The few Xena sites listed here were selected because they are current, comprehensive, long-established and receive wide fan recognition in the form of large numbers of hits and awards from other fan sites:

Whoosh. Better than many an official TV site, it has comprehensive episode guides and series information, active message boards, and a new issue of fan-written articles every month:
www.whoosh.org

Sword and Staff. The ultimate fandom charity site: **www.sword-and-staff.com**

Xenaville. A UK fan page with current news, episode reviews, articles, active message boards and other goodies: **www.xenaville.com**

Australian Xena Information Page. The oldest Australian Xena fan site, featuring news, articles, fan fiction, images and multimedia: **www.ausxip.com**

Xena Virtual Season. Fan written and illustrated scripts for whole new seasons, rigorously selected, and "aired" on a regular schedule, plus message boards: **http://xwpvs.com**

To find all the other Xena fan sites in cyberspace, visit the ultimate list of Xena links, Xena Online Resources: **www.xenite.org/xor/index.html**

sweatshirts, T-shirts, baseball caps, key rings, mugs, trading cards, collectible card games and, yes, illustrated companions. *Xena* episodes are now appearing on DVD and *Xena* video games are available for several gaming platforms. Though licensing of new products has naturally slowed since the show's conclusion, these *Xena* collectibles are still highly sought after, as one can see by a walk through the dealer room of any convention where *Xena* guest stars are in attendance.

Then there's the rarer type of *Xena* collectible — the real thing. Creation Entertainment offers limited edition props and weapons, exact replicas of famed props such as Xena's chakram and gauntlets, or Gabrielle's staff and sais, all created by *Xena*'s prop masters and certified as authentic. Charity

RATINGS FOR XENA: WARRIOR PRINCESS

Each point represents one million US households, for example, a 3.2 rating equals 3,200,000 households. The ratings for each season are the average for the entire year, including repeats:

Season one (September 1995- September 1996): 5.3 average
Highest rated episode: 'Beware Greeks Bearing Gifts', 6.1
Season two (September 1996-September 1997): 6.0 average
Highest rated episode: 'A Necessary Evil', 7.8
Season three (September 1997-September 1998): 5.5 average
Highest rated episode: 'Warrior... Priestess... Tramp', 6.6
Season four (September 1998- September 1999): 4.0 average
Highest rated episode: 'Locked Up and Tied Down', 4.9
Season five (September 1999-September 2000): 3.4 average
Highest rated episodes: 'Fallen Angel', 'Seeds of Faith', 4.1
Season six (September 2000-September 2001): 3.0 average
Highest rated episode: 'A Friend in Need, Part I', 3.9

In its second season, *Xena: Warrior Princess* was the top rated syndicated drama series on American television. For all six years, *Xena* remained in the top five. While *Hercules* won slightly higher ratings during *Xena*'s first year, *Xena* led *Hercules* by a few tenths in every subsequent year that both series aired. *Xena*'s chief ratings rivals were *Star Trek: Deep Space Nine*, syndicated repeats of *ER* and *The X-Files*, and, in the sixth season, Kevin Sorbo's new series *Andromeda*.

auctions of *Xena* memorabilia have commanded small fortunes for autographed shooting scripts and genuine props and costumes that were actually used on the set. Many of these entered the market during the auction of Pacific Renaissance's assets at the wrap of production. A quick search of the internet auction house e-Bay turns up over 2,000 *Xena* items, ranging from videotapes, trading cards and 8 x 10 glossies for a few dollars each, to authentic costumes and props from the show, priced at hundreds or even thousands of dollars. Perhaps the highest price ever paid for a piece of *Xena* memorabilia was the incredible US$31,000 paid for Xena's sword at auction, at the 1999 Creation convention. As usual with such auctions, the proceeds of this sale went to benefit a worthy cause, in this case the Hollywood Horse Show Charities, founded by William Shatner for the benefit of children in need.

Science fiction fans are well known for their generosity. Every convention, no matter how small, seems to have a charity auction or fundraiser, and *Xena* fans are no exception — as the sale of the sword demonstrates. However, some of them have taken this generosity far beyond

the occasional convention. A small *Xena* gathering in New York in 1997 gave rise to a volunteer organisation of *Xena* fans dedicated to helping charitable causes. Sword and Staff, headed by Deborah Cassetta, was named after the weapons of Xena and Gabrielle at the time. Between its inception in May 1997 and the end of 2002, it had raised nearly US$400,000, and its work continues. With ties to other *Xena* fan groups in several countries, Sword and Staff has contributed to a long list of respected charities, including Amnesty International USA, the ASPCA, Oxfam and St. Jude's Children's Hospital. Two of its continuing beneficiaries are charities dear to the hearts of *Xena* fans: the Kevin Smith Trust Fund for the benefit of the late actor's family, and the Starship Foundation, Lucy Lawless' favourite charity, which benefits the Starship Children's Hospital in Auckland. Sword and Staff also assists many other charities by procuring, on request, donations of *Xena* memorabilia for fundraising events.

Ares crashes a press conference in 'Soul Possession'.

With the ending of the show, many people expected *Xena* fandom to fade away in the absence of fresh material to stimulate the fans' imaginations. The official *Xena* magazine and *Xena* website are no more, and many fan websites that were once popular have vanished. But *Xena*'s appeal endures. After all, that you're reading this book is proof in itself that *Xena* fandom is alive and well, years after *Xena: Warrior Princess* ended production!

As further proof, Creation's official *Xena* conventions continue to draw fans by the thousands each year. At the time of writing, *Xena* fandom was abuzz with the news that both Lucy Lawless and Renee O'Connor were scheduled to appear at the February 2003 Pasadena Convention, and the very select (and expensive) Gold Seating category was already sold out. Creation was also advertising its first *Xena* cruise for April 2003, with a pleasant Caribbean itinerary and a clutch of *Xena* guest stars as fellow passengers to enliven the trip.

In fact, *Xena* fans still maintain scores of websites large and small, attend conventions with *Xena* stars, buy large quantities of *Xena* merchandise, raise thousands of dollars for charities, and most important, keep their community of *Xena* friendships alive. Battle on, *Xena* fans! ✄

Here is a rough A-Z guide to the characters, races, places and events in Greek mythology that inspired their namesakes in *Xena*. And you thought the relationships in the show were complicated...

Asclepius: God of Medicine, son of Apollo. He was raised by the Centaur Chiron.

Amazons: a nation of women warriors. They worshipped Artemis and Ares, and were known as skilled archers.

Aphrodite: Goddess of Love and Beauty, wife of Hephaestus. In many myths she is born of the sea foam, in some she is the daughter of Zeus and the sea nymph Dione.

Apollo: God of Music and Truth, son of Zeus and twin brother of Artemis.

Ares: God of War, son of Zeus and Hera. Disliked by both his parents, he is often portrayed as a bully and a coward, and is sometimes the adulterous lover of Aphrodite. The dog is his animal symbol.

Argo: the name of Jason's ship. He and his crew of heroes, the Argonauts, sailed on her in search of the Golden Fleece.

Artemis: virgin Goddess of the Hunt, the Moon and Childbirth, twin sister of Apollo.

Athena: virgin Goddess of Wisdom and War, daughter (and favourite child) of Zeus — she sprang full-grown from his head (the origin of the term 'parthenogenesis').

Bacchus (Greek 'Dionysus'): God of the Vine and Wine, son of Zeus. His dual nature encompasses the opposites of divine ecstasy and savagery. His followers, the Bacchae, were mortal women crazy with wine.

Castor and Pollux: Argonauts, quadruplet brothers of Helen of Troy and Clytemnestra. Castor was mortal and Pollux immortal. In some myths Zeus was said to have fathered Pollux, while a mortal fathered Castor, in other myths Zeus fathered both brothers.

Calliope: Muse of Epic Poetry, daughter of Zeus and Mnemosyne. There are nine Muses of the Arts.

Cecrops: first King of Attica. He earned Poseidon's wrath when he chose Athena over Poseidon to be the patron god of Athens.

Centaur: a race of half man, half horse creatures. In most stories the Centaurs were drunken, violent and especially inclined to ravish women. The exception was the noble Centaur Chiron.

Cupid (Greek 'Eros'): God of Love and Desire. Portrayed as a mischievous youth shooting his arrows. Only in some myths is he Aphrodite's son.

Cyclops: a race of one-eyed giants. Noted for their savagery and their taste for human flesh. The most famous was Polyphemus, who was blinded by Ulysses.

Discord (Greek 'Eris'): sister of Ares and mother of Strife.

The Fates (Clotho, Lachesis, Atropos): divine sisters who were arbiters of destiny. Clotho the Spinner spun the thread, Lachesis assigned each person's fate, Atropos cut the thread at death.

The Furies (Tisiphone, Megaera, Alecto): Goddesses of Retribution. They tormented those guilty of terrible crimes, particularly patricide and matricide.

Hades: God of the Underworld and King of the Dead, brother of Zeus. He was not the same as Death (Greek 'Thanatos'), who was a separate god.

Helen of Troy: the most beautiful woman in the world. Though married to Menelaus, King of Sparta, Aphrodite made her fall in love with Paris, Prince of Troy. When she eloped with Paris, her husband raised an army to pursue her, triggering the Trojan War.

Hephaestus: God of Fire and the Forge, son of Hera. He was legendary for the weapons he made, and was the only Greek god who was crippled and deformed. In some myths he was also Zeus' son.

Hera: Queen of the Gods and Goddess of Marriage, sister and wife of Zeus. She spent much time punishing Zeus and his mortal lovers for his infidelities.

Hermes: Messenger of the Gods, son of Zeus. He wore winged sandals and a winged helmet.

Hestia: virgin Goddess of the Hearth, sister of Zeus.

Mnemosyne: Goddess of Memory, a Titan.

Morpheus: God of Dreams, son of Hypnos, God of Sleep.

Oedipus: solved the riddle of the Sphinx, and unknowingly killed his father, the King of Thebes, and married his mother.

Orestes: punished by the Furies for killing his mother, Clytemnestra, to avenge her murder of his father, Agamemnon.

Pandora: the first woman, given a box by the gods, in which were imprisoned all the troubles of the world. Curious, she opened the box and all the ills escaped, leaving only hope.

Poseidon: God of the Sea, brother of Zeus. In myth, he has a difficult and quarrelsome personality.

Prometheus: a Titan. In some stories he is the maker of mankind, in others he brought humans the gift of fire. The Olympians punished him by chaining him to a rock, but he was freed by Hercules.

Sisyphus: a King of Corinth. He tried to imprison Death, and as punishment was doomed to roll a boulder forever up a hill in Tartarus.

Terpsichore: the Muse of Dance.

Titans: the gigantic progenitors of the Olympians. Led by Cronus, they were overthrown by his children (Zeus, Poseidon and Hades) in a battle for cosmic power. The Titan Hyperion was the father of the sun, the moon and the dawn.

Trojan War: begun when a Greek army besieged the city of Troy to recover Helen, it lasted ten years and led to the deaths of the great heroes Achilles and Hector, and the destruction of Troy. It is the subject of some of the greatest works of classical literature.

Ulysses (Greek 'Odysseus'): cursed by Poseidon after the Trojan War, he spent ten years trying to return home. He was known for his cunning.

Underworld: Greek Land of the Dead, includes the Elysian Fields, home of the blessed spirits, and Tartarus, where the evil suffer torments devised by the gods. Greek burial rites included placing coins with the dead to buy passage across the river Styx from the ferryman, Charon.

Zeus: King of the Gods and God of the Sky and Storms. He is notorious for seducing or raping human maidens; the ancient world was cluttered with his half-mortal offspring.